Food Crops
for the Future

Food Crops
for the Future

The Development of Plant Resources

COLIN TUDGE

Basil Blackwell

British Library Cataloguing in Publication Data

Tudge, Colin, *1943–*
    Food crops for the future: the development of plant resources.
    1. Plant breeding
    I. Title
    631.5'3   SB123

    ISBN 0–631–13907–9   O 864509
    ISBN 0–631–15082–X Pbk

Library of Congress Cataloging in Publication Data

Tudge, Colin
    Food crops for the future.
    Includes bibliographies and index.
    1. Food crops   I. Title
    SB175.T83 1987   630   86–31729

    ISBN 0–631–13907–9
    ISBN 0–631–15082–X Pbk

Typeset in 10 on 11½ pt Sabon
by Columns of Reading
Printed in Great Britain by
Page Bros (Norwich) Ltd

Contents

Contents

Acknowledgements

The author and publishers are grateful to the following for permission to reproduce photographs.

Figure 1.1 International Crops Research Institute for the Semi-Arid Tropics, Hyderabad (ICRISAT); 2.1 Holt Studios; 2.2 International Maize and Wheat Improvement Center, Mexico (CIMMYT); 2.3 ICRISAT; 2.4 ICRISAT; 2.5 ICRISAT; 2.6 ICRISAT; 2.7 ICRISAT; 2.8a ICRISAT; 2.8b ICRISAT; 2.9 Rodale Press, Inc.; 2.10 Dr David Dendy; 2.11 Holt Studios; 2.12 Heather Angel; 2.13 Holt Studios; 2.14 Heather Angel; 5.1 Plant Breeding Institute, Cambridge (PBI); 5.2 PBI; 5.3 ICRISAT; 5.4 PBI; 6.1 Dr R. L. Branton; 6.2 Science Photo Library; 6.3 Food Research Institute, Norwich; 9.1 PBI; 9.2 Professor Nigel Smith; 9.3 PBI; 9.4 Photographie Giraudon; 9.5 PBI; 10.1a International Institute of Tropical Agriculture, Ibadan (IITA); 10.1b IITA

1 The Meaning of Improvement

When our ancestors first learned to cultivate plants, probably between 30 000 and 10 000 years ago, they began a chain of events that was to change the world beyond recognition or revocation. They made it possible for a large and influential animal – the human being – to exist in substantially greater numbers than could be supported by natural forest or savannah. The more that cultivation increased, the greater the numbers of people that were able to survive; and, of course, the more human beings survived, the less room there was for other species.

Now there are five billion (thousand million) of us. We are far and away the most numerous and ubiquitous large animal that has ever lived. By the end of this century there will be more than six billion and sometime in the middle of the next century, the human population is liable to reach ten billion. If our ancestors had not learned to cultivate plants, all those millennia ago, then the human population could never have risen to more than a fraction of a per cent of the figure that is soon liable to be attained. If we do not continue the processes of cultivation more adroitly and efficiently, then we have little chance of feeding the extraordinary numbers of people who will be born into this world in the next few decades, and no chance whatever of doing so without obliterating our fellow species. Efficient cultivation – by which I mean, specifically, cultivation that produces good food but does not obliterate all other living things – is a *sine qua non* if we are to survive in a tolerable world. It is by far the single most important undertaking for the human species.

The cultivation of plants implies two processes which operate in parallel. The first is the care of plants: the ground must be prepared, nutrient and water supplied, and pests and diseases kept at bay. And as plants are protected, so the second component of cultivation comes into play. The forces of natural selection are replaced by those of artificial selection. The cultivated plants are altered genetically so that they come to respond ever more compliantly to cultivation, and evolve characters that are more and more pleasing to the cultivator. Such alterations, desired by the cultivator, are called 'improvements'.

1

This book is about the second of these essential components of cultivation: the conversion of edible plants into food crops capable of feeding 10 billion people.

What is improvement?

'Improvement' can mean whatever people want it to mean. Packers of tomatoes want fruits that will travel well; to them, thick skins are an improvement. Gourmets, however, may well prefer the delicacy of the old varieties that must be eaten direct from the plant. Thick skins to them are an abomination.

There is a research project currently being carried out to change the habit – the form of growth – of the winged bean; this is an extraordinary tropical plant that has nutritious seeds, leaves, and tubers (see page 000). At present it is a straggler, and is grown mainly in gardens, but the intention is to produce a short-stemmed variety that can be grown free-standing in fields, for mass cultivation. But some argue that the winged bean should be grown only in gardens, for personal consumption. If it is turned into a field crop, to sell for cash, then it will merely compete with soya. Probably the answer in this case is to have several lines of winged bean, each being suitable for different circumstances. The point, however, is that the destiny of the winged bean is a matter for debate, and what some consider to be improvement, others feel to be pointless.

Then again, a plant requires more energy to produce one gram of protein than to produce one gram of starch. It follows, then, that the plants with the greatest yield – that is, produce the greatest weight – are the ones that convert the energy they derive from the sun into starch rather than into protein. Thus, a plant with a very high protein content will inevitably yield less (in terms of weight) than one with the same photosynthetic efficiency which produces less protein. High-protein cereals are often considered to be worthwhile and in some circumstances they probably are. On the other hand, it is now widely believed that malnutrition caused by *energy* deficiency is more common than a simple deficiency of protein – and high-protein cereals may be less valuable, in the long run, than those with moderate protein content that contain more starch and yield more heavily.

Yet the most nutritious crop, or indeed the most high-yielding, is of little use unless people are prepared to eat it. Westerners who have not experienced hunger often seem to imagine that people who are hungry will eat anything. This simply is not the case. Even when people are in severe danger of starving, they may find it physically difficult to consume food that is unfamiliar. In addition, the people who are most in danger of starvation are in general those who rely heavily upon a single crop: rice, perhaps, or sorghum or millet. If the flavour or texture of the United Kingdom potato changes, this need not be of very great importance, for potatoes tend to serve largely as vehicles for fat, as in chips or crisps, or serve to soak up gravy. But if the flavour or texture of rice is changed significantly – rice that may supply three-quarters or more of daily calories, and is often eaten virtually alone – then this can create severe difficulties for the consumer. Some new and ostensibly superior varieties of rice have indeed failed simply because people do not like them; and a crop that yields only one tonne per hectare and is prone to fungal attack, is better than one that yields twice as heavily which no-one wants to eat. Indeed, as we will see in chapter 2, the improvement or maintenance of flavour in food crops is just as important as yield or nutritiousness, in the feeding of human beings.

Many crops that are grown for food serve other purposes as well. One and a half billion people in the world rely upon timber for all or most of their cooking fuel; and cooking, for poor people living in the tropics, is by far the greatest consumer of fuel energy. But timber has become scarce. Many people, therefore, rely increasingly upon crop residues, of which a prime example are the stalks of pigeon peas, *Cajanus cajan*, one of the principal food crops of dry tropical countries. Pigeon peas are natural perennials, and though it is sometimes preferable to grow them as perennials, the total yields can be greater if the crop is grown as an annual. If it is grown as an annual, however, the big woody stalks do not fully develop, and its value as a fuel is reduced. In the Sahel, pigeon pea stalks are also used for fencing. The straw of rye is traditionally used for thatch. Coconuts serve for fuel, building, and fibres. In general, where there is possible conflict between various uses, it should pay to increase the most valuable product at the expense of the others. This assumes, however, that the putatively valuable produce can actually be sold, which in countries with undeveloped systems of trade may not be the case; so that sticks that can be burnt may in practice be more 'valuable' than surplus food that simply rots in store. The point in general is that those who would improve crops must be aware of the precise role of those crops within the societies they serve. It is in theory possible to produce new varieties that seem to be better by the most obvious criteria and yet do not serve the society as well as the old.

However, it is not my intention in this book to polemicize, and to argue the merits of particular crops or strategies. I have written other books of polemic, including *The Famine Business* (1977) and *Future Cook* (1980). But two points do require emphasis. The first, as we have seen, is that conflicts arise in the improvement of crops. Sometimes there is a tactical conflict: should a given crop be designed for the garden or the field, raised exclusively for food or for a multitude of purposes? Sometimes the conflict is tactical versus strategic: a high-protein cereal may be useful for raising livestock, but is it necessary for human beings – and is it a good thing to grow cereal specifically for

importance of other use

3

animals? And sometimes the conflict is physical: a tomato cannot be thick skinned and thin skinned at the same time; and the crops with the highest protein content cannot give the highest possible yields.

The second point, however, is that it is quite wrong to assume that crop improvement should proceed only in one direction. If the world's people are to be fed without destroying all other forms of life, then in practice plants must be cultivated in many different circumstances and many different ways. In some regions of some countries – as, perhaps, in East Anglia or the Netherlands – it is appropriate simply to abandon a proportion of the land to farming, and to produce the highest possible yields from the area available. Then, crop improvement implies the provision of plants able to respond to very high inputs of fertilizer, and produce very high yields in return.

In other places it simply is not realistic to think in terms of ultra-high yields. Seven hundred and fifty million people, about one in six of the world's population, live in the areas known as the semi-arid tropics. These areas extend through Asia, including much of India; across the middle of Africa, south of the Sahara, in the region known as the Sahel; and into South America. Part of these regions is irrigated, but most relies entirely upon rain that falls only for a few brief weeks each year. Farming inevitably is small scale, and the ambition is not to feed the cities, as it is in Europe, but for farmers to subsist, with enough left over for a little income. In these regions crops must be bred not for an ability to respond to high inputs, because the inputs inevitably are low. They must be bred above all for resilience.

Arable land, devoted to cereals and other field crops, accounts for about 10 per cent of the world's land surface. Another 23 per cent is permanent pasture – mostly grassland, devoted mainly to cattle, sheep, and goats. This land too makes a vital contribution to feeding the world, and it must also be considered in all conservation strategies. Almost all the world's permanent pasture could be improved, in various ways; it could yield more, and it could contain a greater variety of species. Again, such improvements could be achieved in part by superior management (various forms of rotational grazing, for example), and partly by introducing new and more suitable plants. 'Improved' crops in this case are those that can resist grazing, or indeed thrive on it; those that can enrich the soil by nitrogen fixation (see below); those that are able to resist drought and disease; and those that provide more nutritious forage, for longer periods throughout the year.

In short, it is not just the crops of the high-intensity farms and market gardens of Europe and North America that need improving; and these farms and market gardens are not necessarily the 'best' and certainly not the only proper sources of food. In practice, food plants must be grown in a hundred different ways, in gardens, balconies, greenhouses and farms; on mountains and on the open plain. But wherever they are produced, and in whatever ways, there is scope for their improvement;

Figure 1.1 Up-graded cultivation techniques in the semi-arid tropics should be matched by improvements in crops.

Improvement

for crops that will produce more of what is required, under the conditions with which they are provided.

What is meant by 'improvement', then, is a matter of context. Yet it is possible nonetheless to identify general categories of improvement. Thus, wherever a plant is grown it should be made more responsive to the particular form of cultivation: if it is fertilized, it should be capable of responding to the inputs; if the farmer wants to sow in March and harvest in September, then the crop should germinate, grow, and mature within that time; if he wants to grow a crop in a field and harvest it by combine then he would prefer not to have to provide each individual plant with a stick to grow up. In short, all crops everywhere must be made more compliant to the circumstances pertaining.

Secondly, wherever a plant is grown it should be able to resist the stresses of its particular environment. Sometimes this means drought, sometimes extreme surface heat at the time of germination, sometimes waterlogging, and sometimes excess salinity or other forms of toxicity. Always there will be pests – insects, nematodes, mites, or even birds and rats; and diseases – fungi, bacteria, and viruses. Whatever else 'crop improvement' may mean, it should always imply 'increased resistance to disease and pests'.

The third inescapable line of improvement is in 'quality'. This is the moveable feast: thick skins or thin skins, high or low protein content, red skin, yellow skin, sweet flesh or sour. As we have seen, there can be conflicts of ambition. In general, there are hundreds of crops in the

5

world and the quality of each crop could theoretically be improved in hundreds of different ways.

The fourth line of improvement is in yield. This may mean simply enlarging the mass of plants grown – although in truth this is far from simple. Equally, however, it implies increasing the proportion of the crop that actually is useful: that is, raising the *harvest index*. Thus, cereal yields in recent decades have been increased primarily by raising the weight of grain relative to the straw; and today's high-yielding apple trees are generally much smaller than those of the great orchards of the past.

Finally, many breeders nowadays are endeavouring to increase the ability of plants to *fix* atmospheric nitrogen – that is, to convert nitrogen gas into soluble nitrogenous salts, which the plant can absorb as nutrient. Many plants can perform this feat; or, to be more accurate, they harbour bacteria within or around their roots that have this ability. The most accomplished fixers of nitrogen are members of the Leguminosae, the family that includes the 'pulse' crops, peas, beans and lentils; vetches and clovers; shrubs such as gorse and broom, and trees such as laburnum, leucaena, and acacia. But many other plant families contain individuals or genera with some ability to fix nitrogen, and many grasses (which include the cereals) provide an environment around their roots that encourages the growth of nitrogen-fixing bacteria. Nitrogen fixation could theoretically be increased through various strategies of plant breeding, and the more nitrogen fixation is increased, the less will farmers need recourse to artificial fertilizer.

As far as this book is concerned, it might seem logical to have begun by discussing the kinds of improvement that are being effected. In practice, it proved very difficult to discuss specific lines of improvement without discussing actual methods of improvement first. So the various meanings of 'improvement' are discussed in chapter 9, and nitrogen fixation in chapter 10.

But how are the necessary improvements to be achieved?

The paths to crop improvement

The essence of plant breeding is to select plants with desired characters, to cross them with other plants with other desirable characters, to identify the offspring that combine the attributes of both parents, and to multiply those offspring so that there are enough to supply to farmers, growers, and planters.

If these undertakings were as simple as they sound then this would be a very short book. In fact, heredity is immensely complicated, and if the breeder simply 'crossed the best with the best and hoped for the best', then improvement would at best be erratic and in practice would soon come to a halt. In addition, there are reproductive barriers between plants – within species as well as between species – that complicate many attempts at cross breeding. And the task of multiplying those plants that do contain the required characters – the so-called 'elite' plants – so that there is enough for the farmers and planters, can be just as complicated as the task of combining the required characters in the first place. The main point here is that many plants simply do not *breed true*: that is, when they reproduce sexually, their offspring may be very different from themselves.

Thus, in practice, crop improvement is far from straightforward. It is intricate and time consuming; it must be carried out on a large scale; and it differs in strategy from species to species, depending on the reproductive caprices of each one.

It seemed to me, then, that the only way to give a worthwhile insight into what is involved in crop improvement was to begin right at the beginning. Thus, chapter 3 explores the basis of heredity, and explains why it is indeed complicated; and chapter 4 deals with the reproductive biology of plants, which largely determines the strategy and limitations of plant breeding.

Plant breeding as now carried out is an exercise in applied genetics, and the science of genetics can properly be dated only from the beginning of this century, when the work of Gregor Mendel was rediscovered. But crop improvement did not begin with modern plant breeding. The first people who protected plants from other predators, and deliberately planted the seeds or twigs or tubers of the plants they thought most desirable, were beginning the process of plant breeding. They were altering selective forces. And long before plant breeding became a science, it was a craft of great sophistication. Thus, most crops that are widely grown today were already very different from their wild ancestors by the time the new-found knowledge of genetics was brought to bear on them. We should therefore begin discussion of breeding at the beginning. Accordingly, chapter 5 takes the story of plant breeding from prehistoric times to the present.

Crop improvement, as we have said, is a matter of combining desirable characteristics in one plant, and then multiplying that plant. Traditionally, this has been achieved by manipulating the natural reproduction of plants: combining characteristics by exploiting sexual reproduction; and multiplying the offspring by both sexual and asexual means.

In recent decades scientists have transcended natural processes. Using techniques of cytogenetics, they have effected marriages between plants that normally could not combine, and thus transferred genetic material across natural barriers. These methods are also discussed in chapter 5.

In addition, it is now possible to reproduce plants asexually at a far greater rate than is achieved in nature, and to do this in plants that do not naturally reproduce asexually. This is done by the methods of tissue culture, and is discussed in chapter 6. As we will see, tissue culture has transformed the prospects of several major crops, notably the palms. In addition, tissue culture may be used to produce disease-free stocks, and to produce new varieties and even new species.

The last decade has seen the rise of a quite new science, *genetic engineering*. Biologists can now take an individual gene from one organism and put it into another, thus imbuing the recipient with one at least of the characters of the donor. Furthermore, biologists can in principle take genes from any class of organism and put them into any other; from bacterium into mammal or fish into plant; and from plant into plant, frog, or bacterium.

Genetic engineering is discussed in chapter 7. Its potential is unquestionable. As we will see, however, the technique has theoretical limitations, and it must be seen as an extension to plant breeding, not as a replacement for it.

Finally, modern breeders seek to expropriate genes from plants all over the world to incorporate into their crops: from other varieties, ancient and modern, and from wild plants. Genetic engineers will spread the net even wider. Thus modern programmes of crop improvement must be underpinned by stores, or 'banks' of genes. The world's network of gene banks, and the difficulties of maintaining them, are discussed in chapter 8.

Science and logistics

This book is not polemical: it is about the ways in which things can be done, and why some tasks are easier to tackle than others. But there is a polemical thread. It is that the world's food problems really can be solved, and that crop improvement is part of that solution; but that improvement is difficult and expensive. Solution depends upon world-wide co-operation and science of a very high degree. In the 1970s it was fashionable to argue that the only science or technology that were 'appropriate' to the developing world were of an 'intermediate' kind: better ox-carts, concrete well-heads, small-scale irrigation and so on. Such improvements are indeed vital, and have in the past been grossly neglected. But in addition to these basic requirements, the farmers of the poor world need crops that can resist disease without expensive sprays, that can grow with minimal inputs of fertilizer, and which are able to endure drought and heat. Such improvements are not to be achieved easily, and sometimes can be achieved only by applying some of the 'highest' sciences of all – cytogenetics, tissue culture, genetic engineering. If genetic engineering can produce a fungus-resistant sorghum or a saline-resistant chickpea, then that indeed is 'appropriate' technology. All the farmer needs to care about, after all, is that the crop produces what is required, and is cheap.

But we should begin right at the beginning. In the next chapter we will look at the crops themselves: the food plants that are the objects of improvement.

2 A Survey of Food Plants

Introduction

There are about 250 000 species of flowering plant, and according to the United States National Academy of Sciences, human beings in their time have probably exploited about 3 000 of those species for food, and cultivated about 150 on a commercial scale. However, by far the largest amount of food for human beings is now supplied by only around 20 different kinds of crop.

Many authorities in recent years (not least, the National Academy of Sciences) have pointed out that 150 out of 250 000 is a very small proportion; and that to cultivate a mere 20 species on a world scale seems positively negligent. Three kinds of argument are put forward. The first is that there must be a great many other plants that are not cultivated, but that could be useful. This is unquestionably the case, as we will discuss further in this chapter and in chapter 9. The second argument is that by cultivating only 20 principal crops we are leaving ourselves vulnerable. A change of conditions or an outbreak of disease could have devastating effects – and these would be far less if we had ranks of alternative crops. Again, as a generalization, this seems to make sense: the loss of potato through blight in the 19th century, and because of the eelworm *Globodera* in the 20th; the destruction of maize in the United States in the 1970s by southern leaf blight fungus; and the inability of maize to cope with the recent droughts in vast areas of southern Africa, all suggest that it would be wise to have some alternatives in reserve.

The third argument – still somewhat speculative, but highly intriguing – is that by confining ourselves to a few principal crops we have considerably reduced the range of organic compounds that we now consume. As Dr Michael Crawford points out in *What we eat today* (Crawford and Crawford, 1972), the variety of goods in the supermarket is largely superficial; the 1500 or so 'lines' that may be on display represent variations on only a few basic ingredients. In contrast, hunter gatherers may make regular use of 80 or more different plants and a wide variety of animal foods. In addition, modern cultivars (cultivated varieties) are probably less varied, biochemically, than wild plants because most of the components that are not of obvious nutritional value may well have been bred out of them.

This loss of biochemical variability is probably of no great consequence. For example, many arcane chemical components of plants are simple structural variations of sugars, and the body deals with them as though they were sugars. The loss in other cases may be advantageous: many components of wild plants (and of the fungi that tend to invade them) are toxic. On the other hand, the simplification of our diet *could* have significant nutritional consequences. The possible areas of concern include provision of some polyunsaturated fats, which some authorities allege are deficient in the modern diet; provision of vitamins; and provision of the kind of agents that feature in the 'tonics' of Chinese, Russian, and East European medicine. The human metabolism has evolved to cope with a huge variety of plant-based organic compounds, and clearly has become reliant upon at least some of them, for example, vitamin A and vitamin C. However, we may be more reliant on these plant-based compounds than is yet realized, and perhaps would be a lot better off – less prone to depression, for example, or to chronic disorders such as atherosclerosis – if we consumed a greater variety of plants. This is speculation, but it is not foolish speculation.

On the other hand, there are reasons for suggesting that present-day concentration upon just a few crops is not quite the calamity that has sometimes been indicated. To be a good crop, a plant needs a great many special qualities, and there is no doubt that some plants make better crops than others. We will argue the merits of growing sorghum in this book; it is the outstanding cereal crop of the semi-arid tropics, and could perhaps do more to alleviate famine in the short term than any other single crop. The fact is, however, that sorghum is less versatile than wheat and less tasty than rice; and if people are able to grow rice or wheat, they will. There is a hierarchy among food plants and, broadly speaking, the plants that are now widely grown deserve to be because they have outstanding qualities. This does not mean that we should not make room for others, but it does mean that the final list of cultivars will always be fairly exclusive.

Secondly, it is wise to treat new crops with caution. Thus, the National Academy of Sciences suggests in its 1975 review, *Under-exploited tropical plants with promising economic value*, that the Australian grass *Echinochloa* might make an excellent cereal for very dry regions. So it well might. After all, it produces a fine crop after only one watering. The chief cereal crop of very dry land at present is millet, which is even more drought-tolerant than sorghum. However, millet is not quite drought-resistant enough for the extremely capricious conditions of the semi-arid tropics, and *Echinochloa* might well be a replacement for it. But people know how to cultivate millet, and the people who grow it know how to cook it. *Echinochloa* is an unknown

11

and an improved, super-drought-resistant millet might in the end be more acceptable than the newcomer. The point is, however, that while we should continue to search for new crops, we should also appreciate that the potential of existing crops is far from being fully explored.

There is a third reason too why we perhaps need not be too concerned about the present paucity of cultivated species. The special qualities of wild plants are not necessarily lost simply because the plant itself is not cultivated. Increasingly, genes from wild plants are being incorporated into cultivars to improve their colour, their protein content, their vitamin C content (in the case of tomatoes) and their resistance to pests and stresses – and eventually, perhaps, to increase their ability to fix nitrogen. Thus, the modern cultivar is often a synthesis: a coalescence of several, or even many, different plants. In a few decades' time it will hardly matter whether any one plant is given one species' name or another. Each crop plant will, effectively, be a conglomerate.

In short, we can well expect that more plants will be brought into widespread cultivation, and the increased cultivation of triticale and the 'kiwi fruit' in recent years has shown that there is always room for promising newcomers. But we can also expect to see an increasing concentration of genes from the 250 000 wild species into the few hundred that are grown on a large scale. Agriculture is 10 000 years old but the modern age of plant breeding based on genetics began only in this century, and genetic engineering is only just into its second decade. In a hundred years' time, discussion of possible new species to cultivate might simply seem quaint – for by then the world's principal crops, however many there are, may already contain genes from tens of thousands of species.

The classification of food plants – by family

The 250 000 species of flowering plants (angiosperms) are classified in two main groups: the monocotyledons, or monocots, whose embryos, within the seed, have only one leaf; and the dicotyledons, or dicots, with two seed leaves. The monocots in turn are divided into roughly 57 families, and the dicots into about 250 families: I say 'roughly', and 'about', because different taxonomists classify the plants in different ways. Although only a minority of flowering plant species has contributed directly to the welfare of human beings, most families contribute or have contributed at least one indirectly useful species – if not for food, then for timber, drugs, fibres or dyes. In this respect, at least, human beings throw the exploitative net fairly widely.

However, though most plant families contribute in some way to human wellbeing, only about 35 or so make a significant contribution. Knowledge of taxonomy is of practical use; to some extent, you can get an idea of the kinds of qualities a plant is liable to have from knowledge of its family. Thus, for example, members of the Rosaceae family tend to have succulent fruits; those of the Leguminosae are able to fix nitrogen; and those of the Solanaceae lend themselves particularly well to the rigours of tissue culture and will be among the first to be improved by genetic engineering. A brief discussion of taxonomy, therefore, is well worth while.

The monocots

Monocots include the group that is by far the most important source of food plants: the grasses, alias Gramineae. Many grasses have large nutritious seeds: these are the world's cereals and include wheat, rice, maize, barley, sorghum, the millets, teff, rye, and oats. Grasses have a peculiar habit of growth, in which the growing tip appears far beneath the leaves, which wave overhead. Thus the leaf tops can be removed without damaging the growing point. Grasses can be cut or even burnt without damage, and they provide the principal forage crops. Many grasses have sweet sap, which in the case of *Saccharum* is taken to extreme limits. *Saccharum*, alias sugar cane, is a major source of calories and of wealth worldwide, for good and ill. Finally, the Graminae include bamboo, the shoots of which are almost the sole source of succour for the giant panda, and are a delicacy for human beings.

Second in importance among the monocot families of food plants must surely be the palms, Palmae. The principal food palm is the coconut, followed by the oil palm, then those of the date and sago. Other palms yield toffee-like sugar from their sap and a dozen or so species contribute 'palm hearts' – the central masses of growing tissue, which are eaten as a vegetable, and are regarded as a delicacy. Palms, being trees, are slow to reproduce sexually, and only a few can be reproduced naturally by asexual means. However, as will be discussed in chapter 6, asexual reproduction of palms can now be effected on the grand scale by tissue culture which in the short term will contribute more to the cultivation of the palm than to any other family of plants.

The Araceae, family of the arum lily and the bizarre cuckoo pint, deserve mention here as a source of nutritious tubers. These include taro, cocoyam, and dasheen. Some grow in swamps and some tolerate high salinity; they deserve wider exploitation.

We should mention, too, the Musaceae, the bananas and plantains, important staples for some people and source of income for many others.

Some members of the Liliaceae are characterized by aromatic bulbs in the form of onions, shallots, leeks and garlic; these are sometimes placed either in the daffodil family, Amaryllidaceae, or given their own family, the Alliaceae. The Liliaceae also include asparagus.

Other families of considerable importance are the Bromeliaceae, the pineapples, and the Dioscoraceae, which are known to people in temperate climates as the family of black briony, but which also include the tropical yams.

The dicots

Among the dicots, the most important family of food plants are the Leguminosae. They fix nitrogen and tend, presumably by virtue of this fact, to have a high concentration of protein in their seeds and in their leaves. The large, edible, protein-rich seeds of legumes are known as pulses and the protein-rich leaves of clovers, vetches, lucerne (alfalfa), medicks and acacias are important sources of fodder and are vital to the wellbeing of the world's vast pasturelands; many, notably soya and groundnut, have oil-rich seeds. Legumes are extremely varied in habitat, and include herbs (such as clover and most pulses), bushes (gorse and broom) and trees (acacia). They also tolerate the spectrum of climate, from near desert (bambara groundnut) to extremely wet (runner bean), and from extreme tropics (winged bean) to European winter (broad bean). Legumes are also versatile organic chemists, and are sources of drugs, dyes (indigo), and spices (fenugreek and liquorice), but also of toxins, some of which are potentially useful as pesticides, and some of which tend to complicate attempts to use them as crops (as with broad beans, lupins, and some clovers).

Second among the dicot families are the remarkable Solanaceae. They contain the world's leading non-cereal staple, the potato, plus a formidable and varied array of edible and valuable fruits, including tomatoes, capsicums – both sweet and hot peppers – eggplants, naranjilla, and Cape gooseberries. The Solanaceae are not a major source of green leaves, although the black nightshade serves as a green vegetable in West Africa and Asia. The Solanaceae, like the Leguminosae, includes many notable organic chemists. Many species are toxic, include various species of potato and tomato; and, of course, tobacco. However, several of the toxic agents of the Solanaceae also serve as powerful and useful drugs. Thus deadly nightshade produces belladonna, alias atropine, which is fatal in large amounts and a valuable relaxant in more controlled quantities. Members of this family also lend themselves particularly well to techniques of tissue culture. Many of the pioneering studies were carried out on tobacco and petunia, and the potato will probably be the first major food crop to undergo genetic engineering for serious genetic purpose.

At least three families might vie to be placed third in the hierarchy of commercial importance among the dicots. The Cruciferae certainly have a claim, with their peppery, nutritious leaves, oil-rich seeds, and range of swollen, aromatic taproots. This family includes turnips and swedes, cabbage and kale, rape, mustards, radishes, watercress, and horse-radish.

The Rosaceae, on the other hand, are the source of 'nuts', in the form of almonds, plus some of the world's most valuable fruits: strawberries, plums, gages, damsons and prunes, cherries, peaches, nectarines, apricots, apples, pears, quinces and medlars, blackberries, raspberries, and all their many variants.

The Compositae (the daisy family) also deserve consideration; not so much for the lettuce, which is economically valuable but nutritionally vacuous, as for the sunflower, which has become one of the world's principal sources of edible polyunsaturated oil, and for the less widely grown safflower. Scorzonera, salsify, endive, chicory, and Jerusalem and globe artichokes are minor but delectable members of the Compositae, while tarragon and southernwood, tansy and chamomile, are aromatic herbs and flavourings.

Human beings would also be considerably worse off without the Chenopodiaceae. Some members, notably those of the genus *Beta*, have sweet and valuable swollen tap-roots and include beetroot, sugar beet and mangolds. Some have valuable leaves, including various manifesta-tions of spinach, while the leaves of Good King Henry and fat hen, now known primarily as wayside weeds, may well have served our Iron Age ancestors as important vegetables. Chenopods also include valuable seed plants – including Good King Henry and fat hen, and various species and varieties of quinoa, which was a principal grain crop of the Incas and of various Indian groups of eastern North America.

The Euphorbiaceae is one of the most remarkable of all plant families. Its members range from the candelabra trees of Africa, which resemble cacti although they are not related, to the spurges of Europe; and they include the rubber tree, *Hevea*, and the castor oil plant, *Ricinus*. The Euphorbiaceae is of interest to us primarily as the family of the cassava, the principal tuber of the tropics; also of chaya, also known as tree spinach; and of the mongongo fruit, with its nutritious seeds, discussed below.

The Umbelliferae is remarkable too. It provides sweet roots – carrot, parsnip, and the arracacha of South America. Umbellifers also provide aromatic seeds – coriander, fennel, cumin, dill, and caraway; aromatic leaves, as of dill, parsley, chervil, and samphire; and aromatic leaf stalks, notably fennel, angelica, and celery. Families that provide such aromatics and spices also tend to produce some toxins. Hemlock is an umbellifer.

The Cucurbitaceae provides the world with huge, seedy and fleshy fruits: melons, watermelons, pumpkins, gourds, squashes, marrows, cucumbers, and gherkins; and the chayote of Central America is also a source of shoots, leaves, and fleshy roots. The Moraceae contains breadfruit, figs, and mulberries, as well as the remarkable genus

Cannabis, source of fibres and of drugs. The family of the heathers, lings, and rhododendrons, the Ericaceae, provides food in the form of bilberries, cranberries, and arbutus. The aromatic leaves of the Labiatae seem to provide most of the world's principal herbs: the mints, savory, thyme, sage, basil, balm, rosemary, and oregano.

The world's main staple crops are all members of the Gramineae, Leguminosae, or Solanaceae, but many others that are of great importance to small societies, or are of great potential importance, are widely spread among botanical families. Thus the Amaranthaceae contains the amaranths; these grow in gardens as love-lies-bleeding, but they have also been a valuable source of grain in South and Central America and have great potential importance, as discussed below. The Polygonaceae is the family of pestilential dock, but it also provides the valuable grain, buckwheat, plus rhubarb and sorrel for good measure. Zosteraceae is the family of the eelgrass, another potentially valuable grain. The Convolvulaceae, the bind-weed family, provides *Ipomaea,* the sweet potato.

The Camelliaceae, the camellia family, includes tea; the Rubiaceae gives us coffee, as well as quinine; the Sterculiaceae is the family of cola and cacao, or chocolate. The Myrtaceae, the family of myrtles and eucalyptus, includes the clove, the Pedaliaceae includes sesame, the Piperaceae is the family of pepper, and the Zingiberaceae includes ginger, turmeric and cardamoms.

The Malvaceae, family of the hollyhock and marsh mallow, also includes cotton and – which is of interest to us – the okra, or bhindi. The Anacardiaceae gives us the mango, cashew, and pistachio; the Caricaceae, papaya; the Lauraceae, the avacado; the Oleaceae, the olive; the Vitaceae, the grape; the Grossulariceae, the currants; the Rutaceae contain the citrus fruits; the Sapotaceae provides the tree that produces sapodilla, one of the finest of all tropical fruits, with flesh like barleysugar. It also produces chicle from its bark, source of the world's first chewing gum. The pomegranate has its own family, the Punicaceae.

Trees from a wide range of families contribute nutritious seeds, some of which are known as nuts. Hazels and filberts are from the birch family, Betulaceae; sweet chestnut come from the Fagaceae, family of beeches and oaks; the almond belongs to the Rosaceae; walnut and pecan are from the Juglandaceae; pistachio and cashew belong to the mango family, Anarcardiaceae; brazils are in the Lecythidaceae; and the baobob is of the Bombaceae, also known as the source of the big, fleshy, durian fruit, and of balsa and kapok.

These, then, are the families that contribute most to the human food supply, and to feeding livestock. There are others, including many tropical families with considerable potential. However, although it is the case that useful characteristics do tend to run in families – the Gramineae, Leguminosae, Solanaceae, Rosaceae, etc. – it is also true that economic significance cuts across taxonomic groups. Thus, although the world's grains belong principally to the Gramineae, four other families – Chenopodiaceae, Amaranthaceae, Polygonaceae, and Zosteraceae – also contribute. The world's most valuable tubers are included in the Solanaceae, Diosceraceae, Euphorbiaceae, Convolvulaceae, and Araceae. And nuts (or at least, nutritious seeds of trees and shrubs) come from a very wide range of families.

In short, we should also seek to categorize food plants in terms of function. Function can be defined in various ways: subsistence versus cash crops; arable versus plantation or plantation versus garden; and so on. But the most useful way to categorize food plants for our purposes is according to their role in feeding people; that is, their nutritional function.

Food plants classified by nutritional function

Food crops can be classified by function into five categories. The staples can by themselves provide the bulk of required nutrients and in practice often make up most of the diet. Secondary food crops – fruit and vegetables – supply some nutrients, plus flavour. Tertiary foods – spices, herbs, and infusants – provide few or no nutrients, but do provide flavour and may have additional pharmacological effects. Sugar crops and oil seeds are major sources of energy, and again serve to increase palatability. Finally, we should discuss feed crops – forage and fodder for livestock.

Within each category there are some well-established crop species, and a reserve list of species that deserve to be considered seriously as new crops. Many of those on the reserve list, such as the mongongo nut of Africa, and eelgrass, which is eaten in Mexico, are plants that have served small societies continuously for hundreds, and in some cases for tens of thousands of years, and deserve wider recognition. Others are crops with a fine past that have been neglected more recently to a greater or lesser extent. This has been the fate of amaranth and quinoa. We will look briefly at both groups – the established crops and the promising newcomers – in each category.

The staples: seeds and tubers

Staple crops are plant organs that have evolved to serve specifically as stores of nutrient: seeds, which provide succour for the embryos of the next generation; and tubers and other swollen roots or stems, intended to carry the parent plant through the winter or through drought. These stores evolved to serve the needs of the plant. But many animals, including ourselves, also evolved the teeth and the metabolism necessary

17

to expropriate that nutrient; and human beings, unique among animals, developed means of changing those food stores to suit our purposes more closely.

Staples have always been supremely important among food plants. Strangely, however, it is only in the last 20 years that nutritionists have appreciated just how important staples really are. Thus, 20 years ago, most nutritionists believed that human beings needed a diet that was rich in protein. It seemed that the only way to supply the protein was to consume large quantities of meat, fish, eggs and milk, and that it was perfectly proper to grow cereals, pulses, and tubers specifically as feed for livestock. Since then there has been a radical shift from this attitude – in some ways one of the most momentous changes of mind in all human history. For most nutritionists now feel that human protein requirements in the past were greatly exaggerated. Gross malnutrition is not, it seems, usually caused by a specific lack of protein. Indeed, it seems that all the principal staple crops contain enough protein, or almost enough, to meet the needs of adults, even if growing children may require more. This is unequivocally true of the principal seed crops, wheat and rice, which have a protein content of about 8–10 per cent. Tubers have a lower protein content (generally nearer 2 per cent) but even so, when people have enough of them to eat specific protein deficiency is not common.

Staple foods also, of course, provide energy. This is primarily in the form of starch, with smaller amounts of other carbohydrates, though some staples also provide fat. In addition, most provide at least some vitamins and minerals, though none provides a complete spectrum of these micronutrients.

Thus, staple foods can supply human beings with all the energy and protein that they need – which means that they can supply us with all the nutrients that we need to consume in large amounts. In theory, only a few extra vitamins and minerals need to be added to the principal staples to turn them into 'complete' foods. In practice, an all-staple diet is immensely tedious and on this ground alone is not desirable, as we will discuss in further detail below. It is the case, however, that hundreds of millions of people do live well on diets in which at least four-fifths of the calories and most of the protein are provided by a staple, or mixture of staples; and it is also the case that many modern nutritionists are now urging western people to move back to a more traditional diet, in which staples play a larger part. By far the greatest single task to be undertaken in the feeding of human beings is to grow sufficient staples. If we can do that we will have broken the back of the world's food problems.

The seed staples fall into three main groups: the cereals, which are the most important; the pulses; and a miscellaneous band of grains and nuts (or nut-like seeds) from a wide variety of families.

Seed staples – 1: the cereals

Cereals are seeds of the grass family, Gramineae. Collectively, they are by far the most important food crops in the world. There are nine principal 'kinds' of cereal, though each 'kind' may in practice include several species, and each species may be sub-divided into hundreds of modern cultivars and thousands or tens of thousands of ancient 'primitive' varieties, or *landraces*. These cereals are wheat, rice, maize, barley, sorghum, the millets (including teff, from Ethiopia), rye, oats, and triticale.

The first four of these account for almost 90 per cent of all cereal production. Thus, out of roughly 1 700 million tonnes of cereal worldwide, wheat accounts for 450 million, rice for around 400 million, maize for 350 million, and barley for about 200 million tonnes.

Wheat includes various species of the genus *Triticum*. There are three main types: the primitive einkorn, little removed from the ancestral forms, which now is very little grown; *durum*, grown for pasta; and the many varieties of *Triticum aestivum*, the bread wheats. The difference between these three lies primarily in the number of sets of chromosomes they contain: einkorn, two sets; the durum wheats, four; and bread wheats, six. The subtleties and significance of these differences will be discussed later in chapters 4 and 6. Wheat is grown throughout the world, from the Arctic Circle in Canada, through the temperate lands of the United States, Europe, the Soviet Union, China, South America, Southern Africa, and South Australia, and into the vast sub-tropical wheat belt of India.

There are 22 species of rice, genus *Oryza*, of which two are cultivated: *Oryza glaberrima* is a minor crop, which was first cultivated in Niger about 3 500 years ago, and has remained in the swamps and wetlands of West Africa; and *Oryza sativa*, which is what most people mean by 'rice'.

For both wheat and rice, the most significant improvement in recent decades has been brought about by the introduction of semi-dwarfing genes. These result in plants with short stems. Short-stemmed varieties can be given heavy doses of fertilizer without growing so tall that they fall over; and as the dose of fertilizer is increased, so the yield of grain increases. Thus the most productive wheat lands of the United Kingdom and the Netherlands, and the most productive rice fields of the USA, Japan, and Australia, commonly average more than eight tonnes of grain per hectare, and record yields for both crops stand at more than 14 tonnes. This compares with yields of around one-and-a-half tonnes per hectare, which are common for rice in much of the Third World, and would have been common for wheat in Europe at the turn of this century. More importantly, the semi-dwarf varieties of wheat and rice between them have been responsible for the 'Green Revolution', which in the 1960s and 1970s vastly improved cereal production in much of

Figure 2.1 Rice under test in the Philippines. Worldwide, rice is second to wheat in tonnage, but is eaten by more people.

the Third World. High-yielding crops, requiring high inputs of fertilizer, are not appropriate in all conditions, however, and some high-yielding varieties of rice have been lacking in flavour, and have not proved popular. For this and other reasons the Green Revolution has had its failures. But the new varieties have taken countries such as India from the frontline of famine into a position of relative security.

Wheat and rice are the most important single crops in the world. But the 'value' of a crop cannot be assessed purely in terms of tonnage, or area devoted to it, or market value. On the face of it, for example, wheat is more 'important' than rice. But a large proportion of the world's wheat, especially that grown in the western world, is fed to livestock, whereas almost all the world's rice is eaten by human beings. Furthermore, people who rely on rice as a staple tend to rely upon it more heavily than do people who regard wheat as their staple. So rice undoubtedly feeds more people than does wheat, and makes a greater contribution to those people's diets.

Similarly, maize is a staple for many people in South and Central America and in Southern Africa, but most of the world's crop is used for animal feed or production of alcohol, for drink or fuel. Much of the world's barley production is fed to animals or used in brewing. Barley is a staple only in parts of the Soviet Union and temperate Asia. By contrast, sorghum and various millets account for only 6 per cent of the world's cereal production, but they are the principal cereals for the people who live in some of the world's harshest climates, in the near-

Figure 2.2 Breeders must often pay attention to characteristics that superficially seem of little consequence. When CIMMYT scientists provided Africans with an improved yellow maize the consumers rejected it – because the traditional colour is white.

desert conditions of the semi-arid tropics. These are the people who suffer famine when the rains fail. It could reasonably be argued that the improvement of these apparently 'minor' cereals could do more to insure against future famine than any other single exercise in crop improvement. In the past, these dry land crops have been much neglected. Now they are the principal objects of research at the International Crops Research Institute for the Semi-Arid Tropics, or ICRISAT, which was founded at Hyderabad in India in 1974 and has a new centre in the Sahel.

One incidental advantage of sorghum is that it can be used to make an excellent beer (I know it is excellent, because I have drunk it). It is a mixed fermentation, involving both yeasts and lactobacilli which are the bacteria responsible for making yoghurt. Accordingly, it has only a low alcohol content, and a refreshing acidity. It is also nutritious – particularly rich in B vitamins – because it is sold with the yeast still in suspension; in fact, the finished beer looks like cold Ovaltine. The people who at present drink sorghum beer are often prone to vitamin deficiency, and so, in context, the beer is probably nutritionally significant. More importantly, the production of sorghum beer can provide poor farmers with a source of income; they can grow some sorghum for subsistence, and sell the surplus for brewing. One of the main disincentives for increasing production at present is that it can be extremely difficult to dispose of surpluses, so the increased yields are produced at a loss.

Figure 2.3 Sorghum, one of the two principal cereals of the semi-arid tropics, is now being developed along various lines at ICRISAT.

Figure 2.4 A fine head of sorghum at ICRISAT. Improved disease resistance and still further resistance to drought are breeding priorities.

Figure 2.5 Millet: the most drought resistant of all cereals, and the staple crop of some of the world's poorest people. ICRISAT breeders are now exploring its full genetic potential.

Of the remaining cereals, oats (*Avena*) and rye (*Secale*) really have become minor crops: between them they account for only about 5 per cent of the world's cereal production. They have their supporters, however. Oats can withstand appalling conditions, as has been proved over many a century, in Scotland; though in truth oats grow world-wide, from Mexico to China. They are extremely nutritious, with a higher fat content than most cereals, and an excellent grade of dietary fibre. With the new-found enthusiasm for 'health-foods' in the West – and indeed for cereal-based diets in general – oats could enjoy a revival. Rye, similarly, is able to grow in appalling conditions; it is extremely hardy, and is one of the few cereals to tolerate sandy, acid soils. It is still a staple in parts of Eastern Europe, and produces several specialist forms of dark, heavy bread. Again, as the fashion for more cereal-based diets increases, rye could also enjoy a revival, and surely would repay improvement. Rye also is a cash-earner – the source of rye whisky – and its long, tough straw is traditionally used for thatch.

The remaining cereal is triticale (*Triticale*). This is a hybrid of wheat and rye, and is in fact a man-made species, indeed a man-made genus. It is the only new cereal to join the ranks in several thousand years. The method of its production involved some subtle exercises in cytogenetics, and is discussed in chapter 5. Suffice to say here that the original aim in producing the hybrid was to provide a crop that combined the

23

palatability of wheat with the hardiness of rye. To some extent that ambition has succeeded. Triticale is now grown all over the world. The Soviet Union is the biggest producer at present with around 300 000 hectares, while the United States, China, and Argentina are rapidly expanding their triticale production. It is sold in bread in North America, (where it is something of a gimmick) but would probably serve mainly as animal feed in Britain, and would be grown as a part of rotation, in place, say, of barley. Triticale has had plenty of teething troubles, as will be discussed in chapter 6; not the least of which has been a failure to set seed. But it definitely has a future, both in the rich world where it is grown intensively and harvested by combine, and in the poor world. Mexican hill farmers are already planting triticale with the aid of ox-ploughs, and harvesting it by hand. They say it makes excellent tortillas – the ubiquitous flat bread that traditionally is made with maize.

Seed staples – 2: the pulses

Pulses are the big nutritious seeds of plants of the Leguminosae: beans, lentils, peas, groundnuts and chickpeas. Of all plant foods, pulses are the richest in protein. Soya may contain up to 40 per cent, and many others around 20 per cent protein. Furthermore, two of the established pulses, soya and groundnut, are rich in high-grade edible oil.

However, as with sorghum and millet, the world statistics of pulse production fail to show their true importance. Thus the world's farmers produce less than 200 million tonnes per year of all pulses – roughly the same as the total for barley. Soya and groundnut are the only two pulses to feature among the world's top 25 crops in terms of tonnage, and both of them are grown primarily as oilseeds. In fact, soya alone accounts for half the world's total production of pulses; well over half the world's total of soya is grown in the United States; and 90 per cent of that grown in the United States is used for cooking oil and margarine, while the protein-rich residues go to feed livestock. About a quarter of the world's groundnuts is grown in India.

Yet the small amount of pulse that remains is a vital source of protein for poor people throughout the world. North Americans consume about twelve times as much meat per year as they do pulses, whereas Asians consume more pulses than meat. The pulses are important not only for the amount of protein they contain, but also for the quality of that protein. It is important that protein should contain a good proportion of *all* essential amino acids. Cereal protein tends to be poor in the essential amino acid lysine, but pulses are particularly rich in lysine. Nutritionally, therefore, pulses and cereals are a perfect foil for each other. It is a happy fact that the theme of pulse-with-cereal features in all the world's great peasant cuisines: rice or chapati with dhall (made from various beans, chickpeas, or pigeon peas) in India;

Figure 2.6 Groundnut: one of the most drought-resistant of all pulses and the most valuable of dry-land food crops.

Figure 2.7 Chickpea is one of the three principal pulses of the semi-arid tropics; again being improved at ICRISAT.

25

tortilla with frijoles (kidney beans) in Mexico; beans on toast in the United Kingdom; broad beans or chickpeas with pitta bread in the Mediterranean.

Finally, beans can make several different kinds of culinary contributions, and thus help to alleviate the tedium of simple diets. In China and Japan soya is made into bean curd (tofu), and fermented paste (miso) or sauce (soy sauce). It can also be made into 'milk'. Many other pulses lend themselves to such treatment; tempeh is another fermented paste eaten in South-East Asia, and the Vegetarian Society in the United Kingdom has shown that broad beans can produce excellent tempeh.

As members of the Leguminosae, pulse crops fix nitrogen, and therefore can be grown in very poor soils without fertilizer. However, if very high yields are required, then the crop must be given extra nitrogen. In practice, there is a pulse for every kind of condition, and every climate. Broad beans (*Vicia faba*) in particular are hardy, and may begin their cycle of growth in the North European winter. *Vicia faba* is also grown as a feed crop for livestock in Europe, and when thus grown it is known as the field bean. With a little improvement, field beans could be an excellent food for human beings, but broad beans in general prefer Mediterranean climates, and are an extremely important crop in Southern Europe and the Middle East.

Temperate climates, too, are suitable for the many types of kidney bean (*Phaseolus*), which are of particular importance in South and Central America. Soya (*Glycine*) prefers temperate to sub-tropical climates, while the dry tropics are the home of the chickpea (*Cicer arietinum*) and pigeon pea (*Cajanus cajan*). Groundnuts (*Arachis hypogaea*) can tolerate very dry conditions and produce valuable crops from unpromising terrain. Chickpea, pigeon pea, and groundnut are vital crops in India and have a great future in dry land Africa.

Several other pulses, however, deserve wider exploitation. The remarkable winged bean (*Psophocarpus tetragonolobus*) has attracted wide attention – and is now grown in 80 countries. Its seeds contain up to 40 per cent of protein when ripe – as much as soya. Even the leaves have a 7 per cent protein content and make an excellent vegetable. For good measure, the winged bean produces root tubers – which contain between 3 and 20 per cent of protein. The highlanders of New Guinea regard the tubers as the winged bean's greatest asset and the Thais make the tubers into crisps.

Dr A. S. Wehmeyer, of the National Nutrition Research Institute, Pretoria, has also drawn attention to *Bauhinia esculenta*. This is a vine, up to 18 feet long, that grows on open grassland. Its seeds are rich both in protein and fat – more than 30 per cent of both – and have an excellent flavour. Like the winged bean, *B. esculenta* produces tubers. These may reach a weight of 15 kilograms in 10 years and are an excellent vegetable. Dr Wehmeyer recommends widespread cultivation – for here is a crop that could do well with very little attention.

Figure 2.8a The thick stems of pigeon pea may seem superfluous but are valued for fuel and fencing.

Figure 2.8b Sometimes pigeon pea is best grown as an annual: sometimes it serves best as a perennial. ICRISAT breeders are developing both types.

For very dry conditions there is much to be said for the Bambara groundnut, *Voandzeia subterranea* – another versatile crop. Its oil-rich, protein-rich seeds can be eaten as a vegetable when young, or when dried and mature; and can be made into curds and milk. Its protein-rich leaves can be eaten as a vegetable or fed to livestock. But *Voandzeia* is even more drought-resistant than *Arachis*, and more resistant to pests and disease. It is now grown in South and Central America, Asia, and Australia, as well as its native Africa.

In general, the breeding of pulses has been neglected, compared with that of cereals. Some, including the broad bean and winged bean, have an unruly habit; they do not grow until their seeds are developed, and then stop, as cereals do, but continue to grow until the weather cuts them short. Some, including the broad bean, the kidney bean, and *Lathyrus sativus*, the grass pea, of India, are prone to toxicity – dangerously so, in the case of the grass pea (chapter 9). But if we are truly to feed ourselves without expropriating all the world's land then we should make more use of pulses. They deserve to be among the top priorities.

Seed staples – 3: a reserve list

There is no point in increasing the world's selection of cultivated crops just for the sake of it. There is plenty of work to be done in improving the present ones. There are, however, four good reasons for contemplating new varieties. The first is insurance: a disease that devastates any one crop is not likely, simultaneously, to attack another crop totally unrelated to it. The second is for gastronomic variety: if it is the case (as I believe it must be) that people in future will rely less upon meat for food then they must *ipso facto* rely more heavily upon staples – and those staples should be as varied as possible. The third reason is agronomic. Some environments are extremely harsh; and though some varieties of present-day crops may grow in some of those environments, it is always worth seeking species that are even better adapted. Finally, there are reasons that have to do with ways of life. As the world becomes more crowded, so it becomes imperative to use each stretch of land for more than one purpose. In particular, the few remaining areas of 'wilderness' could serve not only as havens of wildlife and sources of fuel, but increasingly as sources of human food: places where food could be gathered, rather than officiously cultivated. In short, we should forever be seeking nutritious plants that can reasonably be left to look after themselves in the wild – or almost wild.

There are plants, at present underexploited, that meet one or several of these criteria. Six in particular are particularly worthy of discussion as additional staples.

The first of these is buckwheat, *Fagopyrum*, of the Polygonaceae. It is of proven culinary value: the Russians make kasha from it, the

Figure 2.9   The seeds of amaranth, a relative of the garden herb Love-lies-bleeding, were a staple for the Aztecs. With help from breeders, the potential of amaranth worldwide could again be realized.

Figure 2.10   Descendants of the Incas winnowing the non-cereal grain, quinoa: still a staple on the Andes, and with much to offer the rest of the world.

29

Americans make pancakes, and the Indians and Chinese turn it into pasta and noodles. It grows in cool and moist areas, and in tropical highlands.

Two other crops for highland areas are the amaranths, *Amaranthus*, and quinoa, *Chenopodium quinoa*. Amaranths were traditional grain crops of the Aztecs; largely destroyed by the conquistadores, who were anxious to obliterate the culture of the people they vanquished. Amaranth seeds are versatile – they can be popped or parched, and made into gruels or flour. Their merits are now recognized, and more are now grown in Asia, especially India, than in their native Americas. But as the National Academy of Sciences points out, there are many types of amaranth, belonging to several different species; and it is yet to be established which is most suitable for specific conditions.

The Aztecs also grew quinoa, as did the Indians of the Eastern United States, at least 2 000 years ago, and the Incas; indeed quinoa is still grown on the Andes for bread, biscuits and porridge. Again, the conquistadores largely put paid to the crops – unwisely, because it is highly nutritious (12–19 per cent protein, according to the National Academy of Sciences) and extremely hardy. It is, in fact, of potential value to mountain people everywhere.

Desert or semi-desert could well be enriched by a wild grass from Australia, *Echinochloa turnerana*. This is almost untried as a cultivated crop, but even in its wild, unimproved form it produces fine crops – and does so, furthermore, after only one or two downpours of rain, totalling no more than 100 millimetres in a year.

Several kinds of seeds from trees have at times served various societies as staples. The most notable is the coconut, which is a major staple of the Pacific. Dr Wehmeyer recommends two trees that are far less widely known, but have great potential for dry lands: *Sclerocarya caffra*, alias the marula; and *Ricinodendron rautanenii*, alias the mongongo, of the family Euphorbiaceae. The fruit of the marula is prolific, and like a guava. The seeds are hard and the embryos only small – yet they contain 23–31 per cent protein, and 56–61 per cent oil. The Phalaborwa people of the northern Transvaal rely so heavily on the marula that theirs has been called a 'marula culture'. The fruit of the mongongo will keep for months if dried; and its seeds are high in protein (around 28 per cent) and fat (58 per cent), which is highly polyunsaturated. Mongongos grow in Botswana and Ovamboland, and both Bushmen and Bantu rely heavily upon them. Such trees could be allowed to grow wild, or semi-wild, even if they were first 'improved'. And if they were improved, what might be achieved?

Surely, however, the most bizarre environment in which to contemplate the cultivation of staple foods is on the bottom of the sea. But eelgrass, *Zostera marina*, of the monocot family Zosteraceae, grows on the sea-bed all around the world; and Mexican Indians have the sense to harvest its admirable seeds. Others could too.

The list doubtless could be extended. But we should pass on to the second prime group of staples – the tubers.

In general, tubers are less nutritious than seeds, with a higher water content, and a protein content that is nearer to 2 per cent than to 10 per cent. Nevertheless, whole societies have at times subsisted almost entirely on various kinds of tuber, which may not be socially desirable, but demonstrates that they can indeed provide most of what human beings need to stay alive.

Tubers, between them, again span the climatic range; from cool damp mountain or lowland (potato) to wet tropics and even marsh (cocoyam and taro) to tropical dry lands (cassava). We may usefully consider tubers under three headings: potatoes; cassava; and the rest – yams, sweet potatoes, cocoyam and taro.

Tuberous staples – 1: the potato

The world produces around 270 million tonnes of potatoes per year, and yet more could be made of them. The world view of them is changing. In the 19th century they were seen as the desperate fodder of societies that were hopelessly deprived: described as 'the lazy root' by William Cobbett at the beginning of the 19th century; almost the sole item of diet for many Irish and western Scottish people, until devastated by the blight, *Phytophthera infestans*, in the 1840s; depicted by van Gogh as ultimate symbols of degradation in 'The Potato Eaters', at the end of the century. In the 20th century nutritionists largely wrote them off, as being 'fattening', and 'stodge'.

Now it is clear that they are excellent food, with a modest but adequate content of protein of excellent quality. They also provide far more protein per hectare than a field of cereal. And although their content of vitamin C is also modest they are in practice the greatest single source of the vitamin in much of northern Europe because people eat so many of them. They are far from fattening: a kilo of boiled potatoes supplies only 800 kilocalories, which means the average Westerner would need to eat three to four kilograms per day (about nine pounds) to match present calorie intakes. Boiled or baked potatoes do in fact feature in many a modern slimming diet. They become highly calorific only when cooked in fat: chips (what the Americans call 'French fries') are at least three times as calorific as boiled potatoes, weight for weight, with most of the calories supplied by the fat.

There are many directions in which potatoes could develop, some of which we will examine in later chapters. Three points are of outstanding interest, however. The first is the enormous culinary interest of potatoes that has yet to be widely tapped. Westerners grow only one species, *Solanum tuberosum*, which is a descendant of *S. andigena* and also now tends to contain genes from related species. *S. tuberosum*

31

alone provides an extraordinary variety of flavours, textures, and colours – floury, waxy, red, blue, white, white-fleshed and yellow-fleshed, and so on. Yet there are 154 different recorded species of potato in South and Central America, and the people of the Andes cultivate seven of them, of which *S. andigena* is the most important. Within those seven species they have developed thousands of landraces, which offer a quite extraordinary range of flavour, colour, and texture, some of which are highly prized by the few connoisseurs who are aware of them. The new western fashion for high-fibre, high-carbohydrate diets has already raised the status of the potato; and if only a part of its extraordinary culinary potential were exploited, that fashion could be not only beneficial, but also very pleasurable.

Secondly, potatoes lend themselves well to modern techniques of tissue culture (chapter 6). New varieties produced in culture are already being tried in the field; and 'engineered' potatoes, containing various genes from some of the many other species of *Solanum* and perhaps of the closely related tomato, *Lycopersicon*, will soon be grown commercially. In short, potatoes not only have wide potential but are also amenable to very rapid improvement.

Thirdly, potatoes so far have remained crops of temperate lands, and of moist cool highlands – in the Himalayas of Nepal and many other mountain ranges, as well as on their native Andes. But Dr Alan Thomson and his colleagues at the Plant Breeding Institute (PBI) in Cambridge, United Kingdom, are now preparing varieties, or mixtures of varieties, adapted to the tropics. Potatoes are superior to most tropical roots in various ways, and could be a great boon. Again we see that new crops can be developed by extending the range of existing ones, as well as by taming a new species.

Tuberous staples – 2: cassava

Cassava, *Manihot esculenta*, of the family Euphorbiaceae, is also a major crop: more than 120 million tonnes are produced worldwide. *M. esculenta* originated in South America, where is has evidently been cultivated for 4 000 years; Brazil is still the biggest single producer, with 25 million tonnes. But Africa and Asia also now produce around 40 million tonnes each.

Cassava is versatile, both in agronomic and gastronomic terms: it will tolerate drought, and, when harvested, can be fried, roasted, boiled, sun-dried or fermented. One major disadvantage is that some varieties contain hydrogen cyanide, and the crop must be carefully prepared. Another is its low content of protein – a mere 1 per cent. Reducing the toxicity, raising the nutritional value, and increasing resistance to pests are all outstanding priorities for research.

Figure 2.11 Cassava is the second most important of the world's tuberous crops, after potato. This crop is in Thailand.

Tuberous staples – 3: a miscellany

The world's tropical farms and gardens also produce about 130 million tonnes of tuberous roots of about a dozen other species, belonging to three different botanical families. Chief of these is *Ipomoea batata* of the bindweed family, Convolvulaceae. This is the sweet potato: about 100 million tonnes are grown every year, as an annual in temperate countries such as the United States and Spain, and as a perennial in the tropics worldwide.

Yams, of the genus *Dioscorea*, family Dioscoraceae, account for another 20 million tonnes: Nigeria provides well over half of this but yams also feature in South-East Asia and tropical America. Yams are highly varied: several species are eaten, including some wild ones in times of hunger, but they have a tendency to be toxic. Indeed, their use as food competes to some extent with their value as a source of compounds – steroids – for drugs. However, the best varieties have a high protein content, of around 6 per cent. The wide genetic base of the yams offers tremendous scope for improvement and it would be a pity if they were allowed to decline.

The National Academy of Sciences suggests, however, that the most neglected tuberous roots with outstanding potential are those of the cuckoo-pint family, *Araceae*. Two principal genera are involved.

33

Figure 2.12   Sweet potatoes serve both as a staple and as a flavoursome vegetable, throughout the tropics. These are in a Ugandan market.

Figure 2.13   The cocoyam, relative of the taro, is declining in the tropics though its tubers are nutritious and palatable. It deserves more research.

Figure 2.14   Taro is grown commercially only in a few regions, such as Hawaii, as here; but it has great potential for low-lying wetlands throughout the tropics.

Xanthosoma includes about half a dozen edible species known as cocoyams; and *Colocasia esculenta* grows in various forms, including taro and dasheen. Cocoyams will grow by rivers, in land that is too wet for sweet potatoes and yams. Taro, which is widely grown but is a commercial crop only in Egypt, the Phillipines, and parts of the Pacific and Caribbean, can be grown in flooded paddies, like rice. Dasheen is the dry land version of taro: and although it is neglected, it is highly popular in China, Japan, and tropical Asia. It is good food: though low in protein, it produces easily-digestible flour. It even has export potential.

These, then, are the principal crops that serve the world as staples. The seed crops and some of the tubers, taken alone, can provide most of the human diet: virtually all the energy, most of the protein, some fat in some cases, and a variety, though by no means a complete range, of vitamins and minerals. However, a diet consisting only of staples would be tedious in the extreme, and would not be sustaining, because people find it physically difficult to eat sufficient quantities of food that is too boring. Even in times of famine, people may literally be unable to stomach a completely bland diet, however 'nutritious' it may be in theory.

It is essential, then, to augment the basic diet of staples with other food plants, with a variety of flavours. Some of these – spices – make no contribution to nutrition, or at least only a marginal contribution. Some, however, do provide energy, vitamins, minerals, and indeed some protein, in addition to providing flavour. These might be called 'secondary food plants', though they are more commonly known as 'fruit and vegetables'. We will consider them under three headings: leaves, fruits, and roots.

Secondary foods: leaves, fruits and roots

Leaves

That leaves may provide a significant source of protein has been emphasized in particular by N. W. Pirie of the Rothamsted Experimental Station, United Kingdom. There is far more protein in a hectare of green leaves than in a hectare of cereal or potato, and far more than could be produced in that same hectare if it were devoted to livestock. To be sure, as Mr Pirie points out, the protein in leaves tends to be too dilute for human beings – diluted both by water and by fibre. Unlike cattle, we are not equipped anatomically to eat enough leaves to satisfy daily protein needs; and a secondary problem is that many leaves tend to be mildly toxic, and individual types probably should not be eaten in vast amounts. For such reasons Mr Pirie has suggested that the protein-rich pulp should be extracted from leaves, and served as human food, while the fibre-rich residues could feed cattle. There have been and are several enterprises in train for extracting leaf protein.

Even without extraction, however, leaves could be, and for some people probably are, a significant source of protein as well as of vitamins (such as A and C) and of minerals. In addition, there now is evidence that even the fibre in leaves is broken down in the colon by bacteria, to provide volatile fatty acids (VFAs) which can be absorbed by the colon and metabolised as a source of energy. For most people VFAs are at best a marginal source of energy, but for people on marginal diets they could well be a critical source.

The leaves that serve as useful sources of protein for human beings (and as significant sources of vitamin A) are those classed as 'dark and green'. Edible dark green leaves in practice come principally from two families: the Chenopodiaceae, which provide various types of spinach; and the Cruciferae, which contain the astonishing genus *Brassica* – the leafiest examples of which are the cabbages. Other families also contribute, however: the Polygonaceae are the source of sorrel; many legume leaves are extremely nutritious, including those of the winged bean; cassava leaves (Euphorbiaceae) are eaten, and so too are those of amaranths (Amaranthaceae). Other members of the Chenopodiaceae deserve to be considered as sources of good edible leaves, including Good King Henry and fat hen.

The National Academy of Sciences draws attention too to chaya, *Cnidoscolus chaymansa* and *C. aconitifolius*. This is a shrub, which can grow to two metres; another member of the Euphorbiaceae. At present it is to be found in Mexico and Honduras, in thickets and open spaces, and often in rocky places. It endures heavy rain, but also tolerates drought – and springs back to life when the rains return. Chaya, surely, has potential in both Africa and Asia.

Fruits

Fruits are sometimes sweet (apples, pears, apricots) and sometimes savoury (tomato, cucumber, capsicums). In either case they are valuable sources of flavour and of cash for growers, but in western countries their nutritional contribution in general is marginal. They do provide some dietary fibre and some vitamins, but although some fruit may be extremely rich in some vitamins, their overall contribution to nutrition tends to be small, because they are not eaten in large amounts. Thus blackcurrants and oranges are extremely rich in vitamin C, but the greatest single source of vitamin C in Britain is the potato. Its vitamin C content is modest, but it is eaten in large amounts. But of course for babies, and other people in special situations who do not eat large amounts of potatoes, fruits such as orange and blackcurrant can be invaluable.

In poor countries, however, fruit may have far greater nutritional as well as culinary significance. Vitamin A deficiency is a serious problem among children throughout the tropics; it is a major cause of blindness. Fruits such as mango (Anacardiaceae) and papaya (Caricaceae), which grow throughout the tropics, could largely solve this problem, if only people fed them to their children. Many tropical fruits, too, are rich in energy, and could make a significant contribution to a marginal diet. My own favourite is the sapodilla, with its sticky flesh like brown sugar, of the family Sapotaceae. The nutritional contribution is enhanced in general if the seeds are eaten, for they tend to be high in fat and protein. Even the flesh of some fruits is rich in protein; that of the mongongo, for instance.

Fruit trees can be allowed to grow more or less wild: a free resource. Even in the west this tradition is upheld: people feel they have a 'right' to their free autumn harvest of blackberries and elderberries; and the Chinese people of New York gather the fruits of the ginkgo trees in Central Park. In the poor tropics such harvest, from well-chosen trees, can turn a poor and tedious diet into something perfectly acceptable.

The point is, however, that most tropical fruit species are, at present, wild plants. Their yield and nutritiousness could be vastly improved, just as has been achieved with other crops. Here is a potentially very important task, waiting to be tackled.

Roots

Some roots serve as staples. Others, generally lower in their content of protein or concentration of energy, and perhaps too flavoursome to be eaten in large amounts, serve instead as vegetables. Many families contribute: the Umbelliferae gives us carrot and parsnip; scorzonera and salsify are from the Compositae; turnips, swedes, and the various types of radish, from the Cruciferae.

Such roots serve primarily as sources of flavour and interest, but they also make a significant nutritional contribution in much traditional cooking: the carrots in carrot cake and boiled-beef-and-carrots are not simply there for variety. And again, it is in poor societies that such contributions can cease to be marginal. Thus in the highlands of the Andes from Venezuela to Bolivia people grow arracacha, alias the Peruvian parsnip, *Arracacia xanthorrhiza*. It is another umbellifer, with large thick roots. It is less nutritious than the potato, but costs only half as much to plant, and indeed is often interplanted with it. According to the National Academy of Sciences, it could have a fine future in tropical or sub-tropical highlands the world over − East and Central Africa, India, South-East Asia and New Guinea.

Leaves, fruits, and roots contribute both flavour and nutrient. The 'tertiary' foods contribute only flavour − or at least, their contribution of nutrient is so close to zero that it is not significant. They are nonetheless necessary, as well as very valuable in cash terms, and should be considered next.

Tertiary foods: spices and the rest

There is a whole class of foods whose role is purely or principally to provide flavour − plus, in many cases, some extra pharmacological boost. They include spices and herbs, plus tea, coffee, cola, and chocolate. In fact, the seeds of coffee, cola, and chocolate do contain significant amounts of various vitamins and protein, fat, and carbo-hydrate, but they are not consumed in great enough quantities to make a significant nutritional contribution.

Although these 'tertiary' foods make little or no nutritional con tribution, they are extremely important. If the projected world population of 10 billion people is to survive then people must in general subsist on a simple diet − one with a very high proportion of staples. But such diets are not tolerable for long unless they are made interesting, and herbs and spices can make them so. Drinks such as coffee and tea also have an enormous psychological impact, in addition to their contribution of flavour. Many working class people in the United Kingdom at the end of the 19th century and through the early

20th, subsisted largely on bread, with only a little jam. Such diets and the social conditions that led to them are obviously highly undesirable. The point is, however, that they were made tolerable, or just about, because accompanied by tea, which turned virtual prison fare into the semblance of a hot meal. The diets of the future should be better than bread and jam; but however good they are, tea and coffee can make them better. Spices also may have antibiotic properties, and can serve to preserve meat, which is particularly worthwhile in regions where refrigeration is unreliable. Thus Paul Richards in *Indigenous Agricultural Revolution* (Hutchinson, London, 1985) notes that extremely poor people in Africa may spend some of their last few coppers on spices – and comments that this can be a wise investment.

Secondly, tertiary crops are an excellent source of cash, and provide some of the main sources of foreign exchange for many poor tropical countries. It is very obvious that this is not an unequivocal benefit. Production of vital food crops has often been neglected in favour of producing cash crops; research effort has often concentrated upon commodity crops at the expense of essential foods; and the money earned from cash crops has often served only to enrich the elite, and enslave the majority. However, such abuses are not inevitable. Countries that are run benignly and democratically and which do concentrate first upon feeding their own populations, can nonetheless earn foreign exchange from commodity crops; and could, at least in theory, use the income for the benefit of the people. In practice, sale of agricultural produce, plus tourism, are the only possible sources of foreign exchange for many countries. It's as well that the produce should be as highly-priced as possible; and spices, herbs, tea, coffee, cola and cocoa are the most highly priced crops of all.

There is none, however, that cannot be improved. Improvement in these cases means higher yield, of course; but in particular means higher resistance to disease, and a higher concentration of whatever the vital ingredient happens to be.

The fourth category of food crops are also valued largely for their contribution to flavour and texture. But, for good and evil, they also contribute a large proportion of the world's food energy. These are the oil seeds and sugar crops.

Oilseeds and sugar crops

Oilseeds make a vital contribution to world's nutrition and play a crucial role in agricultural economy; there can be no doubt of that. A few years ago nutritionists believed that the greatest single deficiency in world production was in protein. Now it is widely agreed that energy is the greatest single desideratum – and flavour. Fat, whether in the form of plant oil or animal fat, is the most concentrated form of food energy, providing twice as many calories per unit weight as does starch or sugar. A hectare of oil palms provides many times more food calories than a hectare of rice. Fat also enhances palatability and acts as a lubricant. Thus, dry crackers are virtually uneatable, whereas crackers with butter can be eaten indefinitely. The value of fat in poor societies has been admirably illustrated in the Gambia, by nutritionists from the Dunn Nutrition Laboratory, Cambridge, United Kingdom. They found that nursing mothers were unable to consume sufficient calories in a day to sustain lactation, not because food was unavailable, but because the grains and tubers they did have were too bulky and fibrous, and the mothers were physically unable to eat enough. When fat was added, the problem was solved.

On the other hand, there can be little doubt that a large proportion of the world's people eat too much fat. Westerners obtain more than 40 per cent of their calories from fat, while for many Asians the proportion is less than 10 per cent. Many reports in recent years from governments and learned societies have suggested that a very high intake of fat predisposes to coronary heart disease and to certain forms of cancer, including those of the breast and bowel. All these conditions are now common in the West, but are almost unknown in societies with a low fat intake. Plant oil tends in general to be less saturated than animal fat, and may be less likely to predispose to heart disease; but most nutritional reports emphasize that total fat intake is probably more significant than the precise nature of the fat.

In addition, though the world's people may be primarily short of food in general rather than of protein in particular, this does not mean that they do not require protein at all. In general, it seems to be extremely important to maintain a proper ratio of energy to protein in the diet, though nutritionists are far from agreed as to what the proper ratio actually is. Different individuals clearly require different amounts, depending on their age, sex, whether or not they are pregnant, way of life, state of health, and their individual quirks of metabolism. However, if people consume large amounts of fat, which is pure energy, then the question arises as to where they will obtain a correspondingly concentrated form of protein, to balance that energy. One answer, presumably, is 'meat': but most nutritionists now argue that a high-fat, high-meat diet is not desirable.

The answer seems to be that there is definitely a role for fat sources in the diet, and that, in general, animal fats should give way to plant oils. Clearly the fat intake of Westerners is too high; but then, the fat intake of huge numbers of people in the world is probably too low, so on nutritional grounds alone there is room for further expansion.

Already, of course, oilseed production is very big business throughout the world. The world's leader is the soya bean, in temperate to sub-tropical regions. The spectrum of oil crops is widening, however. In temperate regions, major oil sources now are rape and mustard, of the Cruciferae: sunflower of the Compositae, with the related safflower a minor addition; and olive, of the ash and lilac family, Oleaceae. In the wet tropics, oil palm and coconut palm of the Palmae dominate, while groundnut, of the Leguminosae, is an extremely valuable crop in the dry tropics. The prospects for oil palm and coconut are now being transformed by tissue culture, as discussed in chapter 6, while sunflower became a major crop through subtle exploitation of male sterility, as discussed in chapters 4 and 5.

The search for new oil seeds should continue: the National Academy of Sciences suggests that the buffalo gourd, *Cucurbita foetidissima* of the Cucurbitaceae shows promise in barren, dry lands. The Academy recommends species of *Caryocar*, south American trees of the Caryocaraceae, which are little known outside their own countries, but have tremendous promise in the wet tropics; the palm *Jessenia polycarpa*, whose oil is like olive oil; and the babassu palm of South America, *Orbignya* spp., whose seeds resemble coconuts but contain even more oil.

The role of sugar in the world's diet is considerably more equivocal than that of fat. In some countries in the West, sugar accounts for more than 20 per cent of total energy intake. Few nutritionists have anything good to say about it. It is virtually the sole cause of caries, is a major contributor to obesity, and is probably a major cause of adult-onset diabetes. However, it is widely used in food processing not only for its flavour, but also as a preservative and texturizer; its high energy content is almost an embarrassment to the processors. In addition, whereas we might argue that many traditional diets could usefully be augmented by more fat, there are many instances of traditional diets being effectively corrupted by an influx of sugar. In general, fat can be integrated into the diet, whereas sugar, often in the form of soft drinks, is simply superimposed on it.

The fact is, however, that both sugar cane, *Saccharum* spp., and sugar beet, *Beta vulgaris*, are major crops. Cane, from the tropics and sub-tropics, totals almost 800 million tonnes per year, while beet, from temperate countries, totals nearly 300 million tonnes. Out of those crops, more than 100 million tonnes of sugar are extracted.

The contribution of breeders to sugar crops is marvellous and intricate, and we will discuss cane in particular in chapters 5 and 6. It is to be regretted that it does not play a less equivocal role in world nutrition. However, Brazil in particular now grows sugar largely as feedstock for fuel alcohol. This may become its principal role.

The final category of crops is of those that feed livestock.

Crops for livestock

It has often been argued in recent years that to raise animals for food is pernicious. Four kinds of argument are brought to bear. The first is that as the world grows more crowded it is essential to make best use of land: maximum energy and protein must be produced per unit area. In general, the most productive of all livestock systems, which would be dairy cows, produce only a fraction of the calories and energy that could be produced from the same land if wheat or potatoes were raised instead. *Ergo*, the argument runs, livestock production is profligate.

In addition, intensive livestock of all kinds are now raised to a large extent on grain; but the protein content of the meat, eggs, or milk that the animals provide is only a fraction of the protein in the original plants (about a tenth, in the case of beef). Again, livestock production appears to be profligate; and as humans can live on grain, cereal-fed livestock actually may compete with human beings for food. Thus, half the wheat grown in Britain is fed to livestock, plus a high proportion of the barley; and by far the greater share of North American maize and soya is destined to be fed to animals.

Thirdly, as we have mentioned, many nutritionists have suggested in recent years that Western people eat far too much fat. Saturated fat is widely considered to be more pernicious than polyunsaturated: and animal fats are highly saturated.

Finally, more and more people are concerned that livestock farming, and slaughter, are cruel. Highly intensive systems, involving battery cages for poultry or weaner pools for pigs, are chronically stressful. Traditional systems may be no better: sheep die of exposure on the United Kingdom hills, and livestock of all classes may die of hunger and thirst in the dry tropics.

In short, some have argued on economic, nutritional, and moral grounds that livestock production should be severely curtailed, or indeed virtually eliminated. Lacto-ovo vegetarians consume milk, eggs, and in some cases also fish, but eschew meat, while vegans reject all animal products.

All of these arguments are justified to some extent. Livestock production can be profligate, and often is. The production of very fat beasts to over-feed people who are already over-fed, is nonsense. Animals must be kept humanely. When all the arguments are put, however, it remains the case that livestock production, sensibly orchestrated and controlled, must continue to play a large part in feeding people.

Thus, although livestock is often kept on land that could grow crops, and often is given food that could feed people, this is not necessarily the case. Grazing and browsing animals – cattle, sheep, goats, horses, camels – can be kept on land on which it is too dry, too steep, too wet, too cold, too salty or too rocky to grow worthwhile amounts of food crops. If people did not graze sheep on the hills of Greece, or goats and sheep on the commons of India, or cattle, camels, and goats over much of the semi-desert of Africa, then those lands would simply produce nothing. Granted, over much of the world grazing is uncontrolled, and the land is severely degraded. But this is not inevitable. As M. M. Coughenour of the International Livestock Centre for Africa at Addis Ababa and his colleagues recently described in *Science*, pastureland that is properly managed – either by traditional rules, or by imposition of modern grazing practices – can sustain large numbers of animals, and hence of people, indefinitely.

In addition, animals can eat a great many things that human beings find unpalatable, or simply cannot utilize. Thus pigs and poultry were traditionally kept on scraps – and still are, in villages all over the world. Enormous numbers can be kept in this way: thus as Professor Georg Borgstrom pointed out in *The Hungry Planet* (Collier Books, London, 1965) China after its revolution managed to feed as many hogs on scraps as the United States managed by feeding grain. In addition, cattle can utilize straw as a principal source of calories. All grain crops produce straw, which human beings cannot eat to any useful purpose.

Even the feeding of grain to livestock is justified, if not taken to extremes. The world must in general contrive to produce a surplus of staples, to insure against bad years. Most years ther will be a surplus – which can be fed to livestock. In very bad years the livestock are slaughtered, but for most of the time they provide a 'reserve population'. Then again, in countries where fodder production is seasonal, it may be worth feeding animals some grain during the off season so that more livestock may be kept, to make better use of grazing in the good season. Thus United Kingdom hill farmers may feed grain to sheep during the long winters, so they have enough sheep to make full use of the extensive grazing in summer.

Then again, animals may fulfill many other functions, besides that simply of producing food. In India, the water buffalo and zebu provide leather and fertilizer and fuel in the form of dung, as well as milk and meat. But in addition, and crucially, they are the principal form of transport in rural areas; and on small farms they are of far more use than a tractor would be, even if the farmers could afford tractors.

Finally, although it is true that human beings can be healthy on a vegan diet, and true, too, that some people eat too much meat, it is none the less the case that livestock can and does fill important nutritional roles. Nutritionists no longer argue that human beings need vast amounts of protein, as they did in the 1950s and 1960s; staple crops in general provide enough. Nonetheless, it is as well to underwrite the protein supply, and a small amount of meat, fish, milk or eggs can guarantee both quality and quantity. Animal products also provide some nutrients that can be difficult to obtain in adequate amounts from

43

plant sources, including minerals such as zinc, vitamins such as B12 and B2, and some essential fatty acids. Finally, animal products are an outstanding source of flavour, the importance of which we have stressed. A few pieces of pork and cabbage added to the bowl of rice turns a boring exercise in sustenance into a fine meal.

As domestic animals are important, then so too are the plants that sustain them. The provision of suitable grains, food crops that provide nutritious residues, and plants for pastureland of all grades – from the dry lands of Africa to the lush pastures of the United Kingdom and Ireland – is thus an important task for plant breeders everywhere.

In practice, enterprises for producing feed crops are as varied in intensity as those for producing arable crops. In much of Europe grass is often grown as a 'break' crop – part of the rotation, between crops of cereal. In such situations, very highly bred varieties of grass are employed, particularly rye-grass, *Lolium*. The breeding of grass is complicated; a subtle compromise between biomass and hardiness, as discussed in chapter 9.

At the other end of the spectrum, there is much to be done to improve the world's permanent pastures, which cover a quarter of the land mass in the world – two and a half times as much as is devoted to arable crops. Much of this land is severely degraded, and little is used to anything like its full capacity. Improvement is far from simple. Above all, it depends upon good management, including proper rotation of stock. But in India, for example, much of the grazing land is officially common land, and land that is common is under nobody's direct control, so the necessary reforms cannot be made; or, if 'improvements' are made, they are often to the benefit of only a minority.

But even when management is possible, the use of grazing lands is always a subtle exercise in ecology. Often, for example, there would be much to be gained from applying fertilizer. But there may be no point in doing this unless rainfall is adequate, or unless the species present are able to make use of it, or unless there are enough animals to consume the additional vegetation – though not so many as to result in over-grazing.

However, research is being done, in Australia, India, Bangladesh, and the International Livestock Centre for Africa at Addis Ababa in Ethiopia; and principles are emerging. In particular, the value of leguminous plants is that they fix nitrogen, and so effectively fertilize themselves. But it is now becoming clear that many of the world's clovers and medicks could contribute far more than they do if only they were given just a little phosphorus. The provision of legumes-plus-phosphorus has transformed grazing in Australia, and promises now to do so in Ethiopia. Indeed, as L. 't Mannetje and K. F. O'Connor comment in *Advances in Legume Science* (Summerfield and Bunting (eds.), 1980), 'The total beef production of 7.7 million tonnes a year could be doubled if only 25 per cent of the area were improved through the use of legumes and appropriate fertilizer.'

These are early days, however. The wild or semi-wild plants of Ethiopia that people rely upon so heavily have yet to be fully identified. Beyond doubt, too, many new species could with advantage be transferred from their native countries into grazing lands elsewhere. The National Academy of Sciences provides a highly intriguing shortlist. This includes *Acacia albida*, a leguminous tree from Africa, which bears leaves only in the dry season and sheds them during the rains, and whose leaves are enjoyed by camels, cattle, and sheep alike. Then there is the ramon, *Brosimum alicastrum*, from Central America; this is of the mulberry family, Moraceae, a tree of moist forest that also tolerates drought. *Cassia sturtii*, another legume, this time from Australia, is proving to have great potential as a fodder crop in the Negev, in Israel. Salinity is also a problem in much of the world's grazing land. Accordingly the National Academy of Sciences draws attention to various saltbushes of the genus *Atriplex*, of the Chenopodiaceae, which 'excrete' surplus salt through their leaves. Best of all, perhaps, however, is the remarkable tamarugo *Prosopis tamarugo*, another leguminous bush, this time from Chile. It is an evergreen, and flourishes in areas where the salt lies a metre thick on the surface.

If the world's grazing lands were well-managed, and well-stocked with appropriate plants, they could transform the prospects of the whole world. Not only could they support vast numbers of people, but could also serve as important centres for a wide variety of wildlife. At the moment, plant breeders have hardly begun to get to work on them; indeed, as we have seen, the plants themselves have hardly yet been identified. The next hundred years could bring disaster to those vast lands; or they could bring incomparable improvement.

These, then, are the world's principal food and feed crops. The task is to make them better, so that they serve our purposes more precisely. This is done by plant breeding, and plant breeding is an exercise in the acquisition of appropriate genes, and the shuffling of existing ones. In principle, plant breeding is easy. In practice, it is immensely complicated and time consuming. One reason why this is so is that plant reproductive biology of plants is complex, and the breeder must either respect those complexities or else employ extraordinary measures to overcome them. We will discuss those complexities in chapter 4. But the other reason why plant breeding in practice is difficult is that heredity itself is far from straightforward. We will examine the reasons for this in the next chapter.

3   Mendel and After

Introduction

Plant breeding, on the face of it, seems to be a delightfully simple exercise. In the simplest cases of all, it involves two stages. First the breeder produces a plant that has a range of desirable characteristics, or *characters*. Then he multiplies that 'elite' plant to provide a large number of facsimiles or near facsimiles for distribution to the farmers.

The first part of the exercise involves *selection* and *crossing*. In practice, selection normally comes first; the breeder or the farmer selects the best-looking plants from whatever he has available. Then comes crossing; he finds two plants, each of which have some desirable characters but both of which fall somewhat short of perfection, and pollinates one with the other. Some of the offspring inevitably combine the undesirable characters of each parent; most have some desirable characters and a great many undesirable ones; but some will include a fair proportion of the desirable characters of both parents. These, then, are selected, and re-crossed, and re-selected, and so on, until he has the plant he desires.

Nowadays, for the purposes of crossing, the breeder in theory has access to the whole world of plants. If he seeks to produce a plant with resistance to some arcane pest, then he finds a cultivated variety of the crop, or some wild relative, and crosses with that. And in the fulness of time, as all the world now knows, he will not need actually to cross the plants. He will merely expropriate the relevant genes from wherever they occur by means of genetic engineering. Nothing could be simpler.

The second part of the task seems straightforward enough, too. Here the breeder has two alternatives. In some cases, he simply allows his elite plants to breed by sexual means, and so produces copies of the originals in the form of seeds. In other cases – potatoes, apples, strawberries – he makes use of asexual reproduction; taking cuttings or tubers, and offering them to the grower.

The rock upon which all breeding programmes are founded – of dairy cattle and guinea-pigs, as well as of plants – is the fact of inheritance. Parents pass on a selection of their own characters to their offspring; like, by and large, does produce like. Offspring combine some of the characters of both their parents, and then in turn pass on that combination to their offspring. This has been appreciated as an empirical fact for many thousands of years. After all, the ancient Persians were accomplished breeders of horses.

Nowadays this empirical knowledge is underpinned by the science of genetics. We know that each character of each organism is determined by its possession of particular *genes*. The external form of the organism is called the *phenotype*, but the phenotype is determined by the underlying arrangement of genes, the *genotype*. And the reason that different individuals in the same population are different, is that each of the genes that circulate within any one population may exist in more than one version – each version being known as an *allele*. Each parent passes on half of its genes to each offspring. Each offspring, therefore, finishes up with the same number of genes as each of its parents, with half being derived from one parent, and half from the other. But each parent may have different versions of the same genes, so the particular combination of alleles in the offspring will be unique to itself – not exactly the same as in either parent.

Such knowledge makes the whole business of plant breeding much easier, and certainly much more precise. In the past, breeders had to rely purely upon their knowledge of the external appearance, the phenotype, of the plants. The modern breeder can, in theory, think in terms of individual alleles: this plant possesses the allele that produces this character; this other one possesses an allele that will produce another desired character; put the two together – and there's the perfect offspring.

In practice, however, plant breeding is not at all straightforward. Admittedly, a breeder of roses may well produce delightful new varieties simply by crossing two well-established varieties and then multiplying the offspring by cuttings. He may also find that new 'varieties' emerge spontaneously every now and again as some novel plant arises, brought about by a spontaneous alteration, or *mutation* in one of the genes. Many an ornamental novelty has been produced in such ways, by amateurs as well as by professionals. But the *ad hoc* provision of ornamental 'varieties' bears very little resemblance to the business of improving food crops. In this, there are complexities at every stage.

We should discuss these complexities one by one. Because of them, the improvement of commercial food crops cannot be carried out by amateurs on green house benches, and cannot be taken as far as is necessary by farmers working without the aids of modern science. Because of these complexities serious crop improvement is a vast undertaking, that must be pursued on an international scale, over many decades, with enormous inputs of capital and expertise.

The first of the complexities lies in the mechanism of inheritance itself. The modern explanation of inheritance begins with Gregor

Mendel, in the 1850s. It was he who showed that inheritance was guided by simple rules. But he also appreciated full well that those rules cannot always be applied simply.

The beginnings of modernity: Gregor Mendel

Biology in the mid-19th century was very different from today, but it was not a primitive science. Its ideas were rich and subtle; it was then that the foundations of modern understanding were laid. In particular, there was the work of Charles Darwin, who in 1859 published *On the Origin of Species by Means of Natural Selection*. This book can properly be said to have begun the modern era of biology. Darwin's ideas on evolution, sometimes expanded, sometimes criticized, are still at the centre of almost all serious biological discussion.

Evolution is concerned with the ways in which organisms change from generation to generation; in Darwin's own expression, with 'descent with modification'. At the core of evolutionary discussion, then, is inheritance; the fact that although 'like begets like', the offspring are not *exactly* like their parents. Darwin, then, one might imagine, had a very clear idea of how inheritance worked. But in fact he did not. The mechanism of inheritance worried him throughout his life. Indeed, Darwin's book contains a *cri de coeur*:

... no one can say why the same peculiarity in different individuals ... is sometimes inherited and sometimes not so; why the child often reverts in certain characters to its grandfather or grandmother or other more remote ancestor; why a peculiarity is often transmitted from one sex to both sexes, or to one sex alone, more commonly but not exclusively to the right sex.

Gregor Mendel was almost an exact contemporary of Darwin's. By the mid-1860s – 15 years before Darwin's death – he had completed experiments which made it perfectly possible to explain the puzzle so graphically described by Darwin. Many commentators have said what a pity it was that Darwin never knew of Mendel's work. Others suggest that he very possibly did know of it, but failed (as did everybody else at the time) to see its significance. In retrospect, however, such a failure would not be surprising. The simple truth is that Mendel conducted his experiments with a few carefully selected characters in carefully selected plants, under highly contrived conditions. Not even he was able to see that he had in fact discovered universal laws. It would indeed have been stretching credibility too far to suggest that the rules he had worked out using garden peas could also explain the caprices of inheritance in human beings. Here in fact we have the central irony. The basic rules of inheritance are simple, and are universal. But the realities of inheritance are such that the existence of those rules could not be inferred except by exploring deliberately simplified cases, in highly contrived circumstances. Darwin, the greatest observer of the 19th century, could not discern those rules precisely because he observed so widely and was so aware of apparent exceptions.

Mendel was a monk; he conducted his experiments in the garden of the monastery at Brunn, now called Brno, in Czechoslovakia.

As all the world knows, he did his main experiments on peas, *Pisum sativum*. In particular, he explored the inheritance of eight different characters, including stature (whether the plants were short or tall); the colour of the unripe pod – yellow or green; the colour of the cotyledons within the seed – yellow or green; and the behaviour of the seed as it dried – whether it remained round, or became wrinkled.

Here we at once perceive how contrived his experiments really were. Mendel's own parents were growers, and he was very familiar with a wide range of domestic plants. But he chose to work with peas. Peas are *inbreeding.* The stamens, bearing the pollen, and the female stigma which receives it, are enclosed in a complete envelope of petals; no pollen can come in from other plants. And because they are inbreeding they are also *true-breeding.* The offspring are exactly like the parents – unless the breeder does as Mendel did, and deliberately introduces pollen from another plant. The point is, however, that if he works with inbreeding plants such as peas, the breeder can keep their reproduction under perfect control; the plants he is trying to breed are not being constantly assailed with pollen from plants in nearby fields. Mendel would have had much more trouble in demonstrating his laws if he had worked with cabbage which does receive pollen from all quarters – but then he was a good enough observer to know that cabbage is less tractable.

Secondly, he worked only with a few characters within those peas. And he chose those characters very deliberately. As he recalled:

The various forms of peas selected for crosses showed differences in length and colour of stem; in size and shape of leaves; in position, colour, and size of flowers; in length of flower stalks; in colour, shape, and size of pods; in shape and size of seeds; and in colouration of seed coats and albumen. However, some of the traits listed do not permit a definite and sharp separation, since the difference rests on a 'more or less' which is often difficult to define. Such traits were not usable for individual experiments; these had to be limited to characteristics which stand out clearly and decisively in plants.

So – Mendel elected to study the inheritance of a few carefully selected traits, in a well-chosen species. And this is good science; it is a well-established principle that complex issues are often best approached through the study of simple cases. Even when working with this highly simplified case, however, Mendel was able to show how very complicated things become, very quickly.

Intimations of complexity: Mendel's experiments

When left to self-pollinate, round-seeded varieties of peas produce round-seeded offspring, and wrinkle-seeded varieties produce wrinkled-seeded offspring. In one of his first experiments, Mendel set out to discover what the offspring would be like if rounded and wrinkled were crossed.

A cross between two varieties is called a *hybrid*. The first generation following a cross is called the F1 generation; the grand-daughter generation is called the F2 generation; and so on. And the answer to the first question that Mendel asked was that the F1 hybrid offspring of round-seeded and wrinkled-seeded peas all had round seeds.

What had happened to the quality of wrinkledness? Mendel then allowed the F1 plants to self-pollinate. The result of this was that some of the F2 generation had round seeds – but in some, the quality of wrinkledness had miraculously reappeared. This, of course, is exactly the kind of phenomenon that Charles Darwin had drawn attention to; that a quality may miss a generation, and then crop up in a later one.

However, Mendel was not content merely to observe that 'some' F2 plants were round and some were wrinkled. He counted them. And there were 5 474 round ones, and 1 850 wrinkled ones. The ratio is very nearly three to one.

Before Mendel, it was widely believed that inheritance was a rather vague matter: the characters of the parents were mixed in the offspring almost as if different colours of ink were being blended. But such a method of mixing of characters could not explain Mendel's results. The F1 hybrids were not a little wrinkled; they were not wrinkled at all. And the seeds of the F2 generation were not half-heartedly wrinkled or partially round: they were either wrinkled or smooth. There was no mixing of characters, like mixing of inks. But there was no extinction of characters either – merely a temporary suppression.

The explanation that Mendel provided was simple and satisfying. Characters were not determined by vague entities that could be mixed like inks but by distinct 'factors' – the factors that we now call genes. Each true-breeding round pea contains two copies of the roundness gene, and each true-breeding wrinkled pea contains two copies of the gene for wrinkledness. Each kind of pea passes on only one copy of each gene to its offspring. As we have seen, different versions of the same gene are termed alleles; so we can say that each member of the F1 generation inherits one roundness allele, and one wrinkledness allele.

But the roundness allele is <u>*dominant*</u>; so long as it is present, the wrinkledness one is inoperative, or *recessive*. Hence the seeds of the F1 generation are all round – that is, the phenotype is of roundness.

But the plants of the F1 generation can pass on *either* a roundness allele *or* a wrinkledness allele to each of their offspring. Any one offspring, however, may inherit either one wrinkledness and one roundness allele, or two wrinkledness alleles, or two roundness alleles. In practice, as is clear from figure 3.1 the F2s have one chance in four of inheriting two wrinkledness alleles or two roundness alleles; and one chance in two of inheriting one allele of each type. But because the roundness alleles dominate over the wrinkledness alleles, the phenotype of the ones with both kinds of allele is round. Hence there are three round-seeded plants to every one wrinkled-seeded one.

In modern parlance, a plant that has two identical alleles of a given gene, is said to be *homozygous* for that gene: and one that has two different alleles of a given gene, is termed *heterozygous*. In practice, as we have seen, the heterozygous plant may look the same as the homozygous plant; that is, their phenotype is similar. But when the plants reproduce, the difference between them becomes obvious. The homozygous ones can pass on only one kind of allele of the particular gene to their offspring, and the offspring therefore are all the same as the parents – at least with respect to the particular character. Homozygous plants are therefore said to *breed true*. But the offspring of heterozygous plants do not all resemble their parents. So heterozygotes do not breed true. As we will see, a great many crop plants are highly heterozygous, and many 'prefer' to be heterozygous. This fact alone can severely complicate crop improvement programmes, where the aim is to produce large numbers of similar or virtually identical plants.

Mendel did not stop with wrinkledness and roundness. He went on, for example, to show that yellow seed colour dominated green seed colour: when yellows were crossed with greens all the F1s were yellow; and when F1s were crossed with F1s the yellows in the F2s outnumbered the greens three to one, exactly as with roundness and wrinkledness.

Then he tested the inheritance of both characters together. He found, first of all, that whether a pea's seeds were wrinkled or round had no bearing on whether they were yellow or green. The two characters were inherited independently. He also found that when homozygous round-yellows were crossed with homozygous wrinkled-greens the resulting phenotypes were in the ratio of nine round-yellows, three round-greens, three wrinkled-yellows, and one wrinkled-green: 9:3:3:1.

Again, we find that very simple principles in very simple cases none the less lead quickly to great complexities. The ratio 9:3:3:1 is not one that can be spotted easily: only when there are hundreds or thousands of individuals can such a relationship easily be seen. Furthermore, we see that some combinations of characters are rare: only one in sixteen of the offspring are wrinkled green. And the breeder of food crops is not concerned with only one or two characters, but with dozens. If he wanted to produce plants that were homozygous with respect to half a dozen alleles, how many would he have to produce to be sure of finding just one that had the right combination of genes? The answer, in general terms, is 'thousands'. Plant breeding, in practice, is an exercise largely in statistics and book-keeping. In any breeding programme dealing with any major food crop, the breeder must monitor and select from tens of millions of individual plants, to find the ones that have just the right combinations of characters. And that fact is obvious even from a modest extrapolation from Mendel's simplest laws.

Yet, as we keep stressing, Mendel deliberately investigated a case that he knew in advance was very simple. In practice, there are many additional complications.

Mendel with complications

In the characters Mendel chose to study, the pertinent genes were either fully dominant, or fully recessive. This is not always so. Sometimes one allele is only *partially dominant* over another. In this case the phenotype of the heterozygote is intermediate between that of its parents. Thus in some cases a red-flowered plant crossed with a white-flowered plant might produce a pink-coloured plant. In such cases it may look as if the two characters are simply being mixed, like coloured inks, but this is not so. If the pink hybrids are self-pollinated, then the offspring will include some pure reds and some pure whites, as well as pinks.

Sometimes, too – in fact usually – any one character may be influenced by several different genes, each working in concert. This is *polygenic* inheritance.

In 1908, H. Nilsson-Ehle showed both kinds of phenomena taking place within the kernels of wheat. Some wheat strains have dark red kernels, and are true-breeding. Some have white kernels, and are true-breeding. When the two are crossed, the F1s are all medium red. But when the F1s reproduce, the F2s show a range of colours. For every 16 plants (on average) one would be dark red, one pure white, and there would be 14 intermediates: four pink, four fairly dark-red, and six medium-red. The point here is that colour is determined by two alleles, with the red partially but not completely dominant over the white. A plant that contains four red alleles (is doubly homozygous) is dark red, and one that is double homozygous for white alleles is white. Any other combination produces some intermediate colour, depending on the numbers of whites and reds.

Nilsson-Ehle was able to work out what was happening by extrapolating from Mendel's rules. Again, though, if Mendel had not revealed the underlying simplicity by working on simple characters in peas, the interplay of genes that produced the red, pink, and white kernels could not have been discerned. It looks as if the colours are simply being mixed, in a rather random fashion.

Yet another problem is that many important features of crop plants are in fact compounded of several different characters, or may result from any one of several characters. Plants may yield more heavily, for example, because they are bigger, or because they have a higher proportion of useful product: that is, the *harvest index* is higher. If they are bigger, it may be because they have a greater output of some hormone, such as giberellin, or because their cells are more responsive to giberellin, or because they have a longer growing season, or more efficient respiration, or some other reason. Any one of these contributing characters may have a simple genetic basis, or a complex genetic basis.

Then again, any one gene may in practice affect several or many different characters. This is the phenomenon of *pleiotropy*. Thus the semi-dwarfing genes that affect stem-length in wheat also increase the number of seeds in the head. In this case, the same gene has two effects that are both beneficial: both make a positive contribution to yield. But such is not necessarily the case. It is perfectly possible for any one gene to affect one character advantageously, and another disadvantageously.

The phenomenon of *linkage* introduces yet another complication. Mendel observed that characters such as wrinkledness or yellowness could be inherited independently of each other: the form of the seed coat was not necessarily related to its colour. However, genes are not, in fact, passed on entirely separately. They exist within the nucleus of the cell, joined in long chains, each chain being known as a *chromosome*. In practice, if two genes are both on the same chromosome, then they are liable to be passed on together. Whether or not they are passed on together depends on how far apart they are positioned on the chromosome: if they are very close, then they will often be passed on together; and if they are far apart, then there is far less chance that they will be passed on as a duo. Again, however, if it had been the case that the gene for the form of the seed coat had been close to the one for seed colour on the same chromosome, then Mendel would not so readily have perceived his law of independent inheritance. In practice, many of the genes that breeders are interested in are linked to others; and, in practice, desirable genes are sometimes linked to undesirable ones.

The examples of complications so far show that inheritance can be complicated even when it is underpinned by simple Mendelian laws. The final complication, however, is that there are some genes that are not inherited according to Mendelian laws at all. Most of the genetic material of a plant is contained within the chromosomes, which reside within the nucleus. But some genetic material is found within various organelles within the cytoplasm of the cell. Thus, the chloroplasts, responsible for photosynthesis, contain some genetic material; and so too do the mitochondria, which are responsible for respiration within the cell. These *cytoplasmic genes* can have a considerable influence on the life of the plant. Some for example, cause the males to be sterile. As we will see, breeders have turned the quality, or defect, of male sterility to good account; it has played a great part in the development of modern forms of maize and sunflower, in particular. The fact is, however, that cytoplasmic genes can be passed on only through the female line, because only the female contributes cytoplasm to the embryo. All that passes on through the pollen of the male line, is nuclear material. Hence, cytoplasmic genes are not inherited according to the laws of Mendel. They are simply passed from generation to generation, slightly haphazardly, through the female line.

Finally, inheritance is complicated every now and again by the appearance of a *mutation*. A gene may change. Usually such changes are deleterious, and often they are lethal. But sometimes their effects are neutral or beneficial, resulting in some new character that is perfectly compatible with life. Darwin was aware of this phenomenon: new kinds of plant or animal, which suddenly showed some unprecedented feature, were known as 'sports'. In practice, mutations are the ultimate raw material for natural selection to work upon; the source of new variations. In practice, too, the sudden appearance of new mutations has played a crucial part in the development of crop plants, as we will note in chapter 5. The point here, however, is that Darwin was right to be alarmed by the intricacies of inheritance. It can indeed be capricious.

Mendel lost and found

Mendel published his seminal work on peas in 1866 in the *Proceedings of the Brunn Natural History Society*. Then his work virtually disappeared from view until it was rediscovered in a flurry of excitement at the beginning of this century. The new discovery almost immediately generated the new science of genetics. Within a few decades, the ideas of Mendel were fused with those of Darwin to produce a view of living things known as 'neo-Darwinism', in which evolution is explained in terms of the ebb and flow of genes within a population.

But why did Mendel's findings disappear in the first place? Some have suggested that Brunn was simply too obscure; no-one would read such stuff. But it was not as obscure as all that. It was far from being a backwater.

More to the point is that Mendel's peers were not particularly impressed. Several theories of heredity were current at the time; Mendel's was just one more. Besides, his peers did not fail to note the point that we have stressed – that Mendel worked on a few carefully selected characters, in a variety of plant in which he knew before he began that the patterns of inheritance tended to be fairly straight-forward. There was no reason to believe that the rules divined in such circumstances should be universal laws, applicable to all living things.

Indeed, in view of the obvious complexities of inheritance in many other species, there was every reason to suppose that the rules were not universally applicable. Mendel's senior, Karl Wilhelm von Nageli, suggested to Mendel that he should try to make sense of the heredity of the hawkweed, *Heiracium*. Mendel accordingly worked on *Heiracium* from 1866 to 1871, and got nowhere. The reason is now clear: *Heiracium* reproduces by *parthenogenesis* – that is, the eggs develop into embryos without being fertilized by the males. Parthenogenesis is in fact a form of asexual reproduction, even though it is based upon sex cells. Clearly, Mendelian laws of inheritance do not apply to it. Von Nageli would not have known this, however. He was not trying to be mischievous, merely realistic.

Mendel himself was elected Abbé of Brunn in 1868 and became more and more involved in church politics until his death in 1884. It is only in the 20th century that the full power of his work has been appreciated: the fact that the laws of Mendel do apply to every species, but that they do not always, or usually, apply as straightforwardly as in some of the characters of garden peas.

It is partly because the realities of inheritance are far more difficult than the rules suggest, that plant breeding is so complicated. Even when the inheritance of particular characters is simple, only a small proportion of the offspring of any one cross will contain the right combination of characters. If a breeder is trying to combine a dozen of more features in one plant, he may have to choose between many thousands of offspring, over several generations. And since several of the features he is interested in are liable to be of a complicated nature – some brought about by many genes, some of which will be linked to others that are not desirable, some of which will be dominant, some recessive, and some half-way between – breeding in practice involves the careful crossing of scores of parents, and selection from among many millions of offspring.

As if that were not enough, every one character has to be carefully monitored, and not every character that is of significance is immediately obvious. Pest-resistance, for example, is one of the most important characters in all crops; and in general, pest-resistance can be monitored only by subjecting the plants to attack by controlled numbers of pests, which itself can be a highly technical operation.

Yet these are not the end of the breeder's problems. There is the additional fact that some crosses are much more easy to effect than others, and some cannot be effected at all except by employing extraordinary methods. There are various kinds of reproductive barriers both between plants of different species, and between plants of the same species, and the breeder must either respect these barriers, or else impose special means to overcome them. The nature and the reason for these barriers is the subject of the next chapter.

55

4 Populations, Species, and Reproduction

Introduction

Plant breeders generally begin their breeding programmes by crossing two promising parents, and in an ideal world they would simply cross whatever plants they chose, at will. Then they would take the best of the offspring, and produce millions or billions of almost exact copies, more or less instantly.

In the real world the breeders are obliged to fall far short of this ideal. Some crosses cannot be effected at all: the two intended parents simply will not produce offspring. If the initial resistance of the plants is overcome, the offspring may sometimes be outstandingly good, but are sometimes disappointing. They may be sexually sterile, in which case they obviously cannot be multiplied by sexual means; or they may simply be feeble, unable to function as healthy plants. Often, highly desirable offspring cannot be multiplied by sexual means – that is, by seed – because they do not 'breed true'; their own offspring are highly variable, and few have the required combination of characters. Sometimes plants that do not breed true can be multiplied by asexual means – by tubers, bulbs, or cuttings. But some plants do not naturally reproduce asexually, in which case asexual reproduction has to be effected by special means – for example by tissue culture, as described in chapter 6.

The reasons for such caprice and variability lie to a large extent in the reproductive strategies of plants. If we are to understand what it is that plant breeders do in the real world, why some manoeuvres are easy and others that seem straightforward are well-nigh impossible, we must explore those strategies. First we should look at the two modes of reproduction: asexual and sexual.

The advantages of asexual reproduction

Simple organisms, such as bacteria and some protozoa, can reproduce just by splitting in half, producing two organisms where there was one before. More complex practitioners of asexual reproduction, including many plants, produce 'buds' or offshoots of various descriptions, th develop into new individuals.

The first obvious advantage of this mode of reproduction is that it is almost chanceless. Sexual reproduction by constrast is appallingly hazardous, and profligate. Male animals may have to fight for the right to mate with a suitable female – assuming that there are suitable females available. Male plants invest energy in producing pollen, only to surrender it to the four winds, or to some capricious insect. Female plants or animals have to advertise their presence to attract the males, or the bearers of pollen, and so also attract predators. Many an organism that sets out to reproduce sexually fails, because it never makes effective contact with a suitable mating partner – and indeed may be actively thwarted in its attempts to do so. Organisms that reproduce asexually, by contrast, are self-sufficient. For this reason alone, asexual reproduction is all together more efficient.

Then again, the 'point' of reproduction is not simply to produce new individuals, but to produce new individuals that contain the same genes as the parent, or parents. When an individual reproduces asexually, it passes on copies of all of its genes to its offspring. Unless one or other of the genes changes by mutation, then all offspring are genetically identical to the parent. Collectively the offspring of asexually repro-ducing organisms are a *clone*.

But when organisms reproduce sexually, they pass on only half of their genes. However many offspring they have, there is a good chance that some or many of their genes will not be passed on at all. The fate of the genes that are passed on depends largely upon the suitability of those acquired from the other parent. Again, asexual reproduction seems far more efficient than sexual. A hundred per cent of each individual's genes are passed on, rather than only 50 per cent.

Thirdly, there is the question of adaptation. The offspring of asexually reproducing organisms are the same as the parent. If the parent is well adapted to its environment, then it seems to follow that the offspring will be too. But the offspring of sexually reproducing parents are different from either of their parents, because they contain a different combination of genes from either parent. Organisms become adapted to their environment largely by the long and painful process of natural selection. How strange to evolve such adaptedness, and then squander it by producing offspring that are not the same as the parent!

Finally, when organisms that reproduce asexually are in direct competition with ones that reproduce sexually, it seems at first sight that the asexual organisms must prevail for purely statistical reasons. In general, organisms invest as much time and resources in reproduction as they are able. If they invest too little, and produce too few offspring, or offspring that are too small to survive, then their line will become extinct. If they invest too much, then they are likely to die in the attempt. In practice, the compromises that different organisms achieve between what is desirable and what is possible, are very different. Thus codfish lay two million eggs, in the 'expectation' that most will be destroyed, but a few will reach adulthood; while a bat produces a single offspring half the size of herself, with a very high chance of survival. The chances of survival would be enhanced if the codfish laid four million eggs, and the bat's babies were as large as herself, but such investment would overstretch the resources of the parents.

Suppose, however, that a line of codfish emerged in which the eggs did not need to be fertilized; a line, in fact, in which the eggs developed by parthenogenesis, as is the case with hawkweed. Suppose, too, that all the fish that developed from those parthenogenetic eggs were themselves female. At present, the two million eggs produced by the female codfish in fact represent the offspring of two individuals – the female and the male. So there are only one million offspring per parent. But if there were no males, and if the females needed no input from the males, then there would be two million offspring for every adult fish. Suppose, now, that parthenogenetic, all-female fish were sharing the same environment as sexually-reproducing fish; and suppose that the same proportion of offspring of each kind of fish was slaughtered before it reached adulthood. Inexorably, the offspring of the parthenogenetic fish would soon come to outnumber those of the sexual fish, because there are twice as many per individual to start with. Soon the sexual fish would become extinct.

This rarely seems to happen in nature, for reasons we will examine below. The point is, however, that asexual reproduction has several obvious advantages over sexual reproduction. It is hardly surprising, then, that asexual reproduction is so common in nature: it is the usual means of reproduction among bacteria; is common in fungi and in 'lower' animals, such as protozoa and coelenterates; and is common, too, in plants. Only the 'higher' animals have largely eschewed asexual reproduction, but one kind of lizard and several fish are known to reproduce by parthenogenesis, and so, too, can aphids and bees, among arthropods.

Plants are extremely good at asexual reproduction, and achieve it in many different ways. Different species produce new individuals from roots, stems, leaves, or from unfertilized seed, as in hawkweed. The main reason for their efficiency will be explored in chapter 6; the trick is that many of the plant cells remain in an essentially embryonic form throughout the life of the plant, and retain the quality of *totipotency*; the ability to develop into any of the many different kinds of tissue found in the organism. When plants naturally reproduce by asexual means, then the breeder's job can be made much easier. When he has produced an 'elite' plant with the right combination of characters, he can produce exact facsimiles of it at will. Thus potatoes are multiplied as tubers, apple trees are multiplied as cuttings, and new individual strawberries are picked off the runners.

These matters can be left to the next chapter, however, Our task here is to explore the conundrum. We have seen that asexual reproduction is far more efficient than sexual, in several quite different ways; and that asexual organisms ought to be able to out-compete those that reproduce only by sexual means. But although asexual reproduction is common throughout nature, sex is even more common – at least among 'higher' organisms, including most phyla of animals, and among plants. Very few 'higher' animals have abandoned sex all together: both aphids and bees reproduce sexually as well as asexually. Many plants do not reproduce effectively asexually – or at least, do not do so in nature, but very few have lost the ability to reproduce by sexual means. Sex must have advantages, or it could not be as common as it is. Furthermore, those advantages must outweigh the obvious drawbacks. So what are the advantages?

The advantages of sexual reproduction

Biologists have produced two kinds of argument to explain the persistence of sex. The first has to do with long-term, evolutionary advantage. The second suggest that sexual reproduction also produces short-term gains.

To understand the first kind of explanation, we should evoke explanations of evolution based on neo-Darwinism, the modern synthesis of Mendel's ideas with Darwin's.

Darwin pointed out, first, that the offspring of any sexual union are varied. This being the case, some individuals are better adapted to the environment – that is, 'fitter' – than others. The fittest survive, the less fit go to the wall. Thus the organisms change as the generations pass, by 'natural selection'.

Clearly, natural selection could not operate unless the organisms were varied. But the question is, where does variation come from? There are two sources, is the answer. The first is that offspring will be different from their parents because they have a different *combination* of genes from either parent. The second is that every now and again a gene changes, or *mutates*. Clearly, evolution could not proceed very far unless there were a constant source of novel genes being fed in by mutation. Breeders of horses, employing 'artificial selection', are able to produce animals of different sizes and shapes by selecting individuals with particular combinations of genes. But horses could not have evolved from the primitive *Eohippus* unless a great many new genes had been fed into the line by mutation. Evolution needs to be fed with novel genes, produced by mutation, or it effectively comes to a halt.

Consider, however, a group of organisms that reproduce only by asexual means. Every now and again, one of the genes in one of these organisms undergoes a mutation. Most of these mutations are harmful,

59

and the mutant organism dies out. But every now and again – very occasionally – some beneficial mutation occurs. Suppose that one organism in the group undergoes mutation A, which is beneficial; and another undergoes mutation B, which is also beneficial. The offspring of A also contain the A genes, and those of B contain the B genes, so now there are three sub-populations: those with A genes, those with B genes, and those with neither. The three are in competition; both the possessors of A and the possessors of B will presumably oust the originals, as they have an advantage, and, probably, either the As or the Bs will oust each other.

After many more generations, the surviving As undergo the B mutation, or the surviving Bs undergo the A mutation, and in either case they give rise to a super-race of ABs, which ousts the surviving As and Bs. Thus has evolution occurred, by means of natural selection. But beneficial mutations are rare, and this step-wise, stop-go accumulation of beneficial mutations is exceedingly inefficient.

Contrast, now, a population of organisms that is able to share genetic information. Such a population, by definition, is practising sex. If one organism in the group produces beneficial mutation A and another undergoes beneficial mutation B at the same time then there is a finite chance that the ideal combination AB will be produced in the very next generation, by a mating of the two; and if both A and B are beneficial, then it is certain that ABs will be produced far more quickly than would be the case if As had to wait for the B mutation, and Bs for the A mutation.

The contrast in efficiency is obvious if we consider only two mutations, A and B; but if we start to add a little realism it becomes stark. In reality there could be hundreds of mutations jostling for recognition; some of them might be beneficial when in the company of some others, but of no value, or even harmful, on their own. If mutations cannot be added one to another, and combined in different ways, then they can never effect more than the short-term *ad hoc* changes of the kinds that are seen in bacteria.

The degree of evolutionary change that after three and a half billion years has produced human beings, and other animals, and plants, would not have been possible unless those organisms reproduced sexually. The fact that those organisms are so very obviously successful, seems in itself to explain why sex has after all prevailed.

Yet such an explanation, by itself, is not sufficient; as has been pointed out in particular by the British biologist, John Maynard Smith, and the American, George Williams, of the State University of New York at Stony Brook (Maynard Smith, 1978; Williams, 1975). For both have drawn attention to the point noted above: that if organisms that reproduce asexually are in direct competition with organisms that reproduce only by sexual means, then the asexual ones must prevail. True, the asexual ones cannot evolve; or not, at least, to any considerable extent. Lines that breed only asexually are doomed to become extinct, therefore, as soon as conditions change, because they will not be able to adapt. But evolution does not think ahead. The long-term advantage of sexually reproducing organisms is of no relevance, if those organisms are driven to extinction in the short term. Therefore, sexual reproduction must produce short-term advantages in addition to the long-term, evolutionary advantage. If it were not so, then the sexual organisms could not compete in the short term.

So what are the short-term advantages? The answer must lie in a fact that at first seems paradoxical: that the offspring of sexually reproductive organisms are somewhat different from their parents. What we have to explain is why it is an advantage for an organism to produce offspring different from itself.

Biologists have provided two kinds of explanation. The first is that each of the offspring may find that it faces slightly different circumstances from its parent, and that it pays to produce what in effect is many different versions of the same organism, in the 'hope' that one at least of them will find suitable conditions. George Williams offers the example of an elm tree in a wood, producing millions of seeds. Some land in dry leaf litter, some land by the sides of streams, some land in shade and some in full sunshine. No one set of conditions is suitable for all seeds, but if the tree produces a great many seeds that are all a little different one from another, then one at least is liable to land in an appropriate niche.

This first kind of explanation supposes that the environment varies from place to place; that is, varies in space. The second kind of explanation suggests that the environment varies through time: from year to year. But what is it that varies from year to year that is so significant that organisms find it 'worthwhile' to reproduce sexually, and so produce variable offspring?

The strongest hypothesis so far comes from Professor William Hamilton, at Oxford University. And the answer, he says, is – parasites. All large living organisms are attacked by smaller ones. Multicellular organisms such as animals and plants are constantly besieged by viruses, bacteria, and fungi. Those viruses, bacteria, and fungi seek to adapt to their hosts, so that they may invade them more effectively. Although they reproduce primarily by asexual means, they are capable of undergoing the small changes that are needed to increase the degree of adaptation. Often a single mutation, resulting in a small physical change, will turn a non-virulent parasite into a virulent one. In addition, many of the parasites also exchange genetic information to some extent, so they can improve on the crude one-by-one accumulation of mutations described above. In short, parasites constantly change, and natural selection ensures that they tend to become better and better adapted to their hosts. Large organisms therefore need ways of changing as well, to reduce the chances of adaptation. Sex ensures this.

The offspring of two horses are still horses, and the offspring of two cabbages are still cabbages. But because they are also different from their parents, the parasites that lay their parents low cannot attack them with the same virulence and the parasites that adapt to them will not be able to attack their offspring with the same virulence.

A very large proportion of the lives of animals and plants is taken up by sex. Much of the behaviour of animals is concerned with finding mates, keeping them, and warding off rivals; and much of the lives of plants is concerned with broadcasting and receiving pollen. The fact that their evolution has proceeded as far as it has is a consequence of sexual reproduction, for it could not have taken place without the sharing of genes. But the prime motive for sexual reproduction in the first place had nothing to do with evolution, and still less with romance. It was a matter of staying one step ahead of parasites.

Thus we see that both forms of reproduction have advantages and disadvantages. Most flowering plants contrive to get the best of both worlds, by reproducing both sexually and asexually: grasses, onions, potatoes, runner beans, Jerusalem artichokes, strawberries, black-berries, plum trees. In addition, some plants at least seem to have modified asexual reproduction to some extent, to gain some of the advantages of sexuality; and sexuality is modified in various ways, to regain some of the advantages of asexuality. We will look at each of these modifications in turn.

Asexuality modified

The advantage of sex, we have seen, is that it produces variation from generation to generation and the particular reason for that, according to Professor Hamilton, is that such variation helps to defeat parasites. But some individual plants, including many trees, live for hundreds of years – perhaps reproducing asexually to produce an entire coppice, as elm trees may do. And some other plants may occupy the same territory for hundreds or even thousands of years, reproducing asexually from generation to generation. Thus in England, some patches of grass such as sheep's fescue, *Festuca ovina* may have occupied the same corner of their particular field since before the Norman invasion. In mediterranean countries, some clones of fig tree are known to date back to Roman times. If it is necessary to change to avoid parasites, how is it that such plants do not succumb to disease?

One answer is that nature is not one hundred per cent efficient. We may assume that in time, asexually-reproducing organisms must succumb to some slowly adapting parasite. But we need not assume that this will necessarily happen in all organisms, immediately.

The second answer is that long-lived plants, such as trees, seem to alter to some extent as they grow. Thus, as Dr Doug Gill of the

University of Maryland told a meeting of the Population Biologists of New England at Princeton, trees often produce branches that are quite different from other branches. In addition, those altered branches tend to be less badly affected by parasites. Such alteration may occur in several ways. Sometimes it could involve mutation, sometimes simply a re-arrangement of genes, or a suppression of particular genes. In any case, such *in situ* modification would serve the same purpose as the changes wrought from generation to generation by sexual means.

This particular mechanism has considerable significance for crop improvement. As we will see in chapter 6, plants produced by asexual means in tissue culture are often different from the parent plant that originally provided the tissue. This phenomenon is known as *somaclonal variation*, and is now regarded as a potent source of new varieties in the breeding of sugar cane and of potatoes, and it could be useful for providing new varieties of oil palms or coconuts. Somaclonal variation has been regarded as something of a mystery: why should plants produced from the body cells of other plants be different from the parent? But the phenomenon described by Doug Gill could provide some of the explanation. There is biological advantage in varying during growth, as well as in producing different offspring.

Variations of sexuality: inbreeders and outbreeders

One disadvantage of sexual reproduction is that it is chancy. There is a good chance that pollen may fail to land on a receptive stigma. The chances of failure are even greater if the plant is rare, or if the agents of pollen dispersal are rare. For example, wind-pollinated plants may suffer if the air is too still, or the wind too strong, and insect-pollinated plants may suffer if conditions do not favour the flight of insects.

Accordingly, many plants have evolved mechanisms for pollinating themselves. In some, such as the cereals wheat, barley, and sorghum, self-pollination is usual but not invariable. But in the case of the garden pea, as we saw in chapter 3, the pollen-bearing anthers and the receptive stigma are both enclosed within a carapace of petals, and unless this is broached by a breeder or a particularly persistent bee, then self-pollination is almost invariable. In any case, plants that are able to pollinate themselves – or to pollinate other individuals of identical genotype – are known as *inbreeders*.

Nothing is for nothing in nature. Inbreeding has advantages and disadvantages; although features that are an advantage in the wild may not be an advantage to the farmer, and vice versa.

What inbreeders gain, as we have seen, is certainty. Even when it is difficult to transfer pollen from plant to plant, they can still reproduce. On the other hand, the chief advantage of sexual reproduction is to produce variation from generation to generation. Clearly, if a plant pollinates itself, and if the offspring in turn pollinate themselves, then within a few generations the plants become very uniform indeed. Inbreeders thus squander the main reason for being sexual in the first place. On the other hand, uniformity is precisely what the farmer wants. He needs to know that the seed he plants will grow up to be like the parent that produced it. Wheat and barley are therefore very convenient crops, because they 'breed true'.

Wheat, barley, and sorghum are able to in-breed, and in nature they generally do so. Only about 10 per cent of the seed on a sorghum plant will be fertilized by pollen from other plants. But many other plants 'prefer' to be pollinated by other individuals, and some cannot be fertilized by pollen from the same plant, or from another of the same phenotype. The plants that prefer to be pollinated by different individuals are called *outbreeders*; among crops, they include maize, millet, potatoes, and most brassicas. The extreme outbreeders, which have to be pollinated by different individuals of a different phenotype, are said to be *self-incompatible*. Plums are an example.

Outbreeders lose out, in theory, because they are unlikely to flourish unless conditions really do favour the transfer of pollen from plant to plant. But they gain because they drink the cup of sexuality to the full. Because they mate exclusively or almost exclusively with other individuals, their offspring tend to be very variable, and often dissimilar from themselves. Hence, in theory, they provide parasites with their greatest problems. On the other hand, such outbreeders are not 'breeding true'. They therefore provide problems for plant breeders, who want to provide farmers with uniform stock. The way these problems are solved is discussed in the next chapter. Just to anticipate, however, outbreeding crops are sold either as populations of seed that is variable but not too variable, or they are sold as F1 hybrids, or they are reproduced asexually, as is the case with potatoes.

Hence, inbreeding and outbreeding plants provide breeders with different problems, and require different breeding strategies. But both reproductive strategies should be seen as adaptations: attempts to strike a balance between the need to reproduce with certainty on the one hand, and the need to produce variation from generation to generation on the other.

However, the strategies of inbreeding and outbreeding also have genetic connotations, and can be analysed in genetic terms. We must explore these, too.

Sexual strategy and genes: homozygotes and heterozygotes

As we saw in chapter 3, each individual contains two complete sets of genes; one set inherited from the mother, and one from the father. In any one population, any one gene may exist in several versions, known as alleles. If the individual inherits the same version of any particular gene from each of its parents, then it is said to be homozygous for that particular gene. If it inherits a different allele of any particular gene from each parent, then it is said to be heterozygous for that gene.

Two plants of the same species may be perfectly compatible with each other, and yet be very different, because each contains a different complement of alleles. The offspring of their union will therefore be highly heterozygous – many of its genes will be inherited in two different versions. In chapter 3 we saw what happens when heterozygous individuals reproduce. Their offspring may contain many different combinations of alleles, and hence are highly variable. In general, outbreeders tend to be highly heterozygous, because their parents are different one from another and in general their own offspring are highly variable, because heterozygous individuals tend to produce variable offspring.

With inbreeders, things are very different. The two parents are very similar; indeed, they are male and female parts of the same plant. It may well be that some of the alleles that appear in the eggs are different from some of those that appear in the pollen, but there clearly will not be the degree of difference that may exist between two parental maize or potato plants. Thus the offspring will be highly homozygous. The generation after that, produced by inbreeding of homozygous individuals, will be even more homozygous. Hence the uniformity.

However, loss of variability is not the only price that inbreeders must pay for their incest. It is the case, as we have seen, that most mutations are harmful. It is also the case that most harmful, mutant genes are recessive. Therefore they do not make themselves felt unless they are inherited in double dose, one from each parent.

Most organisms that reproduce sexually tend to be outbreeders, and most therefore are highly heterozygous. So long as organisms are heterozygous, then any harmful mutant alleles they contain can be hidden. Human beings tend to be highly heterozygous and it has been estimated that each human being carries an average of five extremely deleterious mutant genes that would be harmful if two carriers of the same mutant allele mated, and produced offspring with a double dose of the gene. Many serious inherited diseases are caused by deleterious alleles. The most common in European people is cystic fibrosis. One in 20 Europeans carries the allele for cystic fibrosis, but heterozygous carriers are not affected because the allele is recessive. However, there is a one in 400 chance that two carriers of the allele will marry (400 = 20 × 20). If they do, there is a one in four chance that any one child will carry a double dose of the gene, and so be affected. Hence the incidence of cystic fibrosis among Europeans is one in 1 600 births. The disease itself is fairly rare – but the proportion of carriers is very high indeed.

Consider what would happen, however, if human beings were

inbreeders, or indeed, if they commonly married their own siblings. Then they would be highly homozygous. Families or 'lines' that included cystic fibrosis gene would have a very high incidence of the disease. Indeed there are many examples of diseases that are caused by single genes appearing in families in which marrying between relatives is common. The most famous is the high incidence of haemophilia among the descendants of Queen Victoria.

It follows, however, that if an organism is to practise inbreeding as a matter of course, then it cannot afford to contain deleterious alleles. If it does, then its homozygous offspring are bound to be seriously affected. Thus, the ability to inbreed is not one that can have been achieved lightly. At some time in the history of all inbreeders there must have been a massive purge of deleterious alleles and we have to assume that the ones that have survived have been in the minority: decandants of those few lines which, by chance, included very few deleterious alleles.

By contrast, habitual outbreeders are not exposed to selective pressure to purge them of deleterious alleles. Occasionally they throw up individuals that are homozygous for some harmful gene, and those individuals die. But the heterozygous carriers, who are unharmed by the gene, persist. It follows, however, that outbreeding organisms inevitably do carry a high proportion of deleterious genes, precisely because there has been no selective pressure to eliminate those genes. Therefore, when habitual outbreeders are obliged to inbreed, their homozygous offspring are very likely to be adversely affected. Indeed, when outbreeders are obliged to inbreed, they show *inbreeding depression*. Their offspring are often extremely feeble.

On the other hand, habitual outbreeders tend to benefit by being as heterozygous as possible. Indeed they show *heterosis*; increased vigour brought about by increased heterozygosity. This phenomenon is partly the reverse of inbreeding depression; in other words, it results partly because the organism contains few double doses of harmful alleles. But there is another possible cause of heterosis, of a more positive nature.

Some genes may be beneficial when present only in single dose, though they are harmful in double dose. Two well-known examples are the genes that cause haemophilia among black people, and the genes that cause thalassaemia among Mediterranean peoples and many Asians. In both cases these genes cause severe anaemia when present in double dose. In single dose they cause minor defects in the blood, but they also confer a considerable degree of protection against malaria, which in the past was extremely common throughout the tropics and sub-tropics, and is still a major disease in Africa. The genes for sickle cell and thalassaemia are extremely common. Because malaria is so damaging, natural selection has favoured their retention. I know of no comparable examples among plants, though it has been suggested to me that some of the genes that produce short stems in cereals − semi-dwarfing genes − may in some cases be more beneficial in single dose than in double dose. In double dose some such genes could be positively stunting. This is a hypothetical possibility, but the general principle, clearly demonstrated by examples in human beings, is that heterozygosity can be innately beneficial.

Breeders therefore may set out with the ideal of producing millions of facsimiles of an outstanding plant. But in practice they find that this may be complicated, because plants are true-breeding only if they are homozygous, and many plants do not do well if they are too homozygous. In practice, breeders can and to a large extent do reduce the difficulties of homozygosity, by purging populations of plants of deleterious alleles. Thus modern varieties of maize or millet tend to be far more homozygous than those of a few decades ago and do not suffer too much from this because deleterious alleles have been bred out of them. However, it may well be that heterozygosity offers special advantages in addition to the mere avoidance of deleterious genetic double-doses, so that even the best-bred homozygous plants are slightly worse off than they would be if they were heterozygous. This is why many crops are now produced in the form of F1 hybrids – the first generation crosses of highly homozygous parents. F1 hybrids are uniform, just as the first generation offspring of Mendel's wrinkled- and smooth-seeded seeds are uniform. But each individual is highly heterozygous. We will see more of F1 hybrids in the next chapter. Even wheat, the inveterate inbreeder, may be better off in a heterozygous form and F1 hybrids are being developed in the United Kingdom, as again is discussed in the next chapter.

However, the point must be made that all strategies in nature carry disadvantages as well as advantages. It is an advantage, in general, to be heterozygous. It is beneficial, in general, to produce offspring that are different from yourself. It is useful, therefore, to mate with individuals that are different from yourself. The inbreeders, that forego these advantages, must be regarded as highly adapted exceptions to the rule, who have squandered the obvious benefits in the interests of efficiency.

On the other hand, organisms must be adapted to their environment. Their offspring cannot be too different from themselves, or they will not be so well adapted – or at least are most unlikely to be as well adapted. So it pays to mate with individuals that are different – but not if they are too different. For example, the offspring of an Arab stallion and a Thoroughbred mare may be more vigorous than either of its parents, because of the benefits of heterozygosity, but in general it will be well adapted to life on the plains, just as its parents are. But a mating between a horse and gorilla, assuming such a thing was possible, would produce a grotesque offspring, adapted neither to plain nor to forest.

In short, variation has to be achieved within limits: always with the proviso that the offspring must be of the same general type as the parents and adapted to the same kinds of environment. However, this raises various questions. How do sexually reproducing organisms contrive to vary from generation to generation, and yet remain recognisably of the same type? How different should the parents be, to strike the right balance between variability and consistency? And how do individuals contrive to find the most appropriate mating partners, neither too similar to themselves, nor too different?

Such questions are relevant to our discussion of crop improvement, and so we should try to answer them.

Barriers to sexual exchange: gene pools and species

Clearly, if organisms are to breed sexually then they have to be of the appropriate sex and age, but even if two organisms are of the appropriate sex, and both are in breeding condition, they may not be able to breed together sexually. There may be barriers between them. These barriers are both specific and non-specific, and they may exist within species or between species.

Barriers to breeding within species

Some plant species are divided into several different breeding types. Individuals of the same breeding type cannot mate. If the pollen from one lands on the stigma of another, then it either fails to germinate, or else the pollen tube aborts as it progresses down the style towards the ova. Such plants are said to be *self-incompatible*. Some varieties of plum and cherry are self-incompatible. Growers therefore may have to plant more than one variety together, to ensure that fertilization occurs and fruit is set. Brassicas, too, tend to be self-incompatible.

Self-incompatibility is brought about by specific genes. The biological advantage of it is that it prevents inbreeding, so that all plants are highly heterozygous.

In addition, however, there are what we might call 'non-specific' barriers to reproduction within species which are natural outbreeders. Thus, as observed in the case of maize, inbreeding may occur, but the offspring tend to be very feeble, mainly because the high incidence of homozygosity ensures that deleterious genes are brought together in double dose.

It does not follow, however, that the best possible crosses within species should be made between individuals that differ most one from another. Certainly if two individuals are very different (which implies that they are genetically different) then their offspring will be highly heterozygous, which should confer some advantage. But genes tend to work in groups. As noted in chapter 3, most characters are influenced by more than one gene, and it is essential that the different genes work well in concert. If the two parents are too different one from another then the offspring may be enfeebled because of a lack of compatibility between their different genes. More likely, the F2 generation – the 'grandchildren' – will be the ones to suffer, because it is when the hybrid F1s form gametes that the various groups of genes which should work in concert, first begin to be broken up by crossing over.

At Cambridge University, Professor Pat Bateson put this idea to the test, through experiments not with plants but with Japanese quail. He proposed that if quail were given a choice of mates, then they would avoid incest, which would lead to inbreeding. But he proposed, too, that if they had a free choice of mates they would also avoid mating with partners that were too dissimilar from themselves. In practice, he found that when either sex was given complete freedom to choose mates from a whole selection of possible choices, each individual tended to choose its own first cousin as mate – birds that were different from themselves, but not too different.

The principle also seems to hold in plants. Thus in 1979 M. V. Price and N. M. Waser reported their observations of a small wild herb, *Delphinium nelsoni* (Price and Waser, 1979). In the wild, the plant scatters its seeds close to itself. In a patch of them, therefore, the plants close together are liable to be siblings, and two individuals that are close together are more likely to be genetically similar than two that are further apart. Price and Waser showed that when plants growing a medium distance apart were mated, they produced more seeds than were produced by matings between plants that were growing very close together and plants that were growing a long way apart. In these plants, the physical distance between individuals corresponds with the genetic difference between them; and, as in Pat Bateson's quail experiments, it was the cousins (or not-too-distant relatives) that produced the most successful matings.

Breeders recognize this principle. Often they will cross plants that are of the same species, but are genetically very different, and sometimes such crosses do produce excellent offspring. But in general breeders seek to cross plants that 'nick' well: and plants that 'nick' well tend to be fairly similar. Thus, the tendency of genes to work in concert, and the need to bring together individuals whose genes can work in concert, to some extent constrain the activities of the breeder.

However, specific barriers to mating within species are the exception rather than the rule. Although it is true that some matings within species are more successful than others, it is generally found that when two individuals are of the same species and the appropriate age and sex, then mating will be successful. The most significant barriers to sexual exchange occur between species.

Barriers between species

Biologists have long recognized that organisms are divided into distinct types, which are known as species. There have been many periods in history when people – even biologists – believed that matings could take place between even the most disparate species: congenital disorders in humans that are now ascribed to deleterious alleles were once blamed upon matings with dogs, or wolves, or monkeys. Now, however, it is widely accepted that dogs mate only with other dogs – or sometimes with wolves and jackals, which are very similar; roses mate with roses and potatoes with potatoes. Indeed, when two organisms can mate to produce fully viable offspring they are said to be of the same species; when they cannot mate at all, or are able only to produce offspring that are not fully viable, then they are considered to be of different species.

Some biologists, notably Ernst Mayr in the United States, suggest that every sexually reproducing organism has evolved specific mechanisms that keep it apart from other species; quirks of behaviour or biochemistry that render each species unattractive to others, or which produce physical barriers between them that prevent mating. However, Professor Hugh Paterson, who recently left the University of the Witwatersrand to return to his native Australia, puts the matter the other way around. He proposes that organisms are of the same species if, and only if, they recognize each other's specific mating signals – biochemical or behavioural. In short, he says, the important fact in the evolution of species is that species have evolved means of keeping members of the same species together – not that they have evolved means of staying apart from other species.

Such discussion is, however, a nicety. The important point for our purposes is that members of the same species effectively belong to a club. They can exchange genetic information with other members of the club, and thus benefit in the ways we have described: short-term variation and long-term evolution. But the other members with whom they exchange information are in essence of the same type of organism as themselves. Thus horses mate with other horses that are also adapted to life on the plains. They do not mate with animals that are adapted to life in the trees, and thus produce offspring that are adapted to neither habitat. Each individual within the species has its own complement of genes, which is known as its *genome*. But together, the species contains a whole library of different alleles, which together constitute the *gene pool* of that species. Often each species is divided into a number of different populations. Then, each population can be said to have its own gene pool.

In genetic terms, the difference between two different species may be minute. Dr Graham White, formerly of the London School of Hygiene and Tropical Medicine, has shown that populations of mosquitoes that previously were regarded as being of the same species, may actually be divided into many different sub-populations that do not and cannot inter-breed. If two populations do not and cannot inter-breed then by definition they belong to different species. Thus Dr White has shown that many 'species' of mosquitoes in fact consist of several or many different species. Yet competent entomologists, closely examining every physical and chemical aspect of those mosquitoes, often cannot tell them apart. It is only their behaviour that reveals the difference between them.

At other times, the differences between species that seem otherwise to be reasonably closely related are revealed not only by discernible differences in their structure and chemistry, but by the structure and number of their chromosomes. Among clovers, for example, some have 14 chromosomes, some have 16, and some have various multiples of 16 – 32 or 48.

However, mating between different species is sometimes possible, both in animals and in plants. The result of such a mating is called an *interspecific hybrid*. Often, such hybrids are extremely tough and vigorous. They are extremely heterozygous, and they sometimes seem to combine the best qualities of both parents. Darwin noted this phenomenon, and called it *hybrid vigour*. But the offspring of matings between species are usually sexually sterile. Thus a mule is the extremely tough progeny of a horse crossed with an ass, but mules, for all their toughness, are infertile.

The reason for the infertility of interspecific hybrids very often lies in the arrangement of the chromosomes. When animals or plants form sex cells, or *gametes*, the chromosomes that they have inherited from one parent must match themselves up with the chromosomes inherited from the other parent. Each chromosome must find the corresponding chromosome from the other parent. But if the chromosomes inherited from the two parents are different, as is the case in interspecific hybrids, then this matching cannot take place. If the two parents each have different numbers of chromosomes, then the miss-matching is obvious: some of the chromosomes from one parent simply have no corresponding partner from the other. But even if the two parents have the same numbers of chromosomes, they may be different in structure if the parents are of different species; so again, the necessary matching cannot take place. Hence interspecific hybrids cannot form gametes and they are sterile.

There are ways of crossing barriers between species, however – ways that result in offspring that are sexually fertile. These methods are an extrapolation of processes that occur to some extent in nature. Insofar as they are natural processes, they will be discussed later in this chapter; though the ways in which barriers between species are crossed for the purposes of plant breeding will be discussed in chapter 5.

In general it is useful to think of the relationships between plants in the terms proposed by Drs Jack Harlan and Jan de Wet from the University of Illinois, in 1971. They proposed that each plant could be thought of as belonging to three concentric gene pools. Plants of the same species, or of closely related species that can inter-breed easily to produce completely fertile offspring, are said to belong to the same *primary gene pool*, or GP1. Genes can be exchanged between them simply by arranging normal crosses. Plants that belong to related species, in which crossing is possible and some at least of the progeny are to some extent fertile, are said to belong to the same *secondary gene pool*, or GP2. When plants can be crossed but only by invoking extraordinary means, and the offspring are infertile or difficult to raise to maturity, then they are said to belong to the same *tertiary gene pool*, or GP3.

Thus a plant breeder can easily derive new genes from other members of the same GP1; can derive those from GP2 with more difficulty; and also has access to the plants of GP3, provided he uses extraordinary measures to obtain them. Perhaps, in these days of genetic engineering, we might invoke yet another gene pool – GP4 – which would effectively include all organisms; because genetic engineering (in theory) enables genes to be brought in from anywhere. The plants of GP3 are already accessible, even without engineering techniques.

Just to give an example, the primary gene pool of the domestic tomato, *Lycopersicon esculentum*, consists of all members of that species, plus members of the wild, ancestral *L. cerasiforme*, *L. pimpinellifolium*, *L. cheesmanii* and two other wild species, which will freely interbreed with *L. esculentum*. The secondary gene pool of the domestic tomato contains three more members of the genus *Lycopersicon* – plus a species of potato, *Solanum pennellii*. The tertiary gene pool of the domestic tomato includes the remaining two members of the genus *Lycopersicon*, plus two more potatoes, *S. lycopersicoides* and *S. tuberosum*, which is the domestic, European potato. In general, the genera of plants were classically defined primarily according to the structures of their flowers, with other considerations being of secondary importance. Now it is clear (as Graham White discovered with mosquitoes) that the ostensible physical differences between plants do not necessarily conform very precisely with underlying genetic similarity, or dissimilarity. It is convenient to think of potatoes as potatoes of the genus *Solanum*, and of tomatoes as tomatoes of the genus *Lycopersicon*. But it is clear that the plants themselves do not necessarily recognize the distinctions made by plant taxonomists.

Sometimes, then, plants of related species may successfully mate simply because they happen to be more similar genetically than appears on the surface. In addition, however, plants of related species that have different chromosomes may sometimes mate successfully. The mechanism involved occurs commonly in nature and is of enormous use to the breeder. It should therefore be discussed.

Crossing the species barrier: polyploidy

Each cell in the body of a plant contains two complete sets of chromosomes, one set inherited from each parent; a cell that contains two sets of chromosomes is said to be *diploid*. When cells divide, the chromosomes first split along their lengths to form four duplicate sets, then a new nucleus forms around each set and finally the cytoplasm splits. Therefore, two new diploid cells are formed, each with a nucleus containing two complete sets of chromosomes. During the formation of sex cells, or gametes, a new nucleus forms around each single set of chromosomes, giving four gametes, each of which contains only one set of chromosomes. A cell containing only one set of chromosomes is said to be *haploid*.

Sometimes, however, the course of cell division does not run so smooth. Occasionally, after the chromosomes have split, a new nuclear membrane forms which encloses both sets of chromosomes, and the cytoplasm fails to divide. Now there is a cell containing four sets of chromosomes; and such a cell is said to be *tetraploid*. More generally any cell that contains more than the standard two sets of chromosomes is called *polyploid*.

Mistakes in cell division are liable to be harmful. Chromosomes need to work in concert and doubling up may disrupt the harmony. However, polyploid cells often do survive and some are particularly vigorous, presumably as a result of their generous complement of genetic material. The fact that polyploids may and do survive has far-reaching consequences, both in nature and for plant breeding.

If polyploidy occurs in an ordinary growing cell — a somatic cell — then this may be of no great consequence. Sometimes a plant throws up a branch that appears different from the rest, and perhaps is more luxuriant. Such a branch sometimes turns out to have originated from a polyploid cell. But polyploidy is of most significance when it occurs during the formation of gametes, or during the first divisions of the newly-formed embryo. In the first instance, provided fertilization and development are able to proceed, then the offspring will have a different number of chromosomes from their parents. In the second case, too, a plant develops whose cells all contain four sets of chromosomes.

Because these new-grown plants have a different number of chromosomes from either of their parents, they are not able to mate with their parents, or with plants similar to their parents — though they will be able to mate with others that also have the same, altered number of chromosomes. In other words, those new-formed polyploid plants, and others like them, constitute a new species. Although accidents of cell division are usually harmful, the particular accident of polyploidy has in practice provided many new natural species and is a powerful source of new plants for the breeder.

When the parents of the newly-formed tetraploid plant are both from the same species, their polyploid offspring are said to be *autotetraploid*. But far more interesting than the autotetraploids are the *allotetraploids*: the offspring of plants of different species.

Normally, as we have seen, interspecific hybrids are infertile, because

73

the chromosomes that the hybrid derived from one of its parents cannot align properly with the chromosomes derived from the other parent and so the hybrid cannot form gametes. But if the early embryo of the hybrid becomes tetraploid and so grows into a tetraploid plant, then this offspring will be fertile, because each chromosome within it now has a duplicate of itself with which to align during gamete formation. In short, allotetraploids are fertile inter-specific hybrids.

Professor Keith Jones, director of the Jodrell Laboratory at The Royal Botanic Gardens, Kew, in London, has suggested that polyploidy (both auto- and allo-) may be far commoner than is often believed. Perhaps a great many plants that appear to be diploid originally arose as polyploids. There may be a continual doubling-up of genetic material, both through polyploidy within species, and through polyploidy in interspecific hybrids. Perhaps whenever we discover a plant whose haploid number is even, we should suspect that the species might have originated as a tetraploid. It is clear, too, that inter-specific allotetraploids do occur in nature. Indeed, Dr Peter Brandham, at Kew, has discovered series of African aloes in which some species appear to be allotetraploid hybrids of others. (Aloes are monocots of the lily family, Liliaceae. They look like pineapple-tops, and are popular ornamental plants, which allegedly have some medicinal uses.)

The accidents that lead to a doubling of chromosomes without cell division may occur more than once. Thus some plants have six sets of chromosomes – *hexaploid*; and some have eight – *octoploid*. Diploid plants may cross with tetraploid plants and the result is a sterile *triploid*, with three sets of chromosomes; or a tetraploid may cross with a hexaploid to produce a sterile pentaploid. Plants that are sexually sterile may survive in nature if they are able to reproduce asexually and they may be useful agricultural crops. Cultivated bananas are sexually sterile triploids, which are multiplied by asexual means. Their fruits contain no seed.

A great many crop plants are polyploids, either auto- or allo-. It has been suggested that all the living species of *Manihot*, which includes cassava, may be allotetraploid hybrids of extinct progenitors. Many commercially important genera include both diploid and polyploid types. Both sweet potatoes and oats include diploid, tetraploid, and hexaploid types. *Oryza sativa*, the principal species of cultivated rice, is diploid (with 24 chromosomes) while several other *Oryza* species are tetraploid. By contrast, many wild potatoes are diploid, with 24 chromosomes, while the principal cultivated types, *Solanum tuberosum* and *S. andigena* are both tetraploid. Wild potatoes also include tetraploids and hexaploids.

Within the genus *Rubus*, some raspberries and some wild black-berries are diploid (with a diploid number of 14) while some cultivated blackberries are tetraploid, hexaploid, or octoploid (28, 42, or 56 chromosomes). Loganberries (a cross between a raspberry and a blackberry) are hexaploid. The brassicas – cabbages, turnips, rapes and mustards – are similarly varied, while the swede evidently occurred first as a tetraploid hybrid of *Brassica oleracea* (the species that includes cabbage, Brussels sprout, broccoli, kohl rabi, and cauliflower) and *Brassica rapa*, the turnip. According to some accounts, swedes probably occurred first in cultivation, in Bohemia, in the 17th century.

The various plants known as wheat are a positive symphony of polyploidy. The primitive, archetypal wild wheat is *Triticum monococcum*, known as einkorn. It is diploid, with 14 chromosomes – two sets of seven. However, sometime in its history, *T. monococcum* was fertilized by a wild goat grass. The precise identity of that grass is still a matter for discussion, but a strong candidate is *Aegilops speltoides*, also known as *Triticum speltoides*. *T. speltoides* also has 14 chromosomes, but they are not directly compatible with those of *T. monococcum*, so the hybrid offspring are generally sterile. Polyploidy may ensue, however, and at some time in the far past one such hybrid emerged as a new species, the tetraploid, 28-chromosome *Triticum turgidum*. The cultivated form of *T. turgidum* is commonly known as emmer, and was chief of the kinds cultivated by the Romans. One 'subspecies' of *Triticum turgidum* is known as *durum*; and durum wheats now provide the world with pasta.

But tetraploid emmer, either in the wild or in cultivation, also effects unions with another wild goat grass, *Aegilops squarrosa*, otherwise known as *Triticum tauschii*. The hybrid offspring, with three sets of chromosomes, are sterile, but they have undergone polyploidy to produce the hexaploid *Triticum aestivum*, with 42 chromosomes. *Triticum aestivum* is bread wheat and it is the thousands of varieties of *Triticum aestivum* that have dominated the arable fields of the temperate world.

The emergence of bread wheat and durum wheat, tetraploid potatoes, swedes and loganberries were natural events seized upon by growers and farmers. Ever since the 1930s, however, breeders have been able to induce polyploidy and so produce fertile inter-specific hybrids artificially. The most notable artifice to date is triticale, the polyploid hybrid of wheat and rye.

This extension of natural processes will be discussed in the next chapter, but here we should note yet another anomaly of cell division that in the wild may generate new species, and which again is exploited by breeders.

Accidents of cell division: aneuploidy

Polyploidy is not the only accident that may occur during cell division. Sometimes the chromosomes fail to divide into two complete sets, so that one daughter cell finishes up with more chromosomes than usual and one with fewer. Occasionally, too, one chromosome or part of a chromosome may become attached to another – an event known as *translocation*. Again, the chromosomes in the daughter cells are anomalous: the chromosomes are arranged differently, even if there is still the same number as before. Organisms that contain the 'correct' number of chromosomes – whatever the 'correct' number may be for the particular species – are said to be *euploid*. Those that contain more or fewer than the euploid number of chromosomes are said to be *aneuploid*.

Usually the loss or addition of a chromosome is fatal, although it may not be in the case of polyploid plants, in which every chromosome has at least one duplicate, so that losses are to some extent covered. And as we will again see in the next chapter, the ability of plants to survive, sometimes, with too many or too few chromosomes is yet another phenomenon of which breeders make considerable use.

It is clear, however, that both in animals and plants, chromosomes do rearrange themselves during the course of evolution. After all, closely related organisms, which may be presumed to have a common ancestor, often have different numbers of chromosomes, so the number must have changed in one or both of them in the course of their descent from that ancestor. Thus, plants of the cabbage species *Brassica oleracea* all have 18 chromosomes. It is at least possible, however, that *Brassica oleracea* originated as a polyploid hybrid from two primitive brassicas that each had a diploid number of 10. So *Brassica oleracea* ought to have 20 chromosomes. But somewhere along the line, it seems, two were lost, or were integrated into the others by translocation.

Polyploidy and aneuploidy might be regarded as accidents of cell division, brought about by the caprices of chromosomes. Accidents or not, however, they have been important in plant evolution and are of great importance to breeders. Before we move on from our discussion of basic reproductive biology we should note one final phenomenon that might reasonably be regarded simply as a genetic disorder. But again, it is one that has been seized upon by plant breeders to great advantage. This is the phenomenon of *male sterility*.

Male sterility

Every now and again, individuals arise among various plant species that are unable to produce pollen. Such individuals have been found among maize, sorghum and barley; cucumber and carrots; tomatoes, sugar beet, onions, and sunflower.

Such male sterility is known to arise in at least three different ways. First, the gene pools of some populations of plants include recessive genes that will produce male sterility if they are inherited in double dose. Male sterility in such cases can be regarded truly as a recessive genetic disease, comparable with cystic fibrosis in human beings.

However, as we discussed in chapter 3, the genetic material of animals and plants is not contained only in the chromosomes, within the nucleus. Both the mitochondria and the chloroplasts, within the cytoplasm, carry genes of their own, which in general work in concert with those in the nucleus. Some of these so called *cytoplasmic genes* also produce male sterility. (Such genes are, of course, passed on only through the female line. If genes that produce female sterility exist, then they could not be passed on.) Such a mechanism causes male sterility in the maize variety Mexican June, which has been extremely important in the recent improvement of maize, as we will discuss in chapter 5 and chapter 9.

The third mechanism of male sterility involves both nuclear (chromosomal) genes, and cytoplasmic genes. This is the case with onions.

The nuclear genes of onions possess a gene that exists in two alleles, one of which is dominant and one of which is recessive. If the dominant gene is present, in single or double dose, then the onion is male fertile. If the onion contains a double dose of the recessive gene, then it may be fertile or it may be sterile, depending on the nature of the cytoplasmic genes. Onions also have two types of cytoplasm; if it has one type, then the onion will be male fertile, whatever the state of its nuclear genes, but if it has the second type of cytoplasm, it will be male sterile if it also possesses a double dose of the particular recessive allele. The dominant allele will 'restore' fertility to an onion whose cytoplasm predisposes it to male sterility; it is therefore known as a *restorer* gene.

Male sterility, as we have suggested, is effectively a genetic disease. It survives among plants partly because it is sometimes caused by recessive genes – and recessive genes can survive indefinitely in populations even though they are harmful. It survives, too, because most flowering plants are hermaphrodite, and a plant that is male-sterile is still fertile on the female side, and can pass on genes. It is hard to imagine that male sterility can ever be of advantage to plants in nature, except perhaps as a device to limit inbreeding. But as we will see in the next chapter, plant breeders find it extremely useful for the production of hybrids. In recent years the phenomenon has had a major influence on the breeding of maize, and has transformed the prospects of sunflowers.

Populations, species, genes and breeders

It is clear from the discussion in this chapter that what taxonomists generally mean by 'species' and what naturalists perceive to be 'populations' may in reality have many different genetic connotations. For example, if a plant is a committed outbreeder, and does not reproduce asexually to any significant extent, then each individual plant will be highly heterozygous, and each will contain a combination of genes that differs from all the others. This would be the case, say, with maize.

But if an outbreeding plant also reproduces asexually, each individual is highly heterozygous, but each individual will also be surrounded by others that are genetically identical to itself. In other words, the population will consist of a number of clones, each containing highly heterozygous individuals. This would be the case among wild, tuber-forming potatoes.

Sometimes asexual reproduction may be more significant in a given context than sexual reproduction. Then, the entire population may consist of a single clone, in which the individuals may tend to be either heterozygous or homozygous, depending on whether the sexual reproduction is carried out by inbreeding or by outbreeding. All the individual plants in the population would therefore be the same as all the others. Patches of grass are often of this type.

If the plants are inbreeding then each individual is liable to be fairly homozygous, though there would be some measure of heterozygosity because most inbreeders do outbreed to some extent. A wild population could be highly variable, however, because each group of inbred siblings may be quite distinct from each other group of inbred siblings. Such might be the case in a patch of wild wheat.

Sometimes, plants may be extremely vigorous and successful in the wild even though they are sexually sterile. This would be the case with asexually-reproducing interspecific hybrids that had not undergone polyploidy.

With cultivated plants, slightly different rules apply. The outbreeding species might remain as heterozygous, variable populations, as in the wild – though the amount of variability would be far less than among wild plants. But the inbreeders and those that reproduced asexually would not be variable, because all would be clones or siblings from one single parent plant. In fact, inbreeders and outbreeders would be extremely uniform. Finally, breeders may produce groups of plants that reproduce sexually and are extremely heterozygous, and yet are also extremely uniform. This is the case with F1 hybrids.

Such discussion, however, belongs in the next chapter.

5 Breeding from the Beginning

Introduction

The modern age of plant breeding began only in the 20th century, when the work of Gregor Mendel was rediscovered. But the moderns inherited crops that were already very different from their wild ancestors – crops that had been developed over thousands of years by farmers, craftsman breeders, and the pre-Mendelian breeders of the 18th and 19th centuries who made the best use they could of the science available in their day. We should look first at the improvements that were made before the modern age.

The beginnings of improvement: the first farmers

The world's first true arable farmers lived in the Middle East about ten thousand years ago, and their crops were wheat and barley. At intervals over the next few millennia, agriculture on a significant scale sprang up in India, China, North, South, and Central America, and in East and West Africa. But according to Dr John Yellen, of the National Science Foundation, Washington, the first conscious acts of cultivation probably took place some 30 000 years ago – perhaps in the forests of West Africa. Someone perceived that seeds sprouted to produce new plants, and so indeed did many a twig, if stuck into the ground. And if a plant is consciously planted, then that is cultivation. No traces are left of those early efforts, but it is hard to see how agriculture could have arisen so often in so many different places as the centuries passed unless there had been a long tradition of informal planting and protection.

It is very easy to see why people might have cultivated particular plants. They increase the numbers by so doing, and ensure that they have the plants they prefer in the place and at the time that they need them. Our ancestors' brains were as advanced as ours, and they could have seen that seeds or twigs would grow into plants, just by observing them doing so on any forest floor.

What is far harder to understand is why people should ever have begun to cultivate on a large scale, eventually to the virtual exclusion of hunting and gathering. It has often been assumed that farming took over from hunting and gathering because people immediately perceived that cultivation was self-evidently superior. But modern anthropologists have shown that this is not the case. Farming, at least when practised without the aid of draught animals, steel-bladed tools, or modern seed, and without knowledge of composting and pest control, is exceedingly hard and often unrewarding. By contrast, hunter-gathering is often rather easy. The !Kung bushmen of the Kalahari live in one of the harshest environments in the world, yet Professor Richard Lee of Toronto University has shown that their life of hunting and gathering is almost leisurely. Small children and old people do not work, and working adults need to put in only six hours' labour a day, two-and-a-half days a week, to provide enough food. The !Kung recognized 23 plants out of the 85 edible species that grew around them, and would eat 54 out of the 223 local animals. John Yellen has found that such bushmen today are perfectly well aware of the arts of farming, and occasionally plant crops and acquire herds of animals. But when their enterprises decline, as they are very likely to do in that harsh environment, they happily revert to the traditional ways. Traditional !Kung bushmen are not materialists. They have very few possessions, and do not traditionally wear clothes. But the !Kung live in one of the harshest environments on Earth and hunter-gatherers in more favoured circumstances do not necessarily live so simply. The ancient cities of Jericho and of Catal Huyuk in Turkey may well have been established before the birth of large-scale farming.

Our ancestors probably did not begin to farm on a large scale because it was easier or intrinsically more 'civilized' than hunting and gathering, but because they forced it upon themselves. Once people start to cultivate, then they obviously can grow more of the plants they require than nature provides. That, after all, is the point of cultivation. Once the food supply has increased, then the population can increase. When the population increases it becomes *necessary* to cultivate, in order to avoid mass starvation. Once cultivation becomes necessary, then more people are needed to work the soil and to harvest the crops, because primitive farming is extremely labour-intensive.

Indeed, it is an intriguing thought that the first farmers may rather have resented the fact that they were obliged to work so hard. Thus it is that when Adam and Eve were in the Garden of Eden, 'the Lord God commanded the man, saying, of every tree of the garden thou mayest freely eat' (Genesis, Chapter 2, Verse 16). But after God has banished the pair for eating the fruit of the tree of the knowledge of good and evil, He tells Adam that from now on, 'In the sweat of thy face shalt thou eat bread, till thou return unto the ground' (Genesis, Chapter 3, Verse 19).

Now that there are five billion of us, the need to sweat is all too evident – albeit now with the help of machines. Once the processes of cultivation were set in train, there was no going back.

Why, though, did the mere act of cultivation begin to cause the kinds of genetic alterations that turned wild plants into recognizable crops?

Domestication and genetic change

Plants in domestication are to some extent isolated from their wild relatives. They also live in different circumstances. For various reasons the gene pool of the quasi-isolated domestic population inevitably begins to diverge from that of the wild. Some alleles are lost from the domestic gene pool; others become far more frequent and a few are added that are not seen in the wild at all.

Two processes serve to remove alleles from the domestic pool. The first and most obvious is *selection*. The farmer begins his crop with only a few plants. These cannot possibly contain all the alleles of the wild species, so the initial gene pool is immediately diminished. Furthermore, the farmer would select the most desirable plants – the biggest, juiciest, sweetest, or least fibrous. Often, these are individuals that would not survive particularly well in the wild, because fibre and thorns and bitterness are part of a plant's natural protection. But with each generation the selection continues. Some alleles are lost and others become more frequent.

Alleles are also lost by *genetic drift*. The rarer alleles within the domestic gene pool are inevitably represented in only a few individuals. Some of these individuals are bound to be eaten or trodden on before they are able to reproduce, and so the alleles they contain die with them. By this process, small populations of organisms rapidly lose a very high proportion of their rarer genes.

If all the alleles of a particular gene are lost except for just one, then that particular allele is the only one that any plant is able to inherit, and all the plants are bound to be homozygous for that gene. At this point, the gene is said to be *fixed* within the population. As selection and genetic drift take their toll, more and more genes become fixed.

If the domestic plants are natural outbreeders, and are not reproduced asexually, then there is a limit to the extent to which the gene pool can be diminished and the variation can be reduced before the plants start to suffer from excess homozygosity. With such plants, such as maize, the farmer needs to maintain a wide variety of individuals, and must avoid selecting too rigorously. But if the plant is a natural inbreeder, such as wheat or barley, or is reproduced by tubers, as in potatoes, then the mere act of selection can produce rapid changes and a high degree of uniformity within a few seasons. After all, a new variety of wheat or of potatoes may begin with a single individual.

However, although the gene pool of the domestic plants is narrowed and refined through selection and genetic drift, it is also added to: by *mutation*, and by *introgression*.

Mutation occurs among domestic populations, just as in the wild. The difference is that some of the mutations that occur in cultivated plants are of a kind that would be positively harmful in the wild and would rapidly be repressed or eliminated, but they may be preserved in cultivation because they are extremely useful to the farmer or grower; and he protects them.

Both wheat and maize have undergone mutations of this type. Each wheat seed is attached to its stem by means of a short stalk known as the *rachis*. In wild plants, the rachis easily shatters when the wheat plant is ripe, so the seed is scattered. In domestic wheat, the rachis remains intact, and the seed remains on the stem while it is harvested – and is then conveniently removed by threshing. It would be extremely difficult to harvest domestic wheat if it still had frangible rachises. Similarly, some time in the pre-history of maize, a mutation took place that locked its seeds into a tight cob. This again is eminently convenient for the farmer. But if such an event occurred in the wild it would be fatal, because seeds that are bound in cobs cannot be scattered.

Tomatoes offer an intriguing example of a mutation or series of mutations that has been inadvertently selected not in the distant past, but over the last few decades. Most of the 8 to 10 wild species of tomato in their native South America are outbreeders, and indeed are self-incompatible. Only the kind that has been domesticated, *Lycopersicon esculentum*, and its close relatives, are self-fertile. Even *L. esculentum* tends to outbreed in the wild, however, for the simple reason that the stigma protrudes well beyond the surrounding circle of anthers, and so it is very hard for pollen to land on stigmas of the same flower.

In the wild, tomatoes are pollinated both by insects and to some extent by wind. Both of these agencies are lacking in modern greenhouses. Tomatoes in greenhouses would therefore tend to remain unfertilized, were it not for the fact that over the years in domestication the styles have become shorter, and in modern varieties are shorter than the stamens. In modern types, therefore, the anthers positively overhang the stigmas, and self-pollination is not only simple but almost inevitable. (See Rick, in Simmonds, 1976.) Modern tomatoes are not of course primitive, and they are bred by the devices of modern science, but the re-structuring of the flower is an example of the kind of change that takes place virtually as an epiphenomenon. Breeders did not consciously set out to select plants with short-styled flowers, but they did seek the ones that bore the most fruit. These inevitably were the ones that could fertilize themselves when conditions were least favourable to outbreeding.

Introgression is the addition of genes from plants that are still growing in the wild, or in other fields of domestic plants. Even natural inbreeders such as wheat are to some extent pollinated by outsiders. Natural outbreeders are particularly prone to influx of foreign pollen. When a plant is growing far from its native land, then it is not liable to be pollinated by wild plants because few of those around will be related to it. But when it is growing in its native land it will be surrounded by its wild relatives, and influx from outside is impossible to avoid. Indeed, primitive wheat fields were and are full of wild wheat-like grasses, and other cereal-like grasses, growing as weeds. Cereals are themselves 'weedy' crops, in the sense that they take readily to freshly cultivated ground and come to maturity in a short time.

In many cases, at least in the short term, introgression would undoubtedly have been an embarrassment. Indeed, William Cobbett recalled a striking example as late as 1822; one recorded not in a primitive agricultural society but in an advanced farming nation. He writes:

This very year, I have some Swedish turnips, so called, about 7000 in number, and should, if the seed had been true, have had about twenty tons weight, instead of which I have about three. Indeed, they are not Swedish turnips, but a sort of mixture between that plant and rape. I am sure the seedsman did not wilfully deceive me. He was deceived himself. The truth is that seedsmen are compelled to buy their seeds of this plant. Farmers save it; and they but too often pay very little attention to the manner of doing it. The best way is to get a dozen of fine turnip plants, perfect in all respects, and plant them in a situation where the smell of blossoms of nothing of the cabbage or rape or even of the charlock kind, can reach them. (From *Cottage Economy*, Oxford University Press, 1979, p. 89)

Turnips and rape are of course both brassicas, and charlock is very closely related, though now placed in a different genus. Brassicas are assiduous outbreeders, and indeed tend to be self-incompatible.

Thus, influxes of foreign genes may destroy decades or centuries of careful selection. But if selection continues, such influx can be very enriching. Modern cereals surely would not be the crops they are if they had not been bombarded over the years by pollen from outside. In addition, and very importantly, if a domestic plant is fertilized by a plant of a different species then the resultant hybrid may undergo polyploidy, and form a new, valuable crop. As we have seen, crops that began as allopolyploid inter-specific hybrids include wheat, swedes, and several crosses of raspberry and blackberry.

Finally, new species may arise in cultivation not by acquiring new genes, but simply by doubling up the ones they already have. In addition to the allopolyploids, some modern crops have arisen as autotetraploids, as described in the previous chapter.

Thus, farmers and growers alone have made tremendous strides in the development of modern crops. By conscious selection, they refined

83

the wild gene pool until it contained a high proportion of desirable genes, and fewer and fewer undesirable wild alleles. By being alert, they took advantage of the various genetic accidents that befell their crops: mutation, introgression, and polyploidy.

The next logical stage was simply to improve upon introgression, and to arrange specific marriages between desirable plants; that is, to make *crosses*. People who consciously organize the reproduction of plants and do not simply select such progeny as occur, can properly be called breeders. As we saw in chapter 3, the skills of plant breeding were well advanced by the 19th century, and if that had not been the case then Mendel could never have discovered his laws.

Varieties developed by farmers by the informal processes of selection and opportunism are known as *landraces*. Although they have often been selected over hundreds or even thousands of years, landraces, particularly of outbreeding species, are inevitably far more variable than modern cultivars. They are adapted to the areas in which they grow, because they have been bred *in situ*. In the fields of Peru, high in the Andes, farmers may grow a different landrace of potato in each field. Each field, after all, is different from all the others, and under such conditions the small differences in altitude, aspect, and incline may be critical. When the breeders begin to take a hand, they generally produce varieties that are less variable than the landraces. But the varieties produced by breeders are the result of conscious crossing, and they would not generally have appeared in the farmer's fields.

In short, farmers and craftsman breeders have taken the process of crop improvement a very long way. Landraces are often very difficult from their wild ancestors. They are highly selected and well adapted to their local conditions. Breeders refined the improvements and provided a wide range of quite new varieties, long before the advent of modern genetics and other modern sciences. So what was there left for scientists to do?

The contribution of science

Modern breeding differs from the craftsman skills of the past in five critical ways.

Firstly, the modern breeder is able to add whatever genes he likes to the pool of his crops, provided only that he can find ways to introduce them into the plants. The farmer begins with the wild gene pool of his local plants, and from then on is more or less obliged to stay with that pool, and the genes that flow into it from outside or arise *in situ*. The traditional breeder may bring in additional material from outside, but his knowledge of the range of such material is limited. But the modern breeder has access to all the genes in the world that might theoretically contribute to his particular crop. They are contained within the world's thousands of landraces, and wild species, and, as described in chapter 8, they are stored in 'gene banks'. Farmers of sorghum in Africa need plants that are resistant to mildew. If the local gene pool happens to contain appropriate genes, well and good. But in practice the local plants do not contain resistance genes. These are to be found only in plants growing in India. It requires the modern international network centred on ICRISAT to identify the African farmers' problems, find an appropriate gene in plants that grow five thousand miles away, and then bring those genes to the fields of the Sahel.

Secondly, because modern breeders have a very fine knowledge of genetics, they knew which crosses, between which plants, are most liable to produce the desired offspring. It is not simply a question of crossing the best with the best and hoping for the best. As we saw from chapter 3, most characters are polygenic, most genes have pleiotropic effects, and many desirable genes are recessive. If breeding programmes are to produce significant advances in a finite time and with finite resources, then they have to be carefully orchestrated; and such orchestration depends upon largely on knowing which characters are inherited to what extent, and what proportion of offspring are liable to have the required combination of characters.

Thirdly, the modern breeder understands the reproductive caprices of plants, as outlined in chapter 4. As we will see later in this chapter, the kinds of crossing and selection programmes that produce good inbreeding plants, will rapidly fail if applied to outbreeders, because the outbreeders are depressed by inbreeding. Before such subtleties were understood the improvement of outbreeders in particular tended to grind to a halt, as further selection was sabotaged by increasing homozygosity.

Fourthly, modern breeders are able to monitor their own activities. As we will see in chapter 9, they *measure* qualities that farmers and old-fashioned breeders had to take on trust, such as specific resistance to particular pathogens, and the composition and physical properties of seed proteins.

Finally, the moderns have added a short but impressive catalogue of techniques which enable them to achieve some ends that are quite out of reach of farmers and craftsmen. Some of these techniques induce changes in plants of a kind that do occur in nature, but only rarely or erratically. For example, modern breeders may induce mutation or polyploidy. Other techniques effect biological changes that could not or do not occur in nature. These would include the cloning of plants that do not normally reproduce asexually, by tissue culture; and the transfer of genes between unrelated organisms by chromosome manipulation or by genetic engineering.

We will discuss tissue culture and genetic engineering in later chapters. Here we should examine the techniques of what is properly called 'breeding': the manipulation and extension of plant reproduction.

Stage one is to establish a suitable gene pool, from which to begin the breeding programme.

The search for new genes

While the crops of primitive farmers were assailed in a random fashion by genes from surrounding plants, the modern breeder seeks to enlarge the available gene pool by precise crosses. And whereas ancient crops were occasionally augmented by chance mutations and polyploidy, the modern breeder seeks to effect such changes to order.

Crossing: GP1, GP2, and GP3

If a breeder can find the genes he requires within plants that belong to the primary gene pool of his crop (GP1) then he will do so. By definition, as described in chapter 4, plants that belong to the same primary gene pool can be crossed by the normal processes of sexual reproduction, and will produce fertile offspring. Only if the primary gene pool fails him will he turn to plants of the secondary pool, GP2. The offspring of such crosses are often infertile. If he can avoid turning to GP3, he will, but often, as we will see, he does have to turn to such distantly related plants. Then he must use extraordinary methods to effect the necessary crosses. Having obtained the hybrids, he must either render them fertile by inducing polyploidy, or – where possible – leave them in their sterile form and multiply them asexually.

Even within the primary gene pool, however, there is a hierarchy of preference. In wheat, for example, most of the steady, year-by-year improvement that is achieved at the Plant Breeding Institute (PBI) at Cambridge, United Kingdom, is achieved by crossing varieties that are already well-adapted to United Kingdom conditions, and already possess many of the characters that the farmer requires. With such crosses, the two parent varieties both contribute a fair proportion of genes to the offspring. In any case, two varieties of the same crop developed in the same country are likely to have a large number of genes in common.

Other varieties within the GP1 may possess one or two features that are desirable, but a great many other qualities that are not. For example, if a wheat is to be grown in the United Kingdom then it is essential that it is adapted to the United Kingdom pattern of winter and summer: it must endure the range of temperature, and respond suitably to changing daylength. It should also have as much resistance as possible to the diseases that occur in Britain, and possess the general characteristics required by United Kingdom farmers and processors. In short, it needs a whole battery of suitable 'background' genes, working in concert. A variety growing in northern Canada or Mexico may have particular desirable characteristics, such as protein quality or disease resistance, and it may be extremely well adapted to conditions in its own country, but would not possess the generality of genes that would produce a plant suitable for England or Scotland. A variety that was even further removed – some primitive variety or even a wild type – would have even less of the necessary 'background', and would undoubtedly possess a great many genes that were positively undesirable.

So even if the two parent plants in a cross are selected from the same primary gene pool, they will not necessarily be allowed to contribute the same number of genes to the final variety. If two established English varieties are crossed to produce a new English variety, then each may be allowed to contribute roughly the same number of genes to the offspring. But if one of the parents does not have an English background, then the progeny must be re-crossed with the established variety, to dilute the genetic contribution of the foreign parent. This is called *back-crossing*. Clearly, the progeny of the first cross derive 50 per cent of their genes from each parent. Those of the first back-cross have 25 per cent of their genes from the foreign parent, and 75 per cent from the native. In the next generation the proportions are 12½ per cent to 87½, and so on. After about five back crosses very few genes of the foreign parent remain. But if the breeder has done his work properly, and selected the appropriate individuals in each generation, then the genes that do remain will be the ones that are required. The parent that provides most of the genes and appears in every back-cross is termed *recurrent* and the one that gives just a few genes is the *donor*.

In practice, varieties advance piggy-back style. At any one time the breeder releases the best of what he has available to the farmer, but he will then continue to cross that variety with others, to provide a new generation of varieties. He will then cross the new varieties with still others, and so on – gradually refining the gene pool and adding to it with each generation.

We can see the process in action in United Kingdom bread-making wheats. Although all domestic hexaploid *Triticum aestivum* is called 'bread wheat' it is not all suitable for making bread. The true bread-making wheats are varieties whose seeds contain a high proportion of the springy proteins known as glutenins. Such wheats are not easily grown under United Kingdom conditions, and though the British grow a great deal of excellent wheat, they have traditionally imported much of what they need for bread from North America.

It was not until 1916 that the PBI released the first high quality bread-making winter wheat for English farmers. It was called Yeoman, and was a cross between Browick, which was an established English wheat, adapted to English conditions, and Red Fife, which was a spring wheat from Canada that contained the appropriate proteins for making bread. Yeoman lasted for 20 years, and was then replaced by Holdfast – which was a cross between Yeoman itself, and another Canadian variety, White Fife. Holdfast was grown until 1958, but in the meantime it was being crossed with Cappelle and Peko, and out of these crosses came Widgeon in the 1960s. The present variety Moulin is a direct descendant of Widgeon – though has acquired additional genes imported from Mexico and semi-dwarfing genes from the variety Hobbit, which we will discuss further in chapter 9.

Along the way, many wheat cultivars have been given new genes by crossing with a wide variety of primitive varieties and wild plants – some of these being in the secondary gene pool, and some in the tertiary. Thus, the wild wheatgrass, *Agropyron*, has contributed genes to Soviet wheat varieties to improve frost resistance, and has been a source of genes for rust resistance. Wild species of rye, *Secale*, have contributed genes to increase the yield of Soviet wheat. Wild and primitive species of *Triticum* itself, belonging to the secondary gene pool of wheat, have also contributed rust-resistant genes. In many cases such crosses have been achieved only by applying special techniques, as described later. At the very least, such crosses involve rigorous programmes of back-crossing, to eliminate undesirable genes. But once the foreign genes have been introduced into modern varieties, and are in the company of the appropriate 'background' genes, then they can be introduced into yet new varieties by simple crossing programmes that need not involve elaborate back-crossing and special intervention. For example, the French wheat line VPM1 contains genes for resistance to the fungus disease eyespot obtained from the goatgrass *Aegilops ventricosa*. These genes have in turn been passed on to Rendezvous, at PBI.

Similarly, rice has acquired resistance to two of its major diseases from the wild *Oryza nivara*: resistance, that is, to blast and grassy stunt virus. Some varieties of barley, *Hordeum vulgare*, have genes for fungus resistance from the wild *H. spontaneum*.

According to Robert and Christine Prescott-Allen, 320 of the 596 cultivars of potato grown in Europe (outside the Soviet Union) possess genes from wild species. Thus, *Solanum acaule* has conferred resistance to potato virus X and potato leaf roll virus. *S. spegazzinii* has donated resistance to five races of cyst nematode, *Globodera*, and to the fungus *Fusarium coeruleum*. *S. vernei* has also provided resistance to *Globodera* and *S. stoloniferum* has given a gene that gives resistance to potato virus Y. *S. demissum* has provided resistance to *Phytophthera*, the blight fungus that caused the potato famine of Ireland in the 1840s.

The world's other principal tubers have also benefited from wild relatives. The sweet potato, *Ipomoea batatas*, has acquired resistance to root nematodes from the wild *Ipomoea trifida*. Cassava, *Manihot esculenta*, has acquired resistance to various viruses from *M. glaziovii*, a tree otherwise known as deara rubber, and from the shrub, *M. melanobasis*.

Legumes do not readily accept genes from alien sources, but the soya

Figure 5.1 Goatgrass, *Aegilops ventricosa*, has contributed genes to wheat that confer resistance to eyespot, a fungus disease.

bean, *Glycine max*, has been given genes from the wild *G. soja* to increase its resistance to cold in the Soviet Union; and at ICRISAT the groundnut has been given genes that confer resistance to leaf spot and rust, from wild relatives still living in South America.

Some crops have not simply been improved, but transformed by importations of foreign genes. These include sugar cane, sunflower and the tomato, which according to Jack Harlan of Illinois could not be grown as a commercial crop without the genes it has acquired from its wild relatives (as listed in chapter 4). Such genes confer most of the tomato's resistance to disease and several qualities relating to colour, nutritional content, and ability to withstand mechanical harvesting.

The mass of cultivated varieties and related species are the best source of new genes in breeding programmes, and the world now has a network of 'gene banks' in which those varieties and species are stored – as discussed in chapter 8. But if no appropriate genes can be found, then the breeder may try another option. He can make new genes.

Genes created: mutation

In the 1920s H. J. Muller showed that genes sometimes mutated if exposed to X-rays. Later it transpired that any short-wave radiation up to ultra-violet would also induce mutation, and so too would a wide range of chemicals of the kind known as alkylating agents. By the 1960s some scientists were suggesting that the creation of new genes was the royal road to crop improvement — just as some are now suggesting is the case with genetic engineering. In practice there have been some successes, including a few notable ones, but there are many snags.

One obvious snag is that the agents that induce mutations also kill. It can be difficult to find a dose that produces mutations without destroying the material. The material that has been mutated often tends to be sickly; sometimes because components other than the genes have been damaged or poisoned, and sometimes for the simple reason that most mutations are harmful. One reason for making new mutations rather than searching for existing genes is that improvements are supposed to be rapid. But if beneficial mutations are rare (as is the case) and if the plants that possess them have also been poisoned, then it can be extremely difficult to identify the few individuals that do have useful mutations, and to obtain them in a condition in which they can contribute to the breeding programme.

Thirdly, unless mutations are induced in gametes — which effectively means in pollen — then they will not easily be incorporated into the breeding line. Finally, most induced mutations are recessive, and therefore will not make themselves felt unless they are present in double dose. Thus, the breeder will not know that he has a useful mutation until he has produced a second generation of mutated plants, some of which will be homozygous. In practice, therefore, inbreeders are most likely to benefit from induced mutation, which means that a very large proportion of crops is unlikely to benefit.

None the less, there have been successes. Several varieties of barley contain artificially mutated genes, which contribute to qualities including high yield, insensitivity to daylength, and resistance to mildew. A mutant gene that induces semi-dwarfing in rice has been produced by X-ray and a gamma-ray mutant rice released in Japan in the 1950s showed widespread improvement including the ability to grow at low temperatures. Groundnuts with thick shells, less liable to crack, have been produced in Carolina, and an inbreeding variety of cherry was produced by exposing pollen to X-ray, in the 1950s. In chapter 9 we will look at the changes produced in the United Kingdom field bean (the same species as the broad bean) by a new mutation from Sweden that changes the habit of growth.

Genes, however, are merely raw material to the breeder, comparable to the pigments used by the painter. The skill comes in combining them in exactly the right proportions and quantities in individual plants, and then multiplying those plants to provide indefinite numbers for farmers and growers. This is generally achieved by arranging the reproductive life of plants; and unless special techniques are applied, it must be done within the reproductive constraints imposed by nature. These constraints vary from species to species, as we saw in chapter 4, and breeding strategies must vary accordingly.

The combination of genes

Plant breeding programmes take many different forms, depending on which plants are being crossed, whether the starting material is primitive or already well-bred, whether back-crossing is necessary, and how much time, space, and labour is available. All plant breeding programmes are a logistic compromise between what is feasible and what is theoretically desirable.

In addition, breeding programmes fall into four distinct categories, depending upon the reproductive biology of the plants. Inbreeders in general require a different strategy from outbreeders, so we immediately have two categories. Sometimes, too, it pays to produce crops in the form of F1 hybrids, making a third category. Finally, some plants are propagated by asexual means – vegetatively. These include potatoes and the fruits of the family Rosaceae. Such vegetative multiplication leads to the production of genetically identical plants which collectively form a clone; this is the fourth category. We shall look briefly at each.

Inbreeders: wheat

Plants that are natural inbreeders do not suffer from being highly homozygous, and this simplifies breeding considerably. All the breeder has to do is to produce one plant that possesses the ideal combination of genes in a homozygous form and he has his new variety. Homozygous plants are true-breeding, and the progeny of such a plant will be uniform, but will not be depressed by their homozygosity. In practice, however, even the simplest breeding programmes of an important inbreeder such as wheat must be conducted on a prodigious scale, as meticulously as a military operation and even if the two original parents are both well-bred plants, it takes 12 seasons to produce a new variety from among their progeny. The 12 seasons may be reduced to less than 12 years, if some of the earlier generations are raised during winter as well as summer, in the greenhouse. But the later phases must be conducted in the field, and it is not possible to reduce the whole cycle by more than a couple of years.

Most breeding programmes begin with a cross between plants of equal merit, whose particular qualities complement each other. A typical cross now under way at the PBI is between Norman, which gives high yields but does not provide grain suitable for bread, and Avalon, which provides very good grain for bread but gives a lower yield.

The progeny of such a cross – the F1 generation – will all be as heterozygous as it is possible for the progeny of two essentially similar plants to be. But they are also uniform. Because each parent is highly homozygous, each of its genes is present in only one version, so there is only one version of each gene available to be passed on to each

91

Figure 5.2 It takes twelve generations to develop a new wheat variety. One way to shorten the process is to grow more than one generation per year, as in this incubator at the Plant Breeding Institute in Cambridge.

offspring. Each individual member of the F1 generation therefore inherits exactly the same genes from each of its parents.

The breeding programme becomes interesting when the F1s are crossed with each other to produce the F2s. These also tend to be highly heterozygous, though less so than the F1s. But they are extremely variable, because their parents, the F1s, are also highly heterozygous, and it is impossible to predict which version of each gene they may pass on. Indeed it is at the F2 stage that the breeder sees the greatest variability that will ever be produced in the breeding programme.

These F2s are exposed to disease (to screen out the susceptible ones) and examined by eye, to see in particular if they are of the right height and have correctly shaped ears. Seeds are taken from an ear of each of the minority that survive this scrutiny, and all of the seeds from each favoured ear are planted in a row, to grow into the F3 generation.

The F3s are more homozygous and more uniform than the F2s; they, after all, are the result of inbreeding, as the F2s are self-fertilizing. Indeed, from F2 until the end of the breeding programme the hybrids become more and more homozygous and uniform, as each generation is inbred and selected. By F6, the plants are highly homozygous.

Selection continues rigorously in each generation. At F5, trials for yield begin, and by this stage there is enough grain to test for milling and bread-making quality. By F9, the plants are ready to go for statutory national trials to see whether they are worthy to be entered in the National List. By the twelfth season after the initial cross, the survivors constitute a new variety, which may be offered to farmers.

Though the improvement of inbreeding plants is conceptually simple, in practice it requires time, expertise, and considerable resources. The number of different genetic combinations that could be produced in the F2 generation is literally astronomical, so the breeder could in theory have a vast number of progeny to examine. In practice, he must compromise between what is theoretically desirable and what is feasible. In any one season at PBI, about 2 000 F2 progeny are examined, from each cross that is made.

However, there is little point in examining the progeny of just one new cross in a season. At PBI, John Bingham and his colleagues make about 1 100 different crosses in a given year. These may involve scores of different varieties. When I visited PBI early in 1985, 2 000–3 000 varieties were being 'actively considered' for inclusion in breeding programmes. In the end, in that particular year, the PBI breeders made about 800 crosses, between pairs of varieties drawn from 87 different types. Between them, the different crosses generate around two million progeny by the second generation – about 2 000 grandchildren from each of around 1 000 original crosses.

Inspection of the F2s invariably show that many of the original crosses are of no value, and those particular breeding lines are simply discontinued. All the F2 progeny from that particular cross are rejected. From other crosses, perhaps only half a dozen F2 individuals are retained and in other cases, several hundred F2 progeny are kept. In total, around 50 000 of the two million F2 individuals are kept: the seeds from one of the heads of each one are sown in a row, to produce 50 000 seed rows of F3s.

In short, the numbers are prodigious and the whole operation is doomed unless the breeder has a very keen knowledge of the different varieties that could usefully be incorporated in the breeding programme. The programme will be unsuccessful, too, unless the breeders are able to make rapid and accurate assessments of the plants at each generation, to decide which should be kept – using the kind of screening methods described below in the breeding of pest-resistant millet. Clearly, such an exercise has to be extremely well organized and conceptual simplicity is not to be equated with practical simplicity.

Outbreeders: an exercise in compromise

Whatever the logistical problems may be, the breeder of an inbreeding plant is essentially home and dry once he has produced a single homozygous plant that has the required combination of genes. All he needs to do at that point is to multiply the plant, which can be done simply by sexual inbreeding. The homozygous offspring are uniform, they are the same as their parent, and they are not depressed by the homozygosity.

The breeder of outbreeders has a conceptually more difficult task. If he produces a plant with a perfect combination of genes in a homozygous form, then that plant will fail, because of inbreeding depression. But if he produces a perfect plant in a heterozygous form, then it will not breed true. He must therefore find a compromise. He must produce a population of plants that is not too variable, otherwise it will not be recognizable as a true variety, will not be easy to manage in the field and will not perform as the consumer requires it to perform. But the population must be sufficiently heterozygous to avoid inbreeding depression: so it must be variable to some extent.

In genetic terms, the breeder of outbreeding plants is aiming to produce a population whose gene pool has four outstanding characteristics. First, the genes that code for critical characters – such as those that determine the number of seeds – should ideally be 'fixed': that is, be present in only one allele so that all individuals within the population possess that allele and exhibit the most important characters. However, genes that code for characters that do not directly affect the value of the crop, should preferably be present in several or many different forms – alleles. This ensures that the plants are genetically variable, and that each individual plant is as heterozygous as possible, at least with respect to those 'non-critical' genes. In general, though (and this is the third requirement) it is as well if each of the different alleles of any one gene tends to produce roughly the same phenotype as the others, so that the plants are phenotypically reasonably uniform, even if they are genetically varied. Finally, the breeder should contrive to purge as many overtly deleterious genes as possible from the gene pool. Whatever steps are taken to keep the population heterozygous, homozygosity is bound to increase, and only the purging of deleterious genes can avoid inbreeding depression.

In practice, there are several different routes by which such a compromise can be effected. By way of illustration, we will look at one technique now being applied to millet, at ICRISAT, and take a broad view of maize development in the United States.

Millet at ICRISAT Millet is an outbreeder that until recently has been bred only by farmers and traditional breeders. Traditional 'varieties' of millet therefore tend to be highly heterozygous, and highly variable.

When a group of plants is highly heterozygous and variable then the plants' true potential is concealed. The gene pool may include a gene that would produce big heads with many seeds and other genes that produce big seeds, but it would also include many other alleles that produce small heads with few seeds, or small seeds. If the genes that produce the big heads and big seeds were recessive, then big heads and big seeds would appear only in those very rare plants that happen to be homozygous for both the relevant alleles. Note, too, that genes that produce big heads and big seeds could well be recessive, because such qualities are not necessarily advantageous in nature and natural

SM[F4]12935

Figure 5.3 Millet at ICRISAT is improved in part by growing plants in groups, and selecting for a particular quality within each group.

selection might select against them if they were dominant.

So when a breeder is faced with primitive varieties of a plant such as millet, the first thing he must do is just to explore its potential. At ICRISAT, John Whitcombe and his colleagues established plots of millet in 1975. Within different plots, they select for different characters. Within some plots they select for short plants, rejecting the tall ones. Within others they select for big heads, and in other plots, for big seeds. The plants within each plot are allowed to breed only with others in the same plot, so that they become increasingly inbred, but any plants that clearly suffer from such inbreeding are rejected, so that the total load of deleterious alleles within each plot is steadily reduced and those that remain are increasingly tolerant of homozygosity. So the plants within each plot become more uniform, but at the same time, become more and more distinct from the plants in the other plots. Every now and again plants from two different plots, each with different desirable characters, are merged to begin a new plot – and that too is refined as the seasons pass.

After just 10 years of such rigorous, formal selection, yield in some plots is now 15 per cent higher than at the beginning, and there is no reason to assume that any plateau has been reached. Some individual plants have heads 30 centimetres long. This is an example of what can be achieved by an orderly examination and refinement of the ancestral gene pool. In essence, the process does not differ from the field-by-field selections made by farmers over millennia, but because the ICRISAT scientists made their selections systematically and rigorously, on small populations that are protected and isolated, they have been able in 10 years to improve significantly on what has been achieved through millennia of traditional practice.

Such techniques are also used in the improvement of maize, again producing distinct strains that are more uniform and tolerant of homozygosity than primitive varieties. Before such order was introduced progress was more fitful. With maize, too, great efforts have been made over the years to combine heterozygosity with uniformity by various degrees of hybridization.

Maize Maize is an ancient crop which was first cultivated by American Indians about 3 000 years ago. It takes many forms, including sweetcorn, which contains sugar instead of starch in its embryos; the ancient pop-corn, which bursts when roasted; the flints, with large floury kernels; and the dents, which have soft starch at their centres and wrinkle (become dented) as they dry.

Europeans in the United States effectively took over from the Indians in the 19th century. In the first half of the century, dents grew in the south, and flints grew in the north. In the mid-19th century farmers in the middle of the United States crossed the two types, and the region where this occurred now forms the corn belt; a swathe across the centre of the country.

The first corn-belt farmers strove to produce better maize, and introduced the corn shows which became an important feature of middle-American life until the early decades of the 20th century. These were traditional shows, comparable to the dog-shows of today – and unfortunately run on much the same lines. The judges had firm ideas on what was desirable. Their principles were firm but arbitrary, and were based primarily on aesthetics. Thus, they favoured cylindrical cobs, typical of the flints that formed the northern component of the corn belt inheritance. They also liked plants with only a single stem and with only one cob per stem, which is more typical of the dents. And of course, the judges favoured uniformity; this being a necessary feature of all crops.

The shows did have some merits. They concentrated the minds of the farmers and led them to select carefully. But they also helped drastically to reduce the rich gene pool that the white farmers had inherited from the Indians, as a very narrow spectrum of features was selected. And those features that were selected were not the most appropriate: yield and pest-resistance are more important than the shape of the cob. Finally, unless the desire for uniformity is tempered by an appreciation of the need to maintain heterozygosity, it leads inevitably to inbreeding depression.

Science was brought to bear in the 20th century. Trials showed that the champion plants of the show bench did not yield particularly well. Maize grown for weight rather than looks out-yielded the handsome show-winners by about one-fifth. The seeds supplied by commercial seedsmen, designed to meet show-bench criteria, produced feeble plants that had been selected for the wrong characters and were deleteriously inbred. By the 1920s the corn shows had passed into agricultural history.

Since the 1920s there have been two outstanding developments. By careful selection in small plots, followed by integration with others, breeders have developed fairly uniform lines reasonably tolerant of homozygosity, as described for millet.

The second development came with the realization that if two uniform, fairly homozygous, but not too enfeebled populations were raised separately and then merged, then the resultant F1 hybrids would be heterozygous and would recover their vigour, but would also be uniform. When this principle was first applied to maize in the early 20th century results were somewhat equivocal. The varieties of those days were not tolerant of homozygosity. If the intended parents were truly homozygous and uniform, then they were so depressed that they could hardly produce enough seed to provide a worthwhile generation of hybrids. On other hand, if the parents were more heterozygous and less uniform, then the hybrids would also be highly variable and probably very little superior to their already heterozygous parents.

The solution to this problem came in 1918, from D. F. Jones, in Connecticut. The cross of A with B might not be economic, nor yet the cross of C with D, but if the F1 progeny of A and B were crossed with the F1 progeny of C and D then the resulting *double cross* could produce very vigorous and reasonably uniform offspring that justified the extra effort of production. By the 1930s such double crosses were economically important and by the 1950s they accounted for practically all the maize grown in the United States corn belt.

However, the main reason for producing double crosses was that single crosses could not be generated in sufficient quantities because the original homozygous breeding lines were too feeble. But as the 20th century progressed the gene pool of maize was progressively stripped of many of its harmful alleles by the kind of selection processes described for millet. By the 1950s there were some relatively homozygous lines that were quite acceptable. When these lines were crossed, their progeny – F1 hybrids – were at least as good as the double-cross hybrids. They are also less trouble to produce and by the late 1950s the new F1 hybrids began to predominate.

All of which brings us to our third category of breeding strategies: the production of F1 hybrids.

F1 hybrids

F1 hybrids ought to be the ideal crops; the only kind of crops that are propagated by sexual means and yet combine heterozygosity with uniformity. Homozygous inbreeding plants are of course uniform, and do not suffer overtly from inbreeding depression, but even they benefit from heterozygosity, which suggests that even the best-adapted inbreeders are depressed to some extent. Nowadays, therefore, F1 hybrids even of wheat are being developed. In the case of wheat however, this may be considered a luxury. In the case of outbreeders, F1 hybrids are a positive boon.

There are, however, three theoretical problems. The first is that the F1 hybrids will not be uniform (which is part of the reason for producing them) unless their parents are homozygous, but outbreeding plants do not generally adapt happily to homozygosity. Thus it was not at first economic to produce F1 hybrid maize because the homozygous parents were too enfeebled and it did not become economical until parent varieties were produced that were reasonably free of deleterious alleles and fairly tolerant of homozygosity.

Secondly, it is theoretically difficult to produce F1 hybrids on a large scale. To produce an F1 hybrid, type A must be crossed with type B. But when plants are grown on a commercial scale there will be thousands of individuals both of A and B. How can the As be prevented from fertilizing other As, and the Bs fertilizing other Bs? By various means, is the answer – which will be discussed below. Until this conceptual problem is overcome, the reliable production of F1s is impossible.

Thirdly, F1 hybrid seed does not breed true. A farmer who grows F1 hybrids cannot simply save some of his seed for next year. At least, if he does, the subsequent, F2 crop would be an extraordinary mixture. For modern farmers, this is no problem since they are used to buying in new seed. For traditional farmers, however, the F1 hybrid has less to offer because it often is not economical to buy in new seed. However, the increased yields should more than offset the cost of new seed, and if the farmer has a market for his increased crops, then F1s should pay their way. ICRISAT has already provided an F1 hybrid sorghum for farmers in the Sudan.

We should return to the second problem, however; how to ensure that each individual in the F1 generation truly has an A parent and a B parent, and is not simply the offspring of two A or two B parents.

One possibility is to make use of the phenomenon of self-incompatibility, whereby two crops of the same phenotype will not interbreed. The disadvantage here is that most commercial crops that are reproduced sexually do not possess specific mechanisms of self-incompatibility. Various members of the species *Brassica oleracea* are self-incompatible, however; so this phenomenon is of use in producing F1 cabbages and cauliflowers.

The second, and more widely applicable, approach is to ensure that one of the potential parents produces no pollen. All the seed it produces must therefore have been provided by the other kind of parent. Thus, one parent provides the seed and the other provides the pollen.

There are several ways to prevent pollen production – that is, to *emasculate* a plant. The first and most obvious way is to remove the anthers physically. For small plants with intricate, hermaphrodite flowers, such an exercise would be ludicrous, at least as an exercise in commercial seed production. But in maize, male and female are in separate flowers, even though both are on the same plant. In fact, the pollen is born on huge, conspicuous tassels, at the top of the plant, while the female flowers, which become the cobs, are on the side of the plant. It has been estimated that at one time, 125 000 people in the United States were involved at the appropriate season in removing the tassels from maize.

A second method is to apply chemical agents that selectively suppress pollen production. This is the method now being employed to produce hybrid wheat in the United Kingdom, for possible sale in the next few years. The F1 hybrids are said to out-yield present pure-bred varieties by around 15 per cent.

The third method is to make use of the phenomenon of male sterility. The genes that produce sterility are in some cases inherited as recessives, and in others are born in the cytoplasm. As described in chapter 4, male sterile individuals have been found in maize, sorghum, barley, cucumber, carrots, tomatoes, sugar beet, onions, and sunflowers.

In the case of maize, genes that produced male sterility – in this case mitochondrial genes – were discovered in the 1940s in Texas, in a variety called Mexican June. If a breeder desired to produce a male sterile line within any particular variety, all he had to do was to cross the variety with Mexican June, and then back-cross with his original variety.

There is one remaining conceptual difficulty. When the F1 seeds are planted and grow up, they are supposed to produce seeds of their own. They will not do this unless male fertility has been restored to them – for pollen must be present. It is necessary, then, to imbue the F1 hybrids with restorer genes and suitable ones were discovered in maize in the 1950s.

So F1 maize hybrids, incorporating the Texas June male sterility gene, became very popular. Indeed, as Major M. Goodman of North Carolina State University records in Simmonds (1976), 'by the late 1960s essentially all US production was based upon male sterile lines using the Texas form of cytoplasmic sterility, except for a few experimental hybrids.'

This might be the end of the story, except that stories in plant breeding never end. The problem was now that all the individuals in the entire United States maize crop had too many genes in common. They were not uniform – or not as uniform as inbreeding crops could be –

but they were similar in respects that proved crucial. They all proved to be susceptible to race T of the southern leaf blight fungus *Helminthosporium maydis*, which in 1970 devastated the corn crop. This setback is not an indictment of F1 hybrids, but illustrates that there are advantages in variability, even in a country such as United States which has ways of controlling disease.

The future for maize is perhaps to become more dynamic. The gene pool will continue to be refined, so that deleterious alleles are purged and plants are able to tolerate greater degrees of homozygosity. On the other hand, more beneficial, or at least harmless, alleles need to be brought back into the overall gene pool, to restore at least some of the variety that existed before Europeans took over the breeding. Hybrids will be generated that are expected to be grown only for a few years, to be replaced by others. The whole process needs to become more fluid, with constant refinement and enrichment of the gene pool.

The phenomenon of male sterility, leading to production of F1 hybrids, has entirely transformed the prospects of the sunflower. Patrice Leclercq discovered a source of cytoplasmic male sterility in France in 1969, in a cross between the cultivated sunflower, *Helianthus annuus*, and the wild *H. petiolaris*. In 1970, Murray Kinman in America discovered a gene that would restore fertility in a wild form of *H. annuus*.

Sunflower hybrids that incorporate the male sterility gene from *H. petiolaris* are now grown over much of the world, including 90 per cent of the North American sunflower area. They are more disease-resistant than the ordinary varieties; they come to maturity all together, not over a period, as ordinary types do; and their yield is greater by 18–25 per cent. Here, in the short term, is an unequivocal triumph for F1 hybrids.

It can be seen that the provision of outbreeding varieties is complicated. Heterozygosity and uniformity are both required, and they cannot be guaranteed in outbreeding plants that reproduce sexually, except by going through the complicated procedures needed to produce F1 hybrids. But if plants can be propagated asexually, then those problems are solved.

Clones

The breeder of an inbreeding species takes two seasons to produce a plant that roughly corresponds to what is required, and spends the next five seasons restoring it to homozygosity, so that it will breed true. The breeder of outbreeders has to manoeuvre the gene pool of entire populations of plants to produce reasonable uniformity without loss of performance. If a plant reproduces asexually, then the breeder merely has to produce the required combination of genes by sexual means, and then multiply the elite possessor of those genes by tubers, cuttings, or whatever means is most convenient. The only problem is that of speed. A breeder of wheat who is multiplying an elite plant for distribution can produce hundreds of copies per season, and within a few years can produce huge numbers of the plant. An elite potato provides only about a dozen plantable tubers at the end of the first season, and 12 × 12 at the end of the second season. It can take several years to produce plants in sufficient number to distribute to farmers. Tissue culture methods will accelerate matters, however, as discussed in chapter 6.

The four categories of breeding strategy we have described so far can be applied only to plants that are entirely sexually compatible. When the intended partners are not completely compatible, the breeder must employ special techniques. In principle, the special techniques fall into three categories. Firstly, cells from different species may simply be fused, by the process of *somatic hybridization*. Secondly, genes may be transported between unrelated species by genetic engineering. These two techniques bypass normal reproductive processes altogether and are discussed in the next two chapters.

However, when plants are reasonably closely related – both members of the same tertiary gene pool – then it is sometimes possible to combine all or part of their chromosomes into one cell. Such techniques extend and exploit normal reproductive processes, and we should therefore discuss them here.

The mixing of chromosomes

There are two main ways in which breeders seek to alter crops by intervening at the level of the chromosome. The first technique, a powerful source of new interspecific and intergeneric hybrids, is by inducing polyploidy. The second is through the various techniques of *chromosome manipulation*, which have been used since the 1960s.

Polyploidy: triticale and sugar cane

Plants sometimes appear naturally in polyploid form. Even if this does not happen in nature, polyploidy can be induced chemically. The original and standard method of doing this is to apply the alkaloid known as colchicine, which was first extracted from the autumn crocus (of the genus *Colchicum*), in 1937, by a Frenchman, Pierre Givaudon. Colchicine interrupts cell division after the chromosomes have doubled, thus producing a cell containing twice the original number of chromosomes. Presumably the alkaloid serves the autumn crocus as a defence mechanism against predators, but whatever its natural role, it has proved invaluable to geneticists and plant breeders.

Some crops, as we have seen, are natural autotetraploids: the potato is a notable example. Virtually every crop has now been produced and examined in tetraploid form, or in some higher ploidy, to see whether the polyploids are superior to the diploids. Sometimes polyploids are more vigorous than the diploids from which they are derived, but usually the advantages fail to outweigh the disadvantages, which can include failures in development. If polyploids were always superior, then we might reasonably assume that they would by now have taken over the world.

However, when polyploidy is induced in inter-specific hybrids, the possibility arises of producing entirely new crop species. The most remarkable success story so far is that of triticale, the fertile hybrid of wheat and rye.

The first recorded attempt to create such a hybrid was made in 1875, by the Scottish botanist Stephen Wilson; he tried to combine the hardiness of rye with the general desirability of wheat. He was disappointed, however, since the hybrid offspring were not particularly exciting, and were frequently sterile. But then, rye has only 14 chromosomes (2×7) whereas durum wheats have 28 (4×7) and bread wheats have 42 (6×7). A hybrid of rye and durum has 21 chromosomes $(7 + 14)$, and one of rye and bread wheat has 28 $(7 + 21)$. In neither case do the rye chromosomes have partners with which to align during gamete formation.

In the mid-1950s, however, Dr F. G. O'Mara of Iowa State University applied colchicine to a hybrid of rye and durum, and so produced the first fertile hybrid – with 42 chromosomes. The new hybrid was not only a new species, but a new genus; and its name, *Triticale*, is also a hybrid, derived from *Triticum*, wheat, and *Secale*, rye. Fertile triticales have also been produced between rye and bread wheat – with $2 \times 28 = 56$ chromosomes.

Problems lay ahead, however. These in part were merely those that beset all cereal breeders and are discussed in chapter 9 such as how to produce short-strawed, high-yielding varieties and how to improve grain quality. But the main problems were those peculiar to allopoly-ploids, those of producing strains in which the enlarged collection of chromosomes behaved as a team.

There are various difficulties. During normal cell division or the formation of gametes, the chromosomes of wheat and those of rye do not necessarily divide at the same rate and hence both development and fertility may be impaired. Secondly, the chromosomes from the two quite different parents may become confused, so that they are unable to divide cleanly to produce gametes. The reason is as follows.

In an ordinary diploid cell, each chromosome has a matching partner, derived from the other parent. Each member of each matching pair is said to be *homologous* with its partner. However, when different but related plants are combined to form an allopolyploid, each chromosome may find that it has not one, but three, possible matching partners. One

Figure 5.4 Triticale (centre) is a hybrid of wheat (left) and rye (right). It is a man-made species, now grown almost worldwide. The particular wheat shown here is a hexaploid bread wheat, though tetraploid durum wheat is the more usual parent.

is its homologous chromosome. The other two are the equivalent chromosomes derived from the other species in the hybrid partnership. Such equivalent pairs of chromosomes from different members of the partnership are said to be *homoeologous*.

During the formation of gametes, each chromosome must align with its homologous partner. During this alignment, the two homologous chromosomes exchange some of their genes, in the process known as *crossing-over*. In allopolyploids, however, it sometimes happens that one or several chromosomes align themselves instead with one of the homoeologous chromosomes. Confusion breaks out, and gamete formation is interrupted.

Often there is no confusion. Sometimes the two parents of the hybrid do not have chromosomes that are particularly similar, even though they are related. In hexaploid wheat, there are specific genes that generally prevent homoeologous chromosomes from coming together. Wheat and rye have comparable chromosomes, and some of the hybrids between them were partially sterile because their chromosomes interfered with each other. Triticale plants produced in the early days often looked marvellous during the summer, with large opulent flowers, but they then failed to produce worthwhile quantities of seed.

These problems have largely been overcome, however. Triticale is

103

now well established in Canada, Australia, the United States, Eastern Europe, the Soviet Union, China, Argentina, Southern Europe and Mexico. It is the first new cereal crop to be introduced in several thousand years and is a man-made genus. But comparable exercises continue to generate new promising species in other crops. There are many examples within the genus *Rubus*, which includes the blackberries and raspberries. Efforts continue too to produce commercially useful polyploid hybrids within the genus *Brassica* and between *Brassica* and the related genus *Raphanus*, the radishes.

Sugar cane is also a successful polyploid, but is a quite extraordinary example, in several ways unique. The original cultivated sugar cane was of the 'noble' kind. This was *Saccharum officinarum*, which has 80 chromosomes, and may well be octoploid – presumably an allopolyploid derived from various wild ancestors. In the early decades of this century breeders began crossing *S. officinarum* with the wild *S. spontaneum*, which has variable numbers of chromosomes – between 40 and 128. When hybrids between *S. officinarum* and *S. spontaneum* were back-crossed with the original *S. officinarum* nobles, the result was a confused mixture of plants. Some of these plants have 100–125 chromosomes, of which 5–10 per cent are derived from the wild *S. spontaneum*. Many of the progeny produced by such back-crossing are aneuploid and sterile. The result may sound disastrous, but in fact the aneuploids grow extremely well and their sterility does not matter as they are reproduced asexually. They displaced the original nobles around 40 years ago and are the only aneuploid hybrids to achieve commercial success as food crops.

These are examples of new crops being produced by combining the chromosomes of one plant with those of another. But breeders can go further than this. For example, in some cases chromosomes can be manipulated so that only parts of them, containing desirable genes, are transferred. Such techniques have produced significant improvements in wheat, the most widespread crop of all. They have been employed since the 1960s, and are effectively a fore-runner of genetic engineering.

Chromosome manipulation

With some species, and in various ways, a breeder can add or substitute a single chromosome of one kind of plant, for another, in another plant. It may then be possible to break down the barriers that may prevent the pairing of homoeologous chromosomes, so that the substituted chromosome aligns with its homoeologous partner, and the two undergo crossing over, just as normally occurs between homologous chromosomes. The offspring of such hybrids therefore contain some, but not all, of the genes from the substituted chromosome, and after a series of back-crossing, progeny result that contain only a few genes from the substituted chromosome. Alternatively, the chromosomes may be broken up by exposure to X-rays after the foreign chromosome is introduced. After such an assault, severed chromosomes then re-form. In some of the damaged cells, pieces of the substituted chromosome will be re-incorporated into the chromosomes of the principal partner. Again, the progeny of a hybrid that has undergone such treatment will contain some, but not all, of the genes from the substituted chromosome and by suitable back-crossing, progeny will result that contain only the genes that are required.

Such techniques have been applied particularly to wheat. One reason is that wheat is one of the world's most important crops, and even the most elaborate manipulations are justified. More important is the fact that if a chromosome is to be substituted, then it is first necessary to remove the homoeologous chromosome from the recipient and only in polyploids is it possible to remove entire chromosomes without killing the plant. Thirdly, wheat has a great many relatives in its tertiary gene pool that have useful characteristics. With wheat, then, chromosome manipulation is both possible and worthwhile.

Various relatives of *Triticum*, including *Aegilops* and *Agryopyron*, have contributed and are contributing a range of valuable genes to wheat: resistance to eyespot from *Aegilops ventricosa*; resistance to stem-rust, which is of great significance in Australia, from *Agropyron*.

The method is as follows. The grass is first crossed with bread wheat. The grass is diploid, with 14 chromosomes, and so the wheat-grass hybrid has 28 chromosomes: 21 from the wheat and 7 from the grass. The hybrid is then treated with colchicine, so that it now contains 56 chromosomes.

The hybrid can in its turn produce gametes containing 28 chromosomes: 21 of which came originally from the wheat, and 7 from the grass. So the hybrid is then back-crossed with wheat – which of course supplies 28 chromosomes. The hybrid offspring of this back-cross should then contain 49 chromosomes – 42 from wheat and 7 from grass. The 49-chromosome plant is then back-crossed again with wheat; but the gametes produced by the 49-chromosome plant are a mixed bag. Some contain only 21 chromosomes (the wheat chromosomes). Some contain as many as 28 (21 from wheat, and all 7 from the grass). In others the numbers are anything in between.

Consequently, the progeny of this second back-cross also have a variable number of chromosomes. Some have only 42, and are in fact pure wheat. Some have 49. Others have any number of chromosomes between 42 and 49: 42 wheat, plus any number between 0 and 7 grass chromosomes.

The progeny that interest the breeder are those that contain 43 chromosomes: 42 wheat chromosomes and 1 grass chromosome. Such plants are called single-chromosome *addition lines*; and it is possible to produce an addition line for each of the 7 different grass chromosomes. With a complete set of addition lines, the breeder is able to see which grass chromosome carries the genes that determine the required character.

Breeders of wheat also keep collections of *monosomics*. These are aberrant plants that have lost a chromosome, and thus only have 41. Again, different monosomics lack different chromosomes. Again, it is only in polyploid plants such as wheat that monosomics can be maintained.

The next task is to cross the addition line that contains the required grass chromosome with a monosomic wheat that lacks the homoeologous chromosome. The result is a 42-chromosome hybrid, in which two of the chromosomes must make do with an homoeologous, rather than an homologous partner. It is possible in some cases to induce these chromosomes to 'make do' with an homoeologous partner by employing a monosomic wheat lacking the particular gene that normally prevents such pairing.

With each generation, further crossing-over occurs between the chromosome pairs as gametes are formed. After a few more generations of back-crossing, progeny are produced which contain only a small proportion of the genes contained in the original chromosomes. In some cases, those genes will include the ones that are required.

By such techniques breeders extend the normal bounds of sexual reproduction. In the next two chapters we will look at ways of bypassing sexual reproduction altogether.

6   Tissue Culture

Introduction

Plants have an advanced capacity for asexual reproduction. They produce a whole host of specialist organs dedicated to this end: modified stems, roots, buds and leaves, manifesting as tubers, rhizomes, stolons, corms, bulbs, suckers, and tillers. Breeders make use of this propensity, multiplying elite strains asexually to obviate the need to produce true-breeding, or relatively true-breeding lines. Farmers and growers of potatoes, apples, strawberries, and ornamental shrubs often prefer asexual means of propagation for the ease and uniformity they provide. Growers do not employ only the specialist organs of asexual reproduction, but take cuttings – pieces of stem or even leaf, that in nature would not normally be expected to take root – and use them as the basis for new plants.

Biologists, using the now established but still rapidly developing techniques of *tissue culture*, are able to take this process much further than the traditional grower and can even regenerate whole plants from single cells. This ability can be and is already being used for several conceptually different purposes.

Firstly, tissue culture can be used to regenerate new lines of particular crops that are free from the diseases of the parent line.

Secondly, breeders may generate huge clones of outstanding plants, each a perfect facsimile of its élite parent, thus creating many thousands or even millions of individuals in a single year. Furthermore – and this perhaps is the most important point – they can do this with plants that do not normally reproduce asexually at all.

In addition, once they have established cultures of plant cells, biologists can begin to manipulate those cells. Thus, the techniques of tissue culture are being used in various ways to create new varieties of plants, or even new species, via the phenomena and techniques of *somaclonal variation*, and *somatic hybridization*, which we will explore in this chapter. Culture techniques are also an essential prerequisite for genetic engineering, the subject of the next chapter.

Finally, once a cell or a collection of cells is established in culture, then in some cases it can simply be maintained as a colony of cells –

producing whatever materials those cells would have produced in nature. Thus, plant cell cultures are providing a new form of biotechnology that is comparable with industrial microbiology. After all, individual, separated plant cells are not conceptually different from single-celled organisms such as yeast, which already are widely used as sources of food and industrial agents.

Before we look at practical examples of all these manoeuvres it is worth asking how they are possible. Cell culture *per se* is not too difficult. Cells of many different kinds of organism can be cultured indefinitely. Some lines of human cells have been maintained in petri dishes for several decades. However, it is not possible to regenerate whole animals from single cells – or at least, not from cells that are past the very early embryo stage. And although a starfish may re-build itself from a few arms, it is not possible to regenerate a sheep from a single hoof, as an apple tree may be created from a twig. So what quality is it that plant cells possess, and animal cells tend to lack?

Totipotency

Every multi-celled organism – snail, carrot, sheep, cucumber – begins life as a single cell: usually a *zygote*, formed by the fusion of the male and the female gamete. This zygote has the power to give rise to every kind of cell that the future body will need: stele, epidermis, mesophyll in the case of the carrot; liver, muscle, and brain in the case of the sheep. Such cells, with the power to become any kind of cell to which their particular species is heir, are said to be *totipotent*.

This quality of totipotency is characteristic of the cells of young embryos, both animal and plant. Each individual cell of a four-cell sheep embryo may develop into a complete lamb, if separated and suitably nurtured. The four together form a clone of identical quadruplets. The cells are still totipotent at the eight-cell stage. In practice, it is not yet possible to produce identical octuplets, but this is only because the initial divisions in the embryo are made without any growth, so the cells from an eight-cell embryo are rather small. Nevertheless, biologists at the Institute of Animal Physiology at Cambridge in the United Kingdom have shown that if the cells from eight-cell embryos are nourished and supported by helper cells, to compensate for their lack of size, then each individual cell does have the capacity to grow into a complete animal.

However, at some point in embryonic development, animal cells lose their totipotency. Exactly when this occurs is hard to define. What is clear, however, is that totipotency diminishes as the cells begin to take on specialist functions – that is, as they begin to *differentiate*.

Totipotency, and the loss of it with differentiation, are easily explained in genetic terms. Each cell in any animal or plant contains exactly the same genes as all the other cells – apart from any mutations that may take place during the life of the organism. This may seem paradoxical, because the cells may differ in size, shape, and function – and size, shape, and function are determined by the genes. The point is that in any one cell at any one time, many or indeed most of the genes are 'switched off'. The genes in a human being's liver cells are the same as those in the white blood cells, but only a selection of the total genes is operative within the liver or the white blood cells – and a different selection is operative in each.

When a cell has lost the power of totipotency, this simply means that the genes that are switched off cannot be switched on again. This is the case with blood and liver cells. A liver cell may divide to form more liver cells, but it cannot produce any other kind of cell. Some white blood cells freely proliferate – but only to form more white blood cells. Once an animal cell is differentiated, then it cannot be de-differentiated.

Plant cells differentiate just as animal cells do. Those of the middle of the leaf, the mesophyll, are very different from those of the stele or the root, or of the epidermis, or the stem. But in plant cells the genes are *not* switched off irreversibly.

The fact that some cells within a plant are totipotent is obvious from simple observation. Behind the growing tip and the root are blocks of tissue known as meristem, and these differentiate to form all the organs of the new shoot, and the various cells of the root. In many plants, pieces of stem demonstrate their versatility by developing roots when thrust into the ground. But as the art and science of tissue culture has progressed it has become clear that *all* growing plant cells may possess this ability. Leaf, root, and stem cells are employed by different culturalists for different purposes. In addition, when a plant is damaged, it heals the wound by producing masses of undifferentiated tissue known as *callus*. Callus is clearly totipotent, and plays an important part in research and in the commercial application of tissue culture.

This difference between animals and plants – the fact that animal cells lose their totipotency quickly and permanently, and plant cells do not – is profound; as profound as any other difference between the two kingdoms. By way of explanation, we might point out that the two kinds of organism have completely different life strategies. Animals survive by moving. They avoid many of life's exigencies by getting out of the way. But the fact that they need to move imposes severe constraints on body shape, and demands that the different parts of the body should be tightly co-ordinated, so the animal can operate as a unit.

Plants stay in the same place and are obliged to endure the insults that animals are able to avoid. They need, therefore, to be both compliant and resilient. At the same time, it is not vital that their body should assume any particular shape, provided only that the roots have access to water and the leaves to the sun. An acorn planted in a park grows into a mighty tree. The same acorn lodged in a crevice of a cliff becomes a twisted shrub. Both are perfectly good oaks and both produce offspring of their own, in due course, but such flexibility of form is possible only because the individual tissues of the plant retain the ability to grow and differentiate as circumstance demands.

In fact, the word 'organism' has different connotations depending on whether it is applied to plants or animals. An individual animal is a unit; no single part of it is capable of life unless it is in the company of all the other parts. An individual plant is in some ways more akin to a colony. Different parts of it, suitably sustained and stimulated, have the capacity to form a new, independent organism.

That, however, is musing; a just-so story. The practical point is that plant cells can not only be cultured, but can in many cases be induced to regenerate into whole plants. With some species – notably the cereals – regeneration of whole plants from culture is not yet possible, but with others it is now routine. However, it has taken most of this century to evolve the necessary techniques, as we shall now examine.

The path to plant tissue culture

Tissue culture is still not a precise science. Tissue culturalists still have a tendency to swap recipes, and are far more successful with some species and families than with others. In general, members of the Solanaceae and Umbelliferae families take to culture far more readily than cereals or legumes.

The general principle, however, is to provide the cultured cells with the same kind of conditions that they would experience in the plant. They must be provided with nutrients and with growth factors, or hormones. The nutrients must include a source of energy, generally sucrose; amino-acids from which to construct proteins; plus vitamins and minerals.

The tissue culturist obviously does not expect any plant cell to perform feats of which it is not biologically capable, but he does expect to evoke qualities that are not normally evidenced in nature. Thus, although a single leaf cell may be able to produce a whole plant, it is not normally called upon to do so in nature. In order to induce cells to perform such feats, the culturist must alter the supply of growth factors in ways that are not normally evident in the whole plant.

The idea that some plant cells are totipotent, and might be cultured and regenerated into whole plants, goes back to the beginning of this century. But the first attempts failed. Culture requires a proper balance of hormones, and the first plant hormone (the auxin indole acetic acid, or IAA) was not discovered until 1934. Other hormones were dis covered later in the 1930s, and the first success in tissue culture came in

1939 when disorganized callus tissue of tobacco (Solanaceae) and carrot (Umbelliferae) were kept alive and multiplying, at least for a time.

The modern era of plant tissue culture properly began in the decade between the mid-1950s and the mid-1960s and in 1957 came the discovery that the *ratio* of hormones could influence events: specifically, F. Skoog and C. O. Miller reported that the ratio of auxin to cytokinin determined the development of organs in tobacco. In 1958, for the first time, a mass of cultured cells gave rise to a complete plant: the plant was the carrot, and the biologist was F. C. Steward. Then in 1960, Georges Morel, in France, produced the first clones from cultured cells. The plants were orchids, of the genus *Cymbidium*.

Morel's work was indeed seminal. Specifically, it gave rise to a flourishing industry. Brave men used to risk their lives to find rare orchids, and laid waste many a tract of forest in the attempt. Now, those same plants are available in the supermarket, often for less than the price of a pint of beer. More generally, Morel suggested that it would be possible to produce enormous clones of many different kinds of plant in a short time: four million a year was the figure he proposed. He also anticipated, correctly, that it would be possible to generate clones that were totally free of virus.

Then, in 1962, T. Murashige and F. Skoog described a medium for the culture of tobacco. This was not a universal formula, for there is no universal formula for the culture of plant cells. But Murashige's and Skoog's principles, for apportioning nutrients and hormones, have since been applied to a wide variety of plants. Finally, in 1965, V. Vasil and A. G. Hildebrandt announced that they had regenerated complete tobacco plants from single cells.

In the modern era, a wide variety of plants has been cultured for a wide variety of purposes, as outlined at the beginning of this chapter. Conceptually, the simplest use of tissue culture is to produce new lines of crops free from disease.

Disease-free crops: cassava

Pathogens – disease organisms – succeed by adapting to their hosts. Crucial among the necessary adaptations are methods of transmission: means of passing from host to host. Infections may be transmitted between members of the same generation, or may be passed from parent to offspring.

In vertebrate animals, few infections are transmitted from generation to generation; the example of congenital syphilis is unusual. But parent-to-offspring transmission is common among plants. Seeds are fine vehicles for all manner of diseases, and so too are the various organs of asexual propagation. Commercial breeders would obviously prefer to begin operations with disease-free stock, but in some species almost all individuals are chronically infected, particularly with viruses. Cassava is severely and chronically affected by a mosaic virus.

Tissue culture provides a way of solving the problem. Cells can be found that are free of all disease, and can be raised in sterile conditions. At San Carlos in California, scientists from the International Plant Research Institute (IPRI) have raised virus-free plants in culture, which can form the basis of disease-free lines. Eventually, they aim to raise present yields of around 10–20 tonnes per hectare to around 40 tonnes. Cassava is not a staple crop in California, as it is in much of Africa; the purpose is to turn the starch from cassava into fructose, for food, and into alcohol, for fuel, but the leap from innate disease to pristine health is an impressive demonstration of one of the powers of tissue culture.

Culture not of single cells but of meristems is now a standard technique for producing disease-free clones, particularly virus-free clones. In India, such *meristem culture* provides the only means of maintaining some important clones of potatoes for breeding purposes.

The production of clones of plants by tissue culture may prove to be of even greater commercial significance. Suitable candidates for such cloning would generally be plants of high value, to justify the costs of developing suitable techniques, which generally have to be adjusted to each kind of plant. Secondly, cloning by tissue culture is of most use when reproduction by more conventional means is difficult or slow, whether sexual or asexual. Orchids fit both these requirements admirably, and were, as we have seen, the first plants to be cloned. Apart from vanilla, however, orchids contribute little in the way of food and are outside our brief. Of greatest interest, at present, are the palms.

The value of palms

There are 2 600 species of palm and many of them are put to good use: for building and roofing, fibre, billiard balls (the ivory palm) and soap. They also provide four outstanding categories of food.

The importance of the date palm, *Phoenix dactylifera*, is somewhat concealed from western eyes, as is the case with sorghum and pigeon peas. Only about three million tonnes are produced world-wide, and only about 10 per cent of that enters world trade; and what does enter, serves merely as an occasional sweetmeat. But to the people who grow dates in the Middle East and North Africa (Iraq and Egypt are the principal producers) they often serve as a staple, as well as a prime source of flavour. In addition to fruits, *Phoenix dactylifera* is the source of palm wine.

The world produces almost 40 million tonnes of the coconut, *Cocos nucifera*. Again this crop is versatile – a source of building material and fibre as well as food. The food it provides includes copra, the valuable flesh of the coconut which for many people is a staple; coconut milk, the liquid endosperm, which is a good drink and has incidentally been widely used as an ingredient in media for tissue culture; and coconut oil. Coconut oil is the favourite cooking oil of people who grow coconuts, for example in the state of Kerala, in south-west India.

The cultivation of oil palm, *Elaeis guineensis*, is one of the world's growth industries. Thirty million trees are planted every year. Soya, sunflowers, or rape can produce about a tonne of oil per hectare per year, and have to be re-sown each season, but the oil palm can produce six tonnes of oil per year, and stand for decades. Already *Elaeis* provides the world with 14 per cent of its vegetable oil, for margarine, cooking and soap. Malaysia is the world's leading producer. There, the value of the oil palm crop is second only to rubber.

Finally, a whole range of palms provide palm hearts – the growing tip, which is eaten as a vegetable. Palm hearts are a great delicacy, with a flavour reminiscent of asparagus, and consumption is increasing worldwide. The National Academy of Sciences (1975) suggest that palm hearts, probably canned, have great export potential.

However, when the growing tip of the palm is removed the tree is killed. At present, palm hearts are taken from the wild, mainly from tropical America and the West Indies: from genera such as *Euterpe*, *Prestoea*, *Guilielma*, *Roystonea*, *Sabal*, *Acronemia*, and many others. Brazil in particular is gobbling up its wild palms. There is a very strong case for widespread cultivation of these highly valued vegetables.

Cultivation of palms is not so difficult. Dates, coconuts, and oil palm are already raised in vast plantations, or are dotted here and there in villages and cities. But to improve these crops by breeding is very difficult indeed. All palms are outbreeders, which raises the kind of conceptual problems discussed in chapter 5: the need to reconcile heterozygosity with uniformity. Furthermore, as discussed below, commercial oil palms more or less have to be grown in the form of hybrids. Yet palms are trees, and the generation time is long. Breeders of palms cannot simply race through the generations, one to three per year, as do the breeders of maize or millet.

The only practical solution to such problems is to identify the elite plants, and then to multiply them asexually; but of the palms we have mentioned, only the date reproduces naturally by asexual means, by producing suckers. The rest produce no organs or twigs or projections that can simply be placed in the ground and grown. The only possible route to asexual multiplication is by tissue culture. Both oil palm and coconut therefore are the objects of intensive research towards that end.

Cloning: oil palms

Breeders of oil-palms are concerned both with yield and with quality. Quality in this context refers largely to the degree of saturation of the oil. In general, nutritionists now suggest that highly polyunsaturated oils are preferable to highly saturated ones; the argument is that the consumption of saturated fats tends to raise the concentration of cholesterol in the blood, whereas consumption of polyunsaturates tends to lower the concentration. The chief component of palm oil, at somewhat less than 40 per cent, is palmitic acid, which is saturated. Second in concentration (and in some individual trees exceeding palmitic acid) is oleic acid which is mono-unsaturated. Mono-unsaturated oils are said to have a neutral effect on blood cholesterol, neither raising it nor lowering it, and most nutritionists consider it acceptable; olive oil, incidentally, is primarily mono-unsaturated. Palm oil also contains about 10 per cent linoleic acid, which is the typical polyunsaturated acid of seeds.

The encouraging point, however, is that the composition of oil in *Elaeis guineensis* differs significantly from individual to individual. In some, the linoleic acid content is above 15 per cent. Such innate variability raises the possibility of breeding or selecting strains that would produce an acceptably unsaturated oil. Improvement is slow, but if one just one individual plant is thrown up with a particularly high content of polyunsaturates, then that plant could in theory be cloned to provide indefinite numbers.

The degree of saturation, however, is of outstanding interest only in the developed world. Westerners tend to consume too many calories, of which about 40 per cent are in the form of fat. People of the Third World generally have a far lower intake of calories, of which 20 per cent or less is provided by fat. Indeed, simple lack of calories is a far greater problem in the Third World than is the quality of individual fats. Though it would be desirable to develop oil palms that produced highly unsaturated oil, the immediate priority is for greater yield.

Unilever is the world's largest processor of fat, and has a very considerable interest in oil palms. In the short term, Unilever breeders envisage an improvement in average yield of at least 30 per cent, this being the difference in yield between the top 5 per cent of present-day trees, and the average yield. Such trees would need to produce 40 tonnes of dry matter per hectare per year, 65 per cent of which would be channelled into the production of oil-bearing fruits.

By the methods of conventional breeding, the task of raising the present average to the level of the best would be very great. The fact that the plants are outbreeders and have a three-year generation time is itself a complication. In addition, the fruits of oil palm are less than ideal unless the plant is produced in hybrid form. The reasons are as follows.

The oil palm fruit consists of a large single seed, surrounded by the fleshy mesocarp, not unlike a plum. The seed comprises the embryo; the endosperm, which feeds the embryo; and the shell, which provides protection. The important palm oil comes from the mesocarp, which should therefore be as fleshy as possible. The endosperm of the seed provides a secondary product, palm kernel oil, which is less important.

What counts is the relative thickness of shell and mesocarp; this is determined by a single gene, known as Sh (standing for shell). This gene exists as two alleles, Sh+, and Sh−. Plants that are homozygous for Sh+ are of the type known as *dura*. These grow semi-wild in groves in Africa. Their shells are thick and their mesocarp is meagre. Plants that are homozygous for Sh− have no shells at all around their seeds, and a very thick mesocarp. These are called *pisiferas*. On the face of it the pisiferas may seem ideal. In practice, however, the Sh− homozygotes are generally female-sterile, and rarely set seed. So planters prefer Sh+Sh− heterozygotes, combining the fertility of the one with the fleshiness of the other. These heterozygotes are called *teneras*.

The production of good Sh+Sh− hybrids would not be so difficult if palm breeders had just one of the basic requirements − good, homozygous parent stocks from which to breed. But they have not. Individual palm trees tend to be heterozygous for a great many genes, and not simply for the Sh gene. So the teneras are highly variable, or in particular, they vary considerably in yield. Furthermore, the breeder cannot see how good a given pisifera will be as a parent just by looking at it. Instead, he must wait for the progeny of the pisifera to grow up, and examine them. Oil palms have marvellous potential, but their biology conspires against improvement.

Overall, the breeder of oil palms must produce trees which in general are heterozygous, to benefit from heterosis; and which in particular are heterozygous for the Sh gene. Such ideal trees should be turned out at the rate of 30 million a year. It is not easy.

The general way to circumvent such problems is to forget about sexual reproduction, with the frustrating intricacies of outbreeding and reproduce the plants vegetatively. Simply find the best individual, and cut it into hundreds of pieces. But oil palms do not provide cuttings. There is only a single stem, within which the growing tissue, the meristem, is well tucked away. There is nothing to cut off that will actually grow.

This is why scientists both at Unilever, in the United Kingdom, and at the Institut de Recherches pour les Huiles et Oléagineux (IRHO) in France are assiduously developing methods of cloning élite palms in tissue culture. Unilever began operations in 1968, and the project continues under Dr Laurie Jones and his colleagues at their research laboratory at Colworth House, Bedford. Dr Jones and his colleagues begin with tissue from the roots of a favoured plant, although other biologists prefer to begin with other tissues, such as leaf vein. The chosen tissue is first treated with disinfectant to remove microbes, and the sterile tissue is then treated with auxins to induce the formation of disorganized callus. The callus is broken up and re-cultured to form secondary callus. This re-culturing evidently serves to re-awaken genes that in the primary callus were quiescent; certainly, secondary callus differs metabolically from primary callus. The process of 're-awakening' evidently continues, because, after about a year of such sub-culturing, cells within the callus begin to organize themselves to form *embryoids*. These embryoids do not form readily, or frequently. As Dr Jones says, conditions can be adjusted to encourage the embryoids to form, but they cannot as yet be switched on to order. Once the embryoids are formed they will proliferate – which again they can be encouraged to do by altering the conditions. Shoots form first; but suitable treatment encourages roots to follow.

The new trees produced by tissue culture have a high degree of uniformity, as would be expected. There is some variation, however. This is *somaclonal variation*, which we will discuss further below. Because of this variation, the offspring must be carefully screened. For the most part, the variants are thrown out. In theory, however, some of the somaclonal variants could form the basis of useful new varieties.

At present, the tissue culture of palms is still at the laboratory stage. It will become commercial when the behaviour of the tissue in culture can be controlled absolutely, to produce embryoids *en masse* in liquid suspension. Already the promise is evident, however. The individuals within any one clone are almost uniform, which is the first requirement. In addition, there are large differences *between* clones, not least in the proportions of the various fatty acids in the oil. There is the promise, then, of providing different varieties of oil palm that serve different purposes – for cooking oil, margarine, soap, or whatever is required.

In short, cloning by tissue culture promises to transform the prospects of the oil palm. The same is true of the coconut.

Cloning: coconuts

Like the oil palm, the coconut is an outbreeder with a long generation time, defying straightforward genetic improvement. Indeed, coconuts do not bear fruit until they are 5 or 6 years old, and it takes 10 years to see whether a coconut has all the qualities required of it. A tree may live for 60 to 70 years. Like the oil palm, the coconut is devoid of suckers or other natural propagules.

As in oil palms, there is enormous variation among coconuts, and a very great difference between the best and the ordinary. The average yield in the important coconut region of Kerala in India is around 35 nuts per tree per year. But individual trees both in Kerala and in the Philippines may yield more than 400 nuts. Scientists at Hindustan Lever in Bombay, to the north of Kerala, are vigorously pursuing methods of cloning coconuts by tissue culture. Comparable work has also been under way at Wye College, of the University of London, since 1970, and is now continued by Drs Richard Branton and Jennet Blake.

Both groups culture leaf tissue of the coconut, which seems to give the best results. The fundamental methods of culture are roughly the same as for oil palm, although of course they differ in detail. One of the bedevilments of tissue culture is that conditions have to be worked out afresh for each species, and palms are among the most recalcitrant of all. But both groups are on the point of commercial success. The Hindustan Lever scientists are now growing coconuts that have been raised in culture in pots. Indeed they have several different lines, cloned from different 'élite' palms. Clones, after all, are the ultimate monoculture; and it would be unwise to base the entire Keralian crop on just one, or only a few, different lines.

It is worth lavishing such research upon oil and coconut palms – and probably on other palms as well – because they are valuable and difficult or slow to propagate by other means. The same applies to two more crops of particular value to India: tea and cardamoms.

Cloning: tea and cardamoms

Cardamoms are the aromatic seeds of *Elettaria cardomomum*, of the monocot family Zingiberaceae; the family of ginger and turmeric. India used to produce around 4 000 tonnes, of which about half were exported. But in recent years the crop has been halved by drought and viruses, and now it must be built up again. The usual way to propagate the crop is by taking pieces of rhizome, the underground storage root. To regenerate the crop in this way would be extremely slow. In this case, new plants are not being generated from single cells, but from small pieces of rhizome raised in culture rather than in the ground. Cultured pieces need be only one tenth of the size that is normally required. Thus, within a few years, the lost hectares will be replaced with élite plants, more resistant to viruses and drought than those that were grown in the past.

Similarly, the tea plants of India are growing old; some are 80–100 years of age. In addition, India's human population is growing at such a rate that by AD 2 000, if present production continues, there will be no tea left over for export. Again, élite clones are being developed by tissue culture that are higher yielding and more aromatic than those that went before. By such means India should stay ahead of its superannuated plants and its growing population, and still have some tea left for earning cash.

Cloning is only one of the advantages offered by tissue culture,

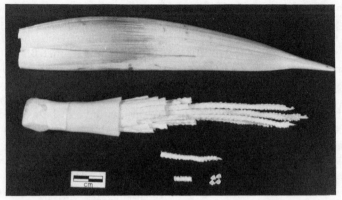

(a) Coconut – inflorescence with spathes removed (explants).

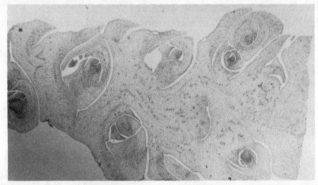

(b) immature inflorescence – coconut showing floral primorthia.

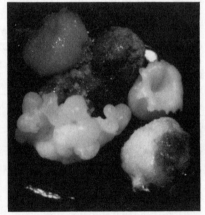

(c) Coconut explants – expansion and growth of primordia.

(d) Explant with calloid. Note abnormal flower.

Figure 6.1 Tissue culture is particularly valuable for producing clones from 'elite' coconuts, as coconuts breed slowly and do not breed true, and cannot be reproduced from cuttings.

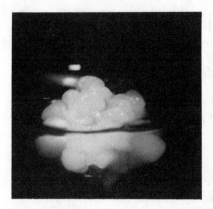

(e) (*above*) Coconut embryoids.
(f) (*right*) Germinating embryoids.
(g) (*below left*) Clonal coconut plantlet.
(h) (*below right*) Clonal coconut plantlet.

however. The techniques provide opportunities to develop quite new varieties, or even species. The first route to this end is by somaclonal variation; the second is by somatic hybrids; and the third is by genetic engineering. We will discuss genetic engineering in the next chapter. Here, however, we should look at the first two possibilities.

Somaclonal variation: potatoes and sugar cane

The idea of cloning plants by tissue cultures is to produce facsimiles of the parent. Occasionally, however, as we noted when discussing oil palms, the progeny differ from the parent. Such variation, *somaclonal variation*, may be an embarrassment to the breeder. But biologists are opportunists, and such variation is now regarded as a valuable source of new crops.

The nature of the changes responsible for somaclonal variation, and the reason for those changes, are unknown. In some cases the change may be due to genetic mutation; a change in one of the nucleotides that constitutes the DNA molecule. In other cases the changes may be more subtle, involving the expression of genes, rather than their actual alteration. Perhaps the changes are brought about by culturing. Perhaps they are of the kind that take place within the cells of plants the whole time, and usually pass unnoticed; in which case they would merely be revealed by culturing. Perhaps – indeed probably – in different cultures, and different species, different mechanisms operate. Whatever the truth of the matter, somaclonal variation occurs. Most of the variations, like most genetic mutations, are undoubtedly harmful, but in the case of somaclonal variation there is a built-in filtering system. Only those variants that have not been irreperably harmed by whatever has altered them, will grow. Thus although the rate of variation is fairly low, and the success rate of variants is even lower, successful cultures are none the less providing a steady stream of variants to explore. Somaclonal variation could generate quite new varieties or it could be used to upgrade existing varieties.

Thus, breeders at PBI are employing somaclonal variation to upgrade the potato, Maris Piper. Potatoes lend themselves readily to culture; and Maris Piper is the leading variety in Britain. It is a splendid variety but it has a few shortcomings, including susceptibility to the fungus that causes common scab, and to some viruses. Already the PBI scientists have found variants of Maris Piper that show increased resistance to scab and to viruses. These variants had their first trials in the fields during the mid-1980s. Any promising variant can be evaluated in 2–3 years and then multiplied by tissue culture for quick release to the farmers.

One of the outstanding problems for growers of sugar-cane is a fungus disease, red rot, which can wipe out entire crops. No resistant lines have been found in the wild. But resistant somaclonal variants have been found in both Fiji and Hawaii, and at Hindustan Lever in Bombay Dr S. Bhaskaran is now searching for comparable variants among the Indian stock. He is also seeking to develop strains resistant to salinity, by the same means. Dr Bhaskaran suggests that somaclonal variation is not only a valuable source of new crops, but perhaps one of the most valuable now available.

Somaclonal variation is not the only source of new varieties that could be provided through tissue culture, however. A tantalizing possibility has been on the horizon for several decades. The idea is to fuse cells from different species or varieties to provide new kinds of hybrid, including kinds that cannot be produced by sexual crossing. Some of this promise is now being realized.

Somatic hybrids

Plants have thick cells walls, made of cellulose. But this cell wall can be stripped away in culture using enzymes derived from fungi, and the result is a naked *protoplast*. If protoplasts are exposed to certain chemicals, including calcium, or organic compounds such as polyethylene glycol, or if they are simply subjected to an appropriate electric field, the protoplasts will fuse; in general, such treatments upset the equilibrium of the cells' surrounding membranes. By such means, cells containing two or more nuclei can readily be produced.

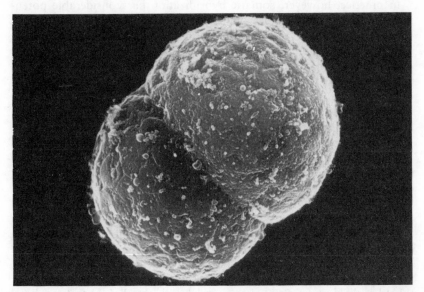

Figure 6.2 Protoplasts – naked cells – can be induced to fuse; and the resulting 'somatic hybrids' can be useful in crop breeding programmes.

Interesting events may then ensue when those nuclei divide, in the course of normal cell division. During cell division, the nuclear membranes break down. If the two nuclei are from varieties of the same species, the two sets of chromosomes may become mixed up one with another, to form one big concatenation of chromosomes. This is a kind of instant polyploidy, achieved not by adding haploid cell to haploid cell and then doubling but by adding diploid cell to diploid cell. Furthermore, this process can generate hybrids between cells of different species – albeit closely related species. Petunia has been fused with tobacco, for example. Such fusions are genuine hybrids, because their genetic material becomes mixed, and operates as one. They are not produced by the fusion of specialized sex cells, but by the coalescence of vegetative, or somatic cells. Hence they are *somatic hybrids*.

When somatic hybridization was first achieved way back in the 1950s (between different cells of tobacco) some suggested that the technique could provide the royal route to hybridization between any two plants. Why not barley and beans, for example, to produce the instant nitrogen-fixing cereal? The immediate answer is that distantly related plants may be so different in the behaviour of their chromosomes and in aspects of metabolism, that the different elements of each cannot possibly work in concert with the other. Some then became disillusioned, and suggested that since somatic hybrids formed viable plants only if both parents were closely related, that they served no real purpose, as closely related parents can generally be combined by sexual means.

In practice, however, somatic hybridization has considerable potential, because some plants whose properties could profitably be combined cannot be crossed by sexual means even though they may be closely related. For example, the wild potato *Solanum brevidens* contains genes that confer resistance to potato leaf roll virus, which is one of the most troublesome of potato viruses in the United Kingdom. But there are reproductive barriers between *S. brevidens* and the domestic potato, *S. tuberosum*. So scientists at Rothamsted Experimental Station in the UK are seeking to form somatic hybrids between the two.

One problem here is that *S. brevidens*, like many wild potatoes, is diploid, with 24 chromosomes, whereas *S. tuberosum* is tetraploid, with 48. So in order to produce a *brevidens–tuberosum* hybrid with compatible chromosomes, the Rothamsted scientists first have to produce a 24-chromosome *S. tuberosum*. This they do by crossing *S. tuberosum* with another wild potato, the tetraploid *S. phureja*. This particular cross can be effected by sexual means. But chromosomes are capricious; and in this particular hybrid the chromosomes that derived from the *S. phureja* parent are rapidly lost as development proceeds. All that's left in the end, then, are the 24 *S. tuberosum* chromosomes. It's this 'diploid' *S. tuberosum* that is fused with the diploid *S. brevidens*.

At Hindustan Lever Dr Bhaskaran and his colleagues have developed a different form of somatic hybrid. They put the nucleus from a cell of one variety of coconut into the cytoplasm of another variety – or even into the cytoplasm of other, related palms.

The main point here is to develop strains of coconut that are resistant to rootwilt, a devastating fungus disease. Some strains of coconut do possess suitable resistance genes, and if breeding was as straightforward in the coconut as it is in wheat, or even in millet, then it would not be difficult to provide resistant varieties, in large numbers. We have seen, however, that in coconuts such breeding programmes would be far too slow. But it seems to be the case that the genes for wilt resistance are carried within the DNA of the mitochondrion, within the cytoplasm. By no means every disease-resistance gene is carried within cytoplasmic genes, but this is one such example. The aim, then, is to take nuclei from cells of élite palms, of the kind that can produce 400 nuts per year, and put them into cytoplasm from resistant palms. If this technique succeeds, and there is every indication that it will, then the Hindustan Lever scientists will produce new super-varieties within a few years. Such improvements would have taken many decades to effect by conventional means.

All the procedures we have discussed so far are intended to produce more or better plants by tissue culture. But tissue culture can also be used to create what is virtually a new class of organism; cultures of free-living, isolated plant cells that are treated and behave virtually as single celled organisms. These already form the basis of what could be promising commercial enterprises.

Dyes and flavours from cultured cells

Plants are the world's most accomplished organic chemists. They provide us with pesticides, perfumes, flavourings, dyes, drugs, unguents and salves – the list is endless. Indeed, a quarter of all the medicines prescribed in the western world are derived from plants – and almost all of those used in traditional medicine. These commodities are sometimes obtained by gathering plants growing in the wild and sometimes by cultivating them.

In general, however, only a small proportion of the cells of any one plant produce the agent of value. Why not simply culture those cells alone, rather than the entire plant? The advantage of such a course is obvious. In a word, it offers control – of supply, of quality, and, in the case of agents such as the opiates, of legalities.

In theory it would be possible to transfer the genes that produce valuable plant commodities into microbes, by genetic engineering. At first sight, such an attempt seems well worth while. Techniques for culturing microbes on the industrial scale are well advanced, whereas those for mass cultivation of plant cells are not. In addition, bacteria such as the highly favoured *Escherichia coli* have a generation time of about 20 minutes, whereas plant cells in culture take 20 to 60 hours between divisions.

In practice, it is probably better to culture the plant cells themselves. Most of the valuable commodities made by plants are produced by complex metabolic processes, whose enzymes are provided by many different genes, all working in sequence. It may be easy enough to put one or two genes into a microbe, and get them to work, but to introduce a whole orchestra of genes and expect them to work in concert is asking a little much. The slow multiplication of plant cells is not such a disadvantage. The aim of plant cell culture is not to produce biomass, but to maintain a fixed number of cells, turning out large quantities of the required product. Cultured plant cells are not like broiler chickens, which are raised and killed. They are like milch cows, maintained for milking.

The mass culture of plant cells for commercial purposes raises four kinds of problem.

First, the culturist must find the most productive cells. This part at least should not be difficult. As we have seen many times in this book, it is often easy to select outstanding individuals in a highly variable population – and once they are found, then the culturist has merely to multiply them. Indeed, it should be easier to find outstanding individual cells, than to find outstanding plants. After all, a plant is a complex organism, and if any one character is over-developed, then others are liable to suffer. But when cells are cultured, all their needs are looked after, and overall viability can to some extent be sacrificed to productivity. Already, individual cell lines have been found in various plants that out-yield their fellows several-fold.

A second theoretical difficulty is that the agents valuable to human beings are of the kind known as 'secondary metabolites'. They are not the kinds of things that every plant cell produces in the normal course of living, in the way that it may generate oxygen. Hence, the genes that produce secondary metabolites may be switched off most of the time, in most parts of the plant. In culture they must be switched on. But it is not always easy to provide a putatively productive cell with conditions in which it will actually produce.

A third problem is that plant cells do not generally release secondary metabolites, once they are produced. These products tend to remain within the cell that made them. But the culturalist wants cells that excrete their products, so that he can harvest them from the medium without killing the cells. This problem is far from insuperable, however. Some cells have leaky membranes, and appropriate types merely have to be selected.

Finally, as we have seen, cultured cells are not immutable. They can undergo profound genetic and cytological changes in culture and indeed may stop producing whatever it is they are meant to produce. On the other hand, somaclonal variants will inevitably be thrown up that actually produce more than the parent tissue. Commercial production lines could serve also as a source of improved varieties.

The difficulties are such that plant tissue culture so far has generally been reserved for commodities of very high value. Indeed the first plant material to be produced commercially by tissue culture was shikonin, which serves both as a red dye and as an anti-bacterial agent in traditional Japanese medicine. It comes from the root of *Lithospermum erythrorhizon*, which, as a member of the Boraginaceae, is related to such plants as borage, heliotrope, and forget-me-not. Shikonin is produced in plant cell culture by Mitsui Petrochemicals Industries in Tokyo, and sells for about £2 000 per kilo.

Biotechnologists now feel, however, that there is promise enough in plant cell culture to contemplate commodities that might retail for a mere £250–500: agents such as digoxin, from foxglove; or vincristine from the Madagascar periwinkle which is used to treat leukaemia; or codeine, from cultured poppy cells.

At the Food Research Institute (FRI) at Norwich, United Kingdom, Drs Brian Kirsop and Michael Rhodes and their colleagues are already producing quinine, from the cultured cells of the *Cinchona* tree. Quinine, which puts the bitterness in tonic water and still has value as an anti-malarial agent, is worth only £50 a kilo. If the FRI scientists succeed, then plant cell tissue culture will surely have moved out of the realms of the exotic into what is almost workaday. A whole host of other flavourings, of comparable middle-order value, might follow in *Cinchona*'s wake.

It is of course the case that high-value plant materials are generally produced in the tropics, and mostly by people for whom they are a crucial source of income. That indeed is a serious objection to the new technologies. There is still a case for horticulture, however. For one thing, the new technologies are highly capital-intensive, and could be very expensive to set up. Horticulture has a head start and is not standing still. For example, scientists with the Central Indian Medicinal Plants Organisation are developing new strains of a whole range of high-value plants, for their aromas and for drugs: various mints, Java citronella, palmarosa, lemongrass, vetiver, rose, clary sage, lavender, patchouli, geranium, linaloe, hops, periwinkle – the list goes on.

In an ideal world, horticulture and tissue culture would flourish side by side. Some plants at least can be regenerated from single cells. New somaclonal variants produced in culture might well simply be put back in the field. In addition, the days are past when it could be assumed that the production of raw material would be carried out in tropical, 'Third World' countries, while the high technology was done exclusively in the West. The West no longer has a monopoly on high technology. Malaysia has also shown, through rubber, that a producer country can

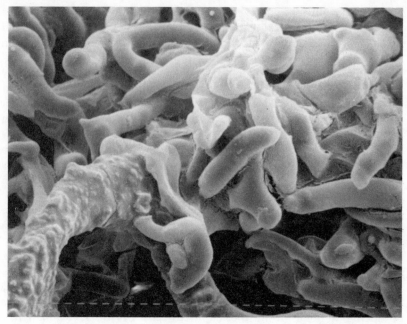

Figure 6.3 The productive cells of some valuable crops may be grown in culture instead of cultivating the crop. These, at the Institute of Food Research in Norwich, are of hops.

exert control over the development and marketing, if it moves astutely. In short, the threat of tissue culture to horticulture, or of rich countries' high-tech to poor countries' intermediate-tech, may be apparent rather than real.

Tissue culture has already proved its commercial worth in horticulture, by providing clones of high-value plants such as orchids. It is about to prove its worth in the high commerce of plantations and agriculture, and is generating a new form of biotechnology comparable to the industrial microbiology that is already well established.

In addition, tissue culture offers various means of producing new varieties and species. We have discussed two of them. The third and conceptually the most exciting possibility is simply to add chosen genes, from any desired source, to the cultured cells. This is genetic engineering, and is the subject of the next chapter.

7 Genetic Engineering

Introduction

Conventional breeders transfer genes between plants that are closely related to each other, and can be crossed by sexual means. By special techniques they can extend the boundaries somewhat, forming hybrids between related species, or transferring pieces of chromosome from one to another. By means of somatic hybridization, it was once thought possible to produce hybrids between species that are not related, but in practice the only successful somatic hybrids are those formed between closely related species, albeit types that cannot readily be conjoined by sexual means. But by the techniques of genetic engineering, genes can in theory be taken from any kind of organism, and inserted in functional form in any other.

Genes might thus be transferred between plants that are quite unrelated; wheat into sorghum, legume into cereal, cereal into brassica. Crops might indeed be given the genes of bacteria, or fungi, or animals; and their genes in turn might be put into any other class of organism. Theoretically, too, it is possible to synthesize quite new kinds of gene. Indeed, as far as the crude chemistry of the operation is concerned this is not particularly difficult. So organisms might in theory be given genes that had never previously existed on earth, endowing characteristics that are quite unprecedented. In the fullness of time, scientists might build living organisms from scratch, as engineers build bridges, or aeroplanes.

Genetic engineering is giving rise to new biological industries. Microbes have been given genes from animals or even humans that enable them to produce valuable proteins for agriculture and medicine: growth hormone to increase the bulk of cattle, and human insulin for the treatment of diabetes. The implications for animal and plant breeding are obvious. At present it may take a decade of crossing and back-crossing to imbue a crop plant with some disease-resistant gene from a wild relative, and to shuffle off all the undesirable genes that are introduced at the same time. By the techniques of genetic engineering, such a transfer might be made in a few weeks.

When genes can be introduced from any source, then in principle we can simply invent our own crops. Vines might trail from the roofs and sills of tower blocks, dripping with tomatoes or passion fruit or anything we cared to envisage. We could produce crops that were insectivorous, like sundews, and fed themselves on the aphids and locusts that came to feed on them. Insectivorous hedgerows might lure pests from the fields they surround. Less whimsical is the possibility of developing cereals that are able to fix nitrogen, as legumes do. This indeed is the subject of serious research, which is discussed in chapter 10. But in practice there are a great many snags.

The hurdles

The age of genetic engineering has not yet dawned in the domain of crop improvement. The problems are of five main kinds.

First, the transfer of genes must not be a gratuitous exercise. The point is to make useful changes in the recipient plant, the host, and if this is to be done the engineer must know precisely which genes achieve which effects. Of all the genes in all the flowering plants on earth (and there are about 250 000 species of flowering plant, each with about 30 000 genes) only a score or so are fully understood (in the mid-1980s): understood, that is, in the sense that their structure and position within the chromosomes is known, and the nature and the function of the proteins they produce. And those genes are not, for the most part, of the kind that most plant breeders would consider to be useful. Until the engineers know which genes they ought to be transferring, then the entire exercise is still-born. The gap in knowledge at present is immense.

Secondly, the problems of inserting genes into intended hosts are far from solved. In particular, there is as yet no certain method of introducing genes into cereals by engineering techniques, and cereals are the most valuable crops of all. As we will discuss later, however, in the mid-1980s this particular problem may be on the point of solution.

The third problem is that of gene *expression*. A gene may fail to function after it is introduced. Alternatively, it may function too well, and be impossible to control. If the gene in question was intended to produce a particularly desirable protein in a seed, then it should not produce that same protein in the leaves, or roots, or flowers. Protein production requires energy, and such prodigality would undoubtedly reduce overall yield. In practice, expression and control may pose greater problems than insertion.

Fourthly, there is a limit to the amount of genetic material that the engineer can introduce – at least at any one time. As we will see, genes in practice are commonly introduced by means of *vectors*, but vectors cannot carry more than one or a few genes at a time. Sometimes a single gene may be all that is required. Disease resistance often has a simple genetic basis (even though, in the mid-1980s the actual nature of that basis is not in general understood). Single genes may also have profound effects on the form and hence on the yield of crops. This is true of the dwarfing genes that reduced the height of wheat and rice and were thus responsible for the Green Revolution, which we will discuss in chapter 9.

But most of the characters of plants that the breeder seeks to influence have a highly complex genetic basis. Yield (dwarfing genes aside) is notoriously complex. So too, are such qualities as the ability to fix nitrogen that is possessed by some bacteria, or the ability to form symbiotic relationships with those bacteria (chapter 10). In theory, the necessary genes that determines a polygenic character could be introduced one at a time. But if those genes became widely separated within the host genome then this could well compromise their ability to act co-operatively.

The largest problem of all is that all the genes within an organism, and all the products of those genes, must work in concert. An alien gene producing some alien protein may simply be disruptive. In practice, then, the genes that are most likely to be transferred across wide species barriers are liable to be those that confer 'ad hoc' qualities that have no great influence on overall performance; genes for pest resistance, for example. In addition, once a foreign gene is introduced, a period of breeding will probably have to follow to select individuals in which the new gene operates most comfortably – one in which the existing background genes have adjusted most smoothly to its presence. Thus, genetic engineering is unlikely to effect the instant improvements that have sometimes been envisaged.

However, the potential of genetic engineering is beyond doubt. We will describe it from the beginning.

The birth of genetic engineering

Modern plant breeding is based upon, and guided by, the science of genetics; and genetics is essentially an abstract pursuit. For the first five decades of this century, indeed, generations of geneticists practised their skills at a very high level – revolutionised the practical crafts of breeding; devised evolutionary hypotheses of enormous subtlety and continuing value – without having any certain idea of what a gene actually is. It was not certain until the 1940s that genes were made of deoxyribonucleic acid, DNA, and were not, in fact, made of proteins. Indeed when Francis Crick and James Watson began their work on the structure of DNA at the beginning of the 1950s, some highly respectable scientists still believed that genes must be made of protein. Only proteins, they felt, had the necessary variability of structure that could provide the code for all the subtleties of life. But for the normal processes of plant breeding it does not matter whether genes are made of DNA, protein, or papier mâché. All the breeder needs to know is whether a particular gene that gives rise to a particular character – whatever it is made of – is dominant or recessive, works on its own or in conjunction with others, and which plants are liable to contain the required genes, as discussed in earlier chapters.

Genetic engineering decidedly is not an abstract pursuit. The genes are physically extracted from one organism, and put into another. It is an exercise in chemistry. If the exercise is to be pursued at all then it is essential to understand the general nature of DNA, and how it behaves. If the exercise is going to be pursued in a useful way – that is, if the genes that are put into a new host are actually going to do anything useful – then it is essential to know which particular pieces of DNA perform which particular function.

The nature of DNA

The important points, for our purposes, are as follows. DNA consists of two long strands that lie exactly in parallel one to another, but are coiled; this structure is the 'double helix', first elucidated by Crick and Watson in 1953. Each strand consists of a chain of nucleotides. Each nucleotide consists of a base, joined to a sugar which in turn has a phosphate group attached; and the sugar is of the type known as deoxyribose. The sugar-phosphate moieties form an external scaffold, and the bases link together across the centre of the two strands.

In fact, the bases are of four kinds: adenine (A), guanine (G), cytosine (C), and thymine (T). Adenine and guanine are of the class of compounds known as purines; cytosine and thymine are pyrimidines. The two purines are very similar in shape, and the two pyrimidines are also much of a muchness, in their overall geometry. In practice the geometry of the four bases is such that when the two strands lie alongside one another, one of the purines, adenine, will always link up with one of the pyrimidines, thymine, while the other purine, guanine, will always link up with the other pyrimidine, cytosine. The two kinds of purine-pyrimidine pairs, A–T and G–C, are known as 'base pairs'.

A point to note in passing, but of great significance to our story, is that the chemical bonds that hold the DNA macromolecule together are of two quite different kinds. Those that hold A to T and G to C, and thus hold the two strands together, are hydrogen bonds. These are very weak; they depend upon the fact that when an A is opposite a T, or a G opposite a C, then the two juxtaposed molecules tend to share the hydrogens that protrude from their surface. Because they are weak, hydrogen bonds are easily sundered: the two strands of DNA are designed to separate, although in living cells an enzyme may be required to effect the separation. But hydrogen bonds also form spontaneously, so that if a single strand of DNA is mixed with another of the appropriate kind (that is, one which has the right bases in the right places) then the two will spontaneously cleave together.

By contrast, the chemical bonds that hold the different nucleotides together *within* each chain are covalent. These are far stronger, and they do not form spontaneously. They can be formed, and broken, only by the intervention of enzymes. In practice, a whole range (what biologists tend to call a *suite*) of enzymes are involved in breaking and re-forming the covalent bonds that keep the individual strands of DNA intact, for the purposes of building DNA, breaking it apart, repairing it, or editing out mistakes. It is these enzymes – many different types, derived from many different organisms – that form the tool-kit of the genetic engineer.

We are running ahead, however. The point to note here is that because A pairs only with T, and G with C, each of the two strands of DNA is, effectively, a mould, or template, of the other. The two strands are, in the language of molecular biology, 'complementary'. If you know the structure of one strand you can infer the structure of the other. More to the point, cell division occurs in such a way that each daughter cell finishes up with the same complement of DNA as its parent cell had. The way this is effected is that before the cells divide, the DNA duplicates itself. And the way it duplicates itself with the necessary precision is that the two strands separate, and then each strand produces, with help from enzymes, a complement image of itself. In addition, (which is something genetic engineers find useful, not to say essential for the purposes of studying the DNA of particular organisms), if two complementary strands of DNA are mixed together in a test-tube, then they will automatically stick one to another, by virtue of hydrogen bonding. But if the two strands are not complementary, then they will not stick.

So much for the structure of DNA. How does it work?

DNA and proteins

DNA operates by making proteins, and that is a useful thing to do partly because many proteins are an important part of the structure of all living cells, and partly because most proteins (whether structural or not) serve in some measure as enzymes, which effectively control the metabolism of the whole cell. Hence the DNA is the director of the cell – which, in plant cells, sits like any good managing director in its office, in the nucleus; and the proteins, acting as enzymes, are the functionaries, carrying out the boss's orders.

In fact the statement that DNA 'makes' proteins is inaccurate in two respects. Firstly, DNA does not 'make' anything. What it does is

131

provide the necessary code, which determines which amino-acids should be incorporated into a particular protein, and in what order. Secondly, DNA does not deal directly with proteins. It operates by an intermediary, a kind of foreman, known as RNA. RNA is similar to DNA, with three differences. The sugar in the sugar-phosphate backbone is slightly different (it is ribose, rather than deoxyribose); the base thymine is absent from RNA, and is replaced by uracil, which does much the same job; and RNA is usually single-stranded, whereas DNA is normally double-stranded, except when the strands have separated for the purposes of replication, or for the construction of RNA.

In practice, then, the production of protein proceeds as follows. First, the two strands of the DNA in the nucleus temporarily separate. One of those strands then makes a complement of itself, not in the form of another DNA, but in the form of RNA – or, more specifically, of a particular kind of RNA known as *messenger*, or mRNA. The process of modelling a strand of mRNA that encapsulates the code of its parent DNA is known as *transcription*. The mRNA, after being cleaned up and edited in ways that need not concern us, migrates from the nucleus into the cytoplasm of the cell, and makes its way to one or other of the *ribosomes*. It is on the ribosomes, attached to the membranes that traverse and interlace the cytoplasm, that proteins are made. In detail, the code encapsulated on the mRNA is *translated* into protein.

But what does 'translation' mean in this context? Cells contain thousands of different kinds of proteins. A whole organism contains hundreds of thousands of different kinds. How can mRNA, or the DNA that gives rise to it, possibly contain enough information to code for all the different varieties?

The genetic code

One reason why early 20th century biologists were reluctant to accept that DNA could provide the code for the manufacture of proteins was that its structure seemed too simple. Any molecule that is to form the stuff of genes must code for all the complexities of life; it must be able to provide the instructions to make each of the many thousands of different materials of which flesh consists. Yet all DNA looked much of a muchness. Indeed the only source of variability in DNA lies in the four bases. And it just didn't seem possible to devise a code that was extensive enough, and comprehensive enough, out of combinations of just four bases.

But this is no more than an extension of the problem that had struck protein chemists from the 19th century onwards. These early organic chemists knew that there were many different kinds of proteins. In 1905 Emil Fischer in Germany showed that proteins were made of chains of amino acids. It seemed, then, that there could well be millions of different kinds of amino acids, from which to fashion that vast array of proteins. But in 1940 (and not until then) it was finally established that there are only about 20 different kinds of amino acid. The immense, even infinite variety of proteins was produced by arranging those 20 different types in different order, in long chains. Yet it is not so surprising that such variation can be produced from such simple elements. Twenty-six letters give us the language of Shakespeare – and indeed of Goethe, Racine, and Dante; a potential infinity of words, languages, and meanings, all out of 26 letters.

However, it has also been clear from the beginning of this century that the prime function of genes, and indeed the thing that makes a gene a gene, is the ability to produce enzymes; the old adage, dating back to the classic observations on inborn errors of metabolism by Dr Archibald Garrod in the first decade of this century, was, 'one gene, one enzyme'. Enzymes are, of course, proteins. So the question of how DNA could function as a gene resolved into a conceptually simpler one: 'how can combinations of four nucleotides code for 20 different amino-acids?'

And the answer to that conceptually simpler question was forth-coming in the 1960s, courtesy of Francis Crick and Sidney Brenner, at Cambridge. They proposed that the four bases in DNA were arranged in groups of three. As there are four bases, and as it is perfectly permissible to use the same base twice, this means that no fewer than 64 different three-base combinations are possible. The bases could be regarded as letters, and the three-letter combinations as three-letter 'words'; although in fact, they called the words, *codons*. Each codon, they proposed, would code for a different amino-acid; and as there are only 20 amino-acids, the 64 possible variants are more than adequate.

Since the 1960s Crick and Brenner's idea has been more than vindicated. The bases in DNA are arranged in a continuous uninter-rupted line. However, some particular sequences do not serve as codes for amino-acids, but instead serve as 'punctuation marks'. They indicate where one gene ends and the next begins.

A summary of molecular biology

In summary, each gene consists of a long sequence of DNA, which may include many thousands of nucleotides. The DNA consists of an uninterrupted chain of nucleotides, but particular base sequences among the 64 codons indicate where any one gene is supposed to begin or end.

Each gene codes for a protein. The way the coding is enacted is that the DNA, in the nucleus, is first re-caste, or, as the expression is, 'transcribed', into the form of messenger RNA. The mRNA travels out of the nucleus to one of the ribosomes, and there its code is read, and 'translated' into a sequence of amino acids. This sequence of amino acids is, by definition, a protein.

Thus have the structure and function of DNA been revealed. But what of manipulation?

DNA manipulated

Although for many years many scientists believed that genes just *had* to be proteins, there was always something deeply unsatisfying about that idea. After all, the function of genes is to *make* proteins. If protein A (the gene) makes protein B (the enzyme) what makes protein A? It is the kind of seven-year-old's conundrum that has kept theologians cogitating for centuries: who made God?

On the other hand, DNA by itself is pretty useless. It doesn't do anything. It needs the enzymes that it produces, to act as handmaidens. It even needs those enzymes to put itself together, and to replicate itself, and indeed to edit out mistakes in its own multiplication and transcription. The symbiosis between DNA and proteins is complete, and is the essential fact of life: proteins need DNA, or they could not come into being; and DNA needs proteins, for its own multiplication and continuance.

It was in the 1940s that the full significance of DNA finally became apparent – that it was the stuff of genes. In the 1950s its structure was revealed. In the 1960s its code was cracked. And in the 1970s its personal retinue of enzymes was first properly investigated; the battalions of functionaries that are employed specifically to marshal its various components into place, bind them there, and uncouple them again, when appropriate. It became apparent, too, that life on the molecular scale is far from tranquil. There is strife. Some organisms produce enzymes with the express function of dismembering the DNA of other organisms. These enzymes, some designed to construct DNA, some to edit the mistakes in it, some actively to destroy the DNA of other species, are the tools of the genetic engineer.

The enzymes that first made it possible even to consider the manipulation of genes are the ones produced for reasons of belligerence, whose task is to destroy the DNA of invading organisms. These are called *restriction enzymes*.

Restriction enzymes

Bacteria are renowned as pathogens, agents of disease. But they are themselves the victims of pathogenic attack, notably by a group of viruses known as *bacteriophages*, or simply as 'phages'. Phages first attach themselves to the outer surface of their victim; and then they release their own DNA into it. The DNA of the virus then takes over from that of the bacterium. It commandeers the machinery of the bacterial cell, and employs it to reproduce its own kind.

Bacteria, however, do not stand idly by and watch this happen. Instead, they attack the DNA of the invading phage. And they do this by means of enzymes that are called 'restriction' enzymes because they restrict the activities of the invader.

The first hint of these activities came from Salvador Luria's observations in the early 1950s, on the conflicts between phage and the bacterium *Escherichia coli*. But the key observation was made by Hamilton Smith at Johns Hopkins University, Baltimore, in 1970. He isolated from the bacterium *Haemophilus influenzae* an enzyme that would break down DNA; not, as it happens, the DNA of a phage, but of the bacterium *E. coli*. However, this particular enzyme did not break down the DNA of *H. influenzae* that produced it.

The crucial point is that the enzyme of *H. influenzae* broke the *E. coli* DNA at a very specific point. It attacked only in the middle of particular sequences of six bases: specifically, wherever it came across the sequence, G, T, any pyrimidine: any purine, A, C.

It is clear now that this particular ability of *H. influenzae* to produce enzymes that sever DNA is widespread among bacteria. At least 200 kinds are known to produce such restriction enzymes. All the restriction enzymes attack DNA at specific points, identified by particular sequences of bases.

But what makes restriction enzymes so extremely useful, collectively, is that they cleave DNA in many different ways. First, they do not all attack at the same sequence. Between them, the known restriction enzymes will recognize about 100 different base sequences at which to attack.

Secondly, whereas some restriction enzymes attack DNA only when they encounter a particular sequence of six bases, other attack wherever they meet a particular sequence of only four bases. Clearly, particular sequences of only four bases will occur far more often than particular sequences of six; so those that require only four will attack a particular molecule of DNA in far more places than those that need a specific sequence of six.

Finally (and it seems sometimes as if nature designed restriction enzymes specifically to make life easy for genetic engineers), some restriction enzymes sever DNA straight across, to produce blunt ends; and some make staggered cuts, which leave two nucleotides protruding on each severed end. These protruding pairs of nucleotides will bind by hydrogen bonding to any corresponding ends of nucleotides protruding from a similarly cleft piece of DNA; and they are, in the crude but sometimes accurate language of molecular biology, known as *sticky ends*. Sticky ends are vital to genetic engineering, as will become apparent.

Incidentally, the reason that bacteria do not attack their own DNA with their own restriction enzymes is that they attach extra chemical groups (specifically, the methyl group, CH_3) to the vital vulnerable spots on their own DNA, and thus mask them.

Restriction enzymes are invaluable. For one thing, in general terms, they enable the genetic engineer to cut out the precise sequences of DNA – the genes – that he wants to transfer to other organisms. For another, they provide a relatively straightforward way of working out the sequence of nucleotides in DNA. In practice, DNA is extracted from the cell, and then different samples of it are cut up, using different restriction enzymes. Each restriction enzyme reduces the long macro-molecules of DNA with which it is confronted into collections of fragments, known as *restriction fragments.*

To reduce the long sequences to more manageable lengths is helpful in itself. In addition, each different enzyme will cut its own particular sample of the same DNA at its own particular site; so each enzyme produces its own characteristic collection of restriction fragments from any one DNA sample. Furthermore, the analyst knows exactly how each fragment in each collection begins and ends, because each enzymes cuts at a particular spot. By analysing the individual fragments produced by any two different enzymes, and then seeing where the two fragments overlap, it is possible to work out the sequence of the entire molecule. This is now done more or less routinely. Indeed, about 40 new DNA sequences are published each week, and a central registry is kept at the European Molecular Biology Laboratory at Heidelburg in West Germany, and by Genbank in the United States.

The genetic engineer cannot begin to operate unless he can extract the particular genes he requires, which entails cutting the DNA in a controlled way. This is where restriction enzymes come in. But the real point of the exercise is not simply to cut up DNA, or even to analyse it, but to introduce the DNA from one organism into another. For this purpose, he needs to be able to join fragments of DNA together; or, as the expression is, to effect *recombination.* The way to do that in an orderly fashion was discovered in 1972 at Stanford University in California, by Janet Mertz and Ron Davis. It is with this discovery that genetic engineering can properly be said to have begun. We began this chapter by listing the present shortcomings of genetic engineering, but those comments should be seen in a historical light. The progress made in a decade and a half has been astonishing.

The recombination of DNA

To effect recombination of DNA, Janet Mertz and Ron Davis employed restriction enzymes that produce a staggered cut in DNA. When such a cut is made, a couple of bases are left sticking out of the ends of each fragment, and these bases will naturally cleave to any complementary bases that might happen to protrude from the end of any other piece of DNA that happens to be nearby. If DNA samples from two different species are mixed, and then cut with a restriction enzyme to produce staggered ends, then each resulting fragment of DNA is just as liable to recombine with a fragment from the other species, as with one of its own species.

In practice, two sections of DNA cannot be joined permanently one to another just by sticking their sticky ends together. The ends of different fragments are initially joined only by hydrogen bonds, which are weak. The covalent links between the nucleotides must also be established. This can be done with the aid of one of the enzymes whose task it is to repair and maintain DNA in a living cell: one known as a *ligase*.

Nowadays, it is also possible to join fragments of DNA together when they have straight ends. Yet another enzyme is employed to attach a couple of nucleotides on to one of the chains, and a complementary pair of nucleotides on to the fragment to which it should be joined. Thus staggered ends are constructed in two steps, rather than in one.

However, cutting up DNA with restriction enzymes, and joining the pieces up to other pieces with ligases, does not, by itself, constitute genetic engineering. It can of course produce some bizarre entities: cat genes may join to those of bacteria; a cactus gene could be joined to one from a human being. But genes floating around in a test tube cannot be functional; they are simply molecules of DNA. The real task is to introduce DNA from one organism into another. This final step was achieved in 1973.

DNA transferred

Most molecular biology has been carried out on bacteria. They are the simplest organisms to study. Not surprisingly, therefore, bacteria were the first organisms to be given DNA from another organism.

The DNA of bacteria is very similar to that of animals, plants, and fungi. At least, the genetic code operates in the same way, and the most significant difference lies in the signals that turn on genes (allow them to express) or turns them off. But the structure of the bacterial cell is quite different from that of fungi or plants or animals. Plants and animals are *eukaryotes*; that is, they have 'proper' cells, in which the chromosomes, containing most of the cell's DNA, are contained neatly within a nucleus. Bacteria are *prokaryotes*. They have no nucleus. Some of their DNA is contained in a single 'chromosome' that lies in the cytoplasm; and the rest is contained in circles of DNA, also lying free in the cytoplasm, known as *plasmids*.

One of the most remarkable feats that bacteria perform in nature is that of passing plasmids from one individual to another. This exchange of genetic information serves the same kind of function in bacteria as sex serves in eukaryotes. But sex, in eukaryotes, is conducted very formally, such that the two parents contribute almost exactly the same amount of genetic information to the offspring. The exchange of plasmids between bacteria is far more *ad hoc*. The amount of genetic information transferred in any one exchange varies enormously.

It seemed, then, that one of the best ways to get a piece of DNA – a gene – into an organism in a form in which it can function, is again to make use of the mechanisms provided by nature: stitch the new gene into a plasmid. This was achieved, in 1973, by Herbert Boyer and Stanley Cohen, again in California. Boyer and Cohen used the same enzyme that Mertz and Davis had used, to create different kinds of DNA with sticky ends, that would cleave together. But one of the pieces of DNA they cut was a plasmid from *Escherichia coli*. And when the plasmid recombined, it contained fragments of the different kind of DNA. Furthermore, plasmids are designed by nature to be taken up by other bacteria, and to multiply as their new hosts multiply. Although the DNA that Boyer and Cohen attached to the *E. coli* plasmids in fact came from other bacteria, any kind of DNA, from any kind of organism, could in principle be so attached. By this means, then, any kind of DNA from any source can be put into a bacterium (which need not necessarily be an *E. coli*). And when that bacterium multiplies, the new DNA that has been put into it will be multiplied as well.

Put the three techniques together: restriction; recombination; and the introduction of fragments of DNA into bacteria, via plasmids, and we have genetic engineering. A fragment of DNA is not necessarily, strictly speaking, a 'gene': it may, for example, have been chopped half-way through a gene, or it may include half of one gene and a quarter of the gene next door. But if the biologist does his work properly then the fragment he extracts could well correspond to a gene. Thus we can say that with this technique any gene can be taken from any organism; put into bacteria; and then multiplied up, in indefinite amounts, as those bacteria multiply.

The applications are obvious, and biologists and industrialists alike have not been slow to exploit them. For example, it is in practice impossible to analyse the DNA from a single cell, but if that DNA is first put into bacteria, and then multiplied, then enough can easily be produced for analysis.

Furthermore, the entire complement of DNA from a cell can be extracted and broken into fragments, and then each of those fragments can be introduced into separate bacteria. This sounds difficult but in principle it is not. Bacteria are obliging. If a solution containing fragments of DNA is simply poured over them then between them they will take up all the fragments. If the different bacteria are then allowed to multiply so that each forms a clone, then the biologist soon has a collection of clones which between them contain the entire genome of the original organism, conveniently broken up into analysable and generally manageable fragments, one fragment per clone. Such a collection is known as a *gene library*.

Gene libraries help to solve the problem of how to find genes that actually perform useful functions. Suppose, for example, that the biologist wishes to transfer genes that code for particular storage proteins from one organism to another. The first task is to identify the relevant genes. To this end, he carries out two procedures. First, he prepares a gene library of the donor organism. Then he finds the particular mRNA that produces the required proteins; and one thing that facilitates the task in this case is that storage proteins are produced in relatively enormous amounts by the cells of the seed, and so, therefore, is the mRNA that codes for those proteins. He then introduces radioactive atoms into that mRNA to act as a 'label', and confronts the various clones of bacteria within the gene library with that labelled mRNA. The mRNA will stick, by hydrogen bonding, to the bacteria that harbour the corresponding DNA. Hence he has found the DNA he requires.

At present, as we have emphasized, there are in practice vast gaps in knowledge. Ideally, if genetic engineering is truly to realize its potential, biologists would need to be able to ascribe a particular character in a plant to the possession of a particular enzyme; and to ascribe that particular enzyme to a particular stretch of DNA. In fact, the metabolic pathways (and therefore the enzymes) that underlie most of the characters of plants are not understood, and even when those enzymes are identified it will be a very long task to find the DNA that produces them.

Nevertheless, biologists do now have the means by which to isolate genes, to analyse them, and to grow them in indefinite quantities. A few plant genes have already been isolated and cloned. It is not then premature to address the final question. Once plant genes are isolated, can they in fact be introduced into other plants?

Putting genes into plants

In theory there are several ways to introduce DNA into new host cells, and some of them seem ridiculously simple. Bacteria will take up fragments of DNA, and incorporate them into their genomes, if they are simply bathed in DNA. It is theoretically possible, though technically difficult, to introduce DNA into plant and animal cells by injecting it; when again, sometimes, it will become incorporated.

A delightfully simple method applicable to plants is that of *electroporesis*. First, the cell wall is removed to reduce the cell to a protoplast. If the protoplasts are then subjected to rapid pulses of electricity – two kilovolts per centimetre at 20 to 50 microseconds – then their cell membranes briefly become porous. If the protoplasts are at the same time steeped in fragments of DNA then some of that DNA will enter and be incorporated into the cell genome.

So far, electroporesis has been used successfully on protoplasts of tobacco which, as we have seen, is in general very amenable to *in vitro* techniques. However, as discussed below, it is now a relatively straightforward matter to introduce genes into plants such as tobacco and potato by means of gene vectors. Dr Mike Jones and his colleagues at Rothamsted feel that the technique of electroporesis has most promise in cereals, which cannot be broached by means of the vectors that are now commonly employed. Indeed, electroporesis may have transformed the prospects for the engineering of cereal, for until the mid-1980s the difficulty of introducing DNA seemed to be the greatest single barrier to progress. Now the greatest problem seems to be that cereal protoplasts, whether genetically engineered or not, cannot yet be induced to regenerate into whole plants. Cereal protoplasts will re-acquire cell walls, and develop into callus, but that callus cannot yet be persuaded to form roots and shoots. There can be little doubt that this problem will be overcome, however, and little doubt that genetically engineered cereals will be with us by the 1990s.

At present, however, the standard method of introducing genes into plants – apart from cereals and similar plants – is to employ vectors: vehicles to carry DNA into the new hosts. In practice, nature has provided several possible vectors. One is that vast and prolific kingdom of quasi-organisms, the viruses, whose normal *modus operandi* is to insert their own nucleic acid (sometimes DNA, sometimes RNA) into their host; and which indeed consist of very little else except nucleic acid. The other promising vector is a bacterium, *Agrobacterium tumefaciens*.

Agrobacterium tumefaciens

Nature is remarkably friendly to the plant breeder, and to the genetic engineer of plants. Having produced, over millions of years of evolution, seemingly unscalable barriers to the union of unrelated plants, she then arranged convenient loopholes in her own laws. Plants with different numbers of chromosomes cannot form fertile hybrids. But wait, there is colchicine, an arcane alkaloid from the bulb of an obscure crocus, which will cause chromosome numbers to double. The genetic engineers need a way of insinuating new genes into the chromosomes of established plants. And there is *Agrobacterium tumefaciens*, supremely equipped to do just that. *A. tumefaciens* was first described about 50 years ago. It attacks wounds of plants. It is fairly catholic in its tastes but prefers some plants to others: for example, it can be a serious pest of raspberries, of the family Rosaceae.

In Australia and the United States it is a pest of vines, from the not-too-distantly related family, the Vitaceae. Once *Agrobacterium* has invaded the wound it infects a cell, and commandeers the cells' genes, much as a virus does. Specifically, it causes the cell to proliferate, to form a tumour; and the common name of *Agrobacterium* is 'crown gall'. It also induces the new-formed tumour cells to manufacture a series of amino-acids, known as opines, which the plant does not normally produce and cannot metabolize – but which the bacterium can metabolize perfectly well. Hence it induces the plant to form a food store; and then induces the plant to stock that store with precisely the provender that the parasite alone can enjoy.

Agrobacterium invades the host's chromosomes by means of a plasmid, known as a Ti plasmid: the Ti stands for 'tumour-inducing'. The plasmid is quite separate from the main genetic apparatus – the 'chromosome' – of *Agrobacterium*, but it is not small by the standards of plasmids. Indeed it contains about 3 per cent of the agrobacterial genome. The Ti plasmid needs to be reasonably substantial. In order to achieve all that the *Agrobacterium* seeks to achieve the plasmid must contain genes to orchestrate three quite separate functions. One function, performed by one set of genes, induces the plant cell to proliferate, to form the tumour. Another gene promotes the production of opines. And a third gene, or group of genes, is the 'vir' region, where vir is short for 'virulence'. This region breaks into one of the plant cell chromosomes and makes an excision in the host DNA, so that its own DNA can insinuate.

In its pristine, parasitic form *Agrobacterium* would be of equivocal use to genetic engineers. They want to insert new genes into their crops, but they do not want to induce the formation of tumours, or the production of opines. Hence they need to identify the genes responsible for the various functions and to eliminate the bits they do not want.

Josef Schell and Marc Van Montagu at the University of Ghent in Belgium, and Eugene Nester at the University of Washington in Seattle, have shown that the plasmid induces the formation of a tumour by prompting the plant to produce, or over-produce, the growth hormones, cytokinin and auxin. At the University of Washington in St Louis, Mary-Dell Chilton and her colleagues have shown that the genes responsible for inducing the tumour can simply be eliminated. That's one problem solved.

For opine production, the *Agrobacterium* carries its own genes, which code for the necessary enzymes. The bacterium provides the genes, and the plant cell provides the materials to make the enzyme that will catalyse the production of opine, for which the host cell also provides the raw materials. This sounds straightforward enough, but it does raise one biological puzzle. It's not difficult to see how the plant cell 'reads' the relevant genes to produce the appropriate enzyme: the genetic code is, after all, universal. But what is not universal is the system of punctuation, which tells the cell where any particular gene begins and ends: the stop-start apparatus. *Agrobacterium* clearly includes plant-like stop-start signals; and it can only be assumed that it must have picked up these signals from plant cells. At some time in its evolutionary history the bacterium must have acquired parts of plant genome, and used those parts to refine its own parasitic technique.

Genetic engineers do not want host cells to produce opines. The plasmid gene that codes for the enzymes that produce opines are of no use to them. But the stop-go signals that the plasmid contains within it are of outstanding value. Any new gene that they want to introduce can be inserted in place of the gene that codes for the enzyme production; and the necessary stop-go punctuation is already in place.

In the early 1980s Professors Schell and Van Montagu showed that this could indeed be done. The plant they used as a host was one of great commercial importance, though not destined to feed the world; it was tobacco. Tobacco, as a member of the Solanaceae, is extremely compliant to tissue culture and to genetic engineering, and hence is a common laboratory 'model'. The gene they introduced was not of any great use: it was one that conferred resistance to an antibiotic, chloramphenicol. The point, however, is that it's one thing to get a gene into a plant cell, and quite another to see whether it is actually working when it's in. It is very easy to tell whether a plant that confers resistance to antibiotic has been successfully inserted. Just expose the cell to the antibiotic, and see whether it survives. In fact, Schell and Van Montagu's engineered tobacco cells were resistant to chloramphenicol. There can be few more useless contrivances on the face of this Earth than a chloramphenicol-resistant tobacco plant. But as a demonstration that foreign genes could indeed be inserted into plants, and that, once in, they could work, Schell and Van Montagu's work deserves to be recognized as one of the pivotal pieces of research of the late 20th century.

The gene that codes for chloramphenicol resistance came from a bacterium. It may be useful in practice to endow plants with bacterial genes. Bacteria produce hosts of substances that might help to protect plants against all kinds of pests and parasites. But for the most part, genetic engineers will probably be seeking to transfer genes from one kind of plant to another. In November 1983, Norimoto Murai at the University of Wisconsin, and his colleagues, announced that they had done just this. They put a gene that codes for a particular protein in beans – phaseolin – into a Ti plasmid, in place of the *Agrobacterium*'s opine-producing enzyme gene, and inserted the plasmid into a sunflower. Beans, of course, are of the family Leguminosae; and sunflowers are of the daisy family, Compositae, and they do not normally produce phaseolin. But they did produce detectable amounts of it after being engineered. The protein was somewhat degraded, however, which, as Murai and his colleagues comment, perhaps raises one of the problems that we noted at the beginning of this chapter. Perhaps plants will sometimes object to the production of foreign proteins within their midst, even when they have been successfully engineered. Meantime, however, the principle that genes can be transferred between plant families is well established. By the mid-1980s, about seventy genes had been transferred between plants by genetic engineering.

At the time of Murai's paper, however, *Agrobacterium* was known to have one great drawback as a vector of genes. It did not, apparently, attack monocotyledenous plants. The wide variety of plants it was known to attack, such as raspberries and tobacco, were all dicotyledenous. But the most important group of plants in the world, the ones that agriculturalists would most like to influence, are, of course, the cereals. The cereals belong to the family Gramineae, and the Gramineae, of course, are monocots.

It now seems, however, that *Agrobacterium* does attack monocots after all. What it does not do in monocots is induce the formation of crown galls. It does induce production of opines, and if you set out to look for opines after infecting a monocot with *Agrobacterium*, then you may indeed find them.

The research was reported in 1984 by Dr G. M. S. Hooykaas-Van Slogteren and her colleagues at the University of Leiden and the hosts they employed were not of the commercially important Gramineae: one was a *Chlorophytum*, a relative of the spider-plant, which is one of the Liliaceae; and the other a *Narcissus*, of the family Amaryllidaceae. After wounds of these plants were infected with *Agrobacterium*, they did indeed swell slightly. But it was the fact that they produced opines that confirmed infection.

Is it possible to induce *Agrobacterium* plasmids to carry genes into grasses? As we have seen, the Ti plasmid represents only about 3 per cent of the total *Agrobacterium* genome. But the other 97 per cent, including that of the chromosome, also contributes to the parasitic process. One thing it must contribute is the ability to recognize a particular plant cell as a suitable host, and also the ability of the bacterium to bind to that host. The apparent failure of *Agrobacterium* to attack grasses lies with this process of recognition, which in turn implies that there is something inhospitable about the structure of the cell wall of grasses. The cell walls of grasses differ from those of most plants in that they contain a great deal of silicon. Perhaps this is at least part of the answer.

Secondly, the vir genes of the Ti plasmid need to be switched on, if they are to carry out their function of breaking into the host DNA. What switches them on is some kind of feedback from the host cell itself. It may be that grasses do not produce the right kind of signals, that would bring the vir region to life and so allow plasmid DNA to insinuate. If the breakdown in communications between *Agrobacterium*

143

and the Gramineae is as basic as this, then it could indeed prove difficult to apply this vector to cereals.

However, what emerges from the work at Leiden is that the only reason biologists did not realize that *Agrobacterium* does indeed infect monocots is that they did not know how to look for it. It produced no crown galls in monocots, so they did not know it was there – or not, at least, until Dr Hooykaas-Van Slogteren and her colleagues looked not for gross tumours, but for opines. It is at least possible, then, that there are other, comparable parasites in nature, which also insert into plant chromosomes, but which are not apparent because they do not produce any obvious signs. There may, in short, be other possible vectors, that will fill in the gaps left by *Agrobacterium*. However, as biologists have now ways of knowing how to look for organisms whose presence is not apparent, this may be only of theoretical interest. In any case, as noted above, the problem of introducing foreign DNA into cereals may be solved by electroporesis.

Thus, the state of play at the end of 1984 is that *Agrobacterium* has been used to transfer a gene between different plants of quite different families, and that gene was expressed; and it has been shown to infect monocots, but not grasses. In short, the problems have been breached. It is only a matter of time, and probably a few years rather than decades, before genes that really are of commercial use are put into commercially useful species. Before we speculate on what these might be, it is worth looking briefly at the other main category of potential gene vectors, the viruses.

Viruses as vectors

Bacteria do not keep all their genes in their 'chromosome'; and neither do eukaryotes. To be sure, eukaryotes keep by far the majority of their genes in chromosomes, but they also have some DNA, including functional genes, within the cytoplasm. Specifically, these genes are contained both within the mitochondria, which contain enzymes concerned with respiration, and thus provides the cell with its energy; and the chloroplasts, which contain chlorophyll and the other pigments and enzymes necessary for photosynthesis. The fact that there is functional DNA within these organelles supports the hypothesis of Professor Lyn Margulis. She suggests that these organelles originally were prokaryotic parasites, which stayed to become symbionts, and finally became essential components of the eukaryotic cell.

Viruses operate, in general, by insinuating themselves into their host's genome. But there is no evidence that any of the many hundreds of plant viruses actually infiltrate the chromosome, within the plant nucleus. They get no further than the cytoplasmic genes, within the organelles.

The organelles, however, and in particular the chloroplast, might be a very good place indeed to put certain plant genes. For one thing, although the genes of the organelles do work in co-operation with those of the nucleus, they do have some measure of independence. They are not as likely to be repressed, as a nuclear gene would be. For some genes constant ubiquitous self-expression would be an embarrassment; no-one wants high-value seed proteins produced in the roots, for example. But for other genes, constant unharried expression would be an advantage. Such might be the case with genes that confer resistance to disease.

Accordingly, to take just one example of such work, Dr Roger Hull and his colleagues at the John Innes Institute in Norwich are now endeavouring to persuade cauliflower mosaic virus to carry useful genes into plants. Cauliflower mosaic virus is, of course, an unwholesome parasite and if it is to be useful as a vector, then its teeth must be drawn. Accordingly, Dr Hull and his colleagues have developed strains that are able to infect, but cannot be transmitted, plant to plant.

There are other reasons, too, for favouring the cytoplasm rather than the nucleus as a site for the introduction of new genes. One is simply a matter of commerce. When genetic engineering truly becomes a commercial proposition, the engineers will want to protect their property. If the genes they have introduced are in the plant's chromosomes, then this is difficult. The changes made are permanent; and the farmer can simply save the seed of the engineered plant. But if the new genes are introduced into the cytoplasm, then their heredity is far more haphazard, and it should be possible to include other genes alongside the required ones, to ensure that they are not passed on at all. Of course, the astute grower could always multiply up his plants by tissue culture.

No vector can yet be used routinely to carry desirable genes into valuable crops. But it is not too early to ask how the new techniques are likely to be applied, when the technical problems are solved.

How might genetic engineering be applied?

In theory, genetic engineers might expect to operate in one of three different ways. They could simply synthesize the genes they require; they could remove genes from plants, alter them in required fashion, and reinsert them; or they could introduce existing genes taken from other organisms — which would normally mean from other plants, though genes could in theory be obtained from any kind of organism.

The first possibility, gene synthesis, is in some ways less difficult than it might seem, and in some ways more difficult. It is not difficult to effect the synthesis: that is, to join nucleotides together in the required sequence. The genetic code is now understood. Genes could be synthesized to produce proteins with any required sequence of amino acids.

There are two problems, however. The first is to ensure that the synthetic gene, when once introduced, is expressed and regulated. The most likely fate of such a synthetic sequence is that it would sit within the genome, but remain inoperative. The second problem is more profound. In effecting crop improvements, the genetic engineer would generally be seeking to introduce genes that code for particular enzymes, that have a particular effect upon the plant's metabolism and structure. The behaviour of enzymes depends upon their physical structure, and that in turn depends upon their chemistry – the sequence of amino acids within the protein chain or chains of which they are composed. However, protein chemists cannot yet predict the physical properties of a protein simply from knowledge of the sequence of amino acids within it. Still less are they able to synthesize a totally novel protein with predictable but novel properties just by stringing amino acids together. The possibility of producing a novel protein that would function predictably as an enzyme seems extremely remote.

Method two – removing a gene from a plant, altering it, and putting it back in an altered form – is known as *controlled mutagenesis*. Here, the engineer seeks only to make small but perhaps crucial changes in enzymes or other proteins that are already well-studied, by making small changes in the genes that code for those enzymes. In chapter 9 we will see two examples of this that are already in progress: the first is an attempt to alter the gene that codes for the springy storage proteins, or glutenins, that are so necessary in bread-wheats; and the second is an attempt to improve the efficiency of photosynthesis by improving the behaviour of the most important enzyme.

In general, however, the method of crop improvement that holds greatest promise is simply to obtain genes from existing organisms. In particular, there is much interest in equipping crops with genes that confer resistance to pests and diseases – genes that may in principle be obtained from plants quite unrelated to the crop in hand. One reason for this interest is that pest and disease resistance is such an important quality; but another is that such resistance often has a simple genetic basis, and in the immediate term engineers will at best be able to transfer single genes between plants. The task discussed in chapter 10 – how to endow wheat and other cereals with the ability to fix nitrogen – will have to wait, because nitrogen fixation is genetically complex, and it will be many years before engineers can transfer entire suites of genes while retaining their ability to function.

But if engineers, or indeed breeders in general, are going to be able to make use of the many thousands of potentially useful genes that are to be found within wild species and primitive landraces, then those species and landraces must be saved from extinction, and indeed made constantly available. How this can be done is the subject of the next chapter.

8   Genes in Store

Introduction

Breeders spend much of their time re-arranging the genes in the gene pool with which they begin. If they begin with a wild plant, a primitive variety, or a small group of varieties, then simple selection and judicious crossing between the individuals that are immediately to hand can produce enormous improvements. As breeding proceeds, some alleles are eliminated, some that were uncommon in the original plants become frequent, or even 'fixed', and eventually individuals emerge that are quite different from the starting material.

But there is a limit to the improvements that can be made in this way. For the cultivars produced only by working upon the original gene pool contain only those genes that were present in the original pool. Sooner or later the breeder will feel the need to incorporate new qualities, not present in the original plants. He will need to add genes from elsewhere.

As we have seen, there are several ways of doing this. One is to create novel genes by inducing mutation, and though this in principle is a hit-and-miss approach, many a modern crop has been improved by this technique (see chapter 5). Somaclonal variation also throws up useful novelties, which may or may not involve the creation of new genes by mutation. In theory, too, breeders may one day improve on this approach by creating new genes to order.

The third, and by far the most fruitful way to acquire new genes, is to search for them in other plants. The required genes may sometimes be found in other, advanced cultivars, and if that is so, so much the better. Such cultivars are liable to contain fewer unsuitable alleles than wild plants or primitive landraces, and there will be less need for rigorous back-crossing to eliminate the undesirables. Suitable cultivars are increasingly available, because many now already incorporate genes from wild plants or primitive cultivars. As we saw in chapter 5, the French wheat cultivar Roazon contains a gene from the goat grass *Aegilops ventricosa*, that confers resistance to eye spot.

Often, however, there is no suitable cultivar with which to cross, in which case the breeder turns to primitive landraces. Collectively, indeed, such landraces are by far the biggest source of new genetic material. They, after all, have been developed in tens of thousands of locations all over the world over centuries or millennia, and each contains a fair selection of the genes from the original primitive stock and acquired from local plants by introgression, plus whatever mutations have occurred *en route*. It is not the case, however, that any one landrace will contain all the genes from which it could benefit, which is one reason why landraces themselves are in need of improvement.

If no landrace is available then the breeder turns to the wild ancestors of his crop, if those wild ancestors still exist. If they are of no use, he turns to closely related wild species. Some of these close relatives will belong to the primary gene pool (GP1) of the crop, because the way they are classified by taxonomists (and the way they behave in the field) does not necessarily coincide precisely with the exclusiveness of their respective gene pools. Inevitably, however, as he searches more and more widely for suitable genes the breeder must seek out plants in the secondary and tertiary pools, which greatly complicates the task. Yet as we have seen in chapters 5, 6, and 7, breeders can now stretch the net very widely, and at least in crops such as wheat can make regular use of plants from the secondary or tertiary gene pools. The techniques of genetic engineering will in theory make all genes available, from all organisms.

The only question is whether suitable genes still exist. Landraces are the biggest single source of them; and landraces are rapidly being obliterated as modern cultivars take over. There is an irony here, indeed, as pointed out by Professor J. G. Hawkes, in *The Diversity of Crop Plants* (Hawkes, 1983). The breeders have themselves helped to eliminate the varieties that they themselves need. Thus, new varieties of wheat have been introduced to much of the Third World in the course of the Green Revolution. 'At their best', says Professor Hawkes, these varieties 'have helped solve many food problems. At their worst they have caused a catastrophic genetic erosion, especially in Turkey, Iraq, Afghanistan, Persia, and India. In those countries it is now quite difficult to find the older bread-wheat varieties, even though they were still common some 20 years ago.'

And what is true of the primitive varieties, is at least as true of the wild relatives. The International Union for the Conservation of Nature (IUCN) in Geneva estimates that at least 10 per cent of all the world's quarter million flowering plants are in imminent danger of extinction. Beyond doubt, many of those species that survive are rapidly losing a great deal of their natural variety – including, of course, such plants as wheat. Furthermore, the wild relatives of modern crops are of the kind that farmers tend to regard as 'weeds', not least because they tend to grow alongside the cultivated crops. These, then, are among the kinds that have been most assiduously eliminated. Other wild relatives simply find themselves living in areas that are densely inhabited, albeit seasonally. Thus the plants of the Mediterranean in general are under great pressure from tourists.

Conservation has many justifications, of which the aesthetic and the ethical must be considered most important. But it has material connotations too. If wild plants and primitive landraces are eliminated then crop improvement, sooner or later, will shudder to a halt. In the shorter term, it will at least be sadly compromised. How, then, can the wild plants and landraces be conserved?

Conservation

There are four basic ways to conserve wild plants and primitive landraces. The first is simply to maintain them where they are: in wild places, or on old-fashioned farms. The second is to hold them in botanical gardens. The third is to feed them into the horticultural trade, so that they are cultivated by people at large. And the fourth is to preserve them in the form of seeds, or some other storable material, in a 'gene bank', or 'germplasm bank'.

Maintaining plants in wild places or old-fashioned farms is the ideal, but there are two provisos. The first is that wild places have already been dramatically eroded through farming and the spread of towns, and the sad reality is that they can be maintained in the future only if the human species re-assesses its scale of values, or if the wild places can to some extent be made to pay their way. The latter is a possibility. Wilderness in the semi-tamed forms of national parks and game reserves does play an increasing role in the economies of many develop ing countries. In addition, more and more techniques are emerging for exploiting the wild for food and for plants that are valuable for drugs or other purposes, without doing irreperable harm. Game reserves can pay their way at least in part by providing entertainment for tourists, though tourists, with their motor cars and hotels, tend to destroy what they are paying to preserve. There is a case, too, for maintaining old-fashioned farms as centres of education and entertainment – but only if tax-payers or visitors are prepared to pay, for the old-fashioned farm can rarely compete with the modern.

Botanical gardens have a role both in conservation and in education. But few can maintain more than a few thousand species, and they tend inevitably to preserve just a few of each kind, which between them contain only a small selection of the genes encompassed by the species as a whole. In addition, gardens tend to keep plants that are most attractive to look at, and to keep the most attractive specimens of each. By selecting for attractiveness, the gardener inevitably jettisons many of the original alleles.

The third option, of feeding rare plants into the horticultural trade, possibly has more promise than is often realized. Several rare animals are now sustained in worthwhile numbers by consortia of amateur. David Jones, director of London Zoo, suggested in a recent radio programme that rare species of fish could be better served by enthusiastic amateurs, breeding them at home in tanks and ponds, than by zoos – precisely because amateurs do not need to concentrate upon the most spectacular species. Some plants, such as the primitive ginkgo tree, are now common – simply because they have been taken up by gardeners. People could do more than they know to conserve worthwhile species.

All such methods are flawed, however. In all cases, only a selection of the original gene pool is maintained. In the wild, the selection is random. All we can be certain of is that a national park is bound to contain fewer species, and fewer variants of those species, than once were present in the whole country. In botanical gardens and within the horticultural trade, conscious selection reduces the number and variability of species still more.

But the breeder of plants requires access to the entire library of genes available in any one species. The only practical way even to come close to achieving this is to scour the world for variants, and then store them not as entire plants, but in the form of germplasm. Stores of germplasm – 'gene banks' – have thus become an essential adjunct of all major programmes of crop improvement.

Gene banks

Plant breeding is an ancient craft, but the idea that crop improvement programmes needed to be complemented by stores of germplasm has only recently been acted upon on a worthwhile scale. The Food and Agriculture Organization of the United Nations (FAO) first began to take an interest shortly after the Second World War. Throughout the 1950s and 1960s expert committees met to establish guidelines on the kinds of areas that should be searched for plants, and the ways in which seeds should be gathered and stored. There were national initiatives, too. Notably, the United States established its National Seed Storage Laboratory at Fort Collins in Colorado in 1958.

The 1970s was a decade of consolidation. In 1971 the FAO and World Bank established CGIAR, the Consultative Group on International Agricultural Research. Its aim is to increase food production in developing countries – by encouraging and training scientists to do the research and extension work in those countries. CGIAR is now funded by the United Nations Development Program (UNDP), by various foundations including Ford, Rockefeller, and Kellog, and by regional development programmes and donor countries. And in 1973 CGIAR combined with FAO to generate a body specifically concerned, worldwide, with preserving the genes of plants. This is IBPGR, the International Board for Plant Genetic Resources.

The world's gene banks themselves are of several types and fulfil several functions. Some contain only one crop and its wild relatives. Some contain several crops of a particular region. Some serve as 'base collections' for long-term storage, while others serve the particular needs of particular institutes. The gene bank at Kew Gardens (or, rather, at Kew Gardens's country home at Wakehurst in Sussex, England) is unusual in that it is exclusively concerned with conserving wild plants, although many of its 5 000 species have known or presumed commercial significance. Different institutions co-operate with each to exchange genetic material and, in general, IBPGR knows who has what, and encourages particular institutions to undertake particular projects. Kew, for example, at present, is co-operating with IBPGR to collect forage plants from Ethiopia.

Of crucial significance is the network of international crop institutes, nine of them, overseen by CGIAR. These are devoted either to specific crops or to the crops of particular kinds of terrain, and most, but not all, of the institutes have responsibility for conserving the world collections. The International Rice Institute (IRRI) in the Philippines aims to collect all of the world's varieties of rice by 1987: 100–120 000 different types are recognized. The International Maize and Wheat Improvement Center (CIMMYT) in Mexico oversees the world's central collection of maize. The International Potato Center (CIP) in Peru stores 12 000 lines of primitive landraces; and the International Crop Research Institute for the Semi-Arid Tropics, ICRISAT, in Hyderabad, India, keeps the world's main collections of sorghum, millet, chickpea, and pigeon peas, and one of the main collections of groundnuts.

The International Center for Tropical Agriculture (CIAT), in Colombia, among other things looks after the world's base collection of cassava (*Manihot*), and *Phaseolus* beans; the International Institute of Tropical Agriculture (IITA) at Ibadan, Nigeria, looks after genetic resources of African rice, root crops, and tropical groundnuts. The International Center for Agricultural Research on Dry Areas (ICARDA) at Aleppo, Syria, and Beirut, Lebanon, is concerned with those crops from the Mediterranean and Near East that are adapted to dry conditions – including barley, lentils, vetches, durum wheat, and chickpeas. The Asian Vegetable Research Development Center (AVRDC) at Taiwan is associated with CGIAR, and is responsible for such crops as tomatoes, soyabeans, Chinese cabbage, sweet potatoes, and mung beans.

There are also several national gene collections, among which we might note CENARGEN, recently established in Brazil, and the collaborative Netherlands/German potato bank in West Germany. Finally, many breeding institutes maintain their own lines of germ-plasm. For example, the PBI in the United Kingdom maintains 3 000 breeding lines of wheat. These are used in PBI's own breeding programmes, and lent out for others elsewhere.

With the world's growing collection of gene banks, then, the picture is not entirely black. But it is far from perfect. The world's main crops and their wild relatives are probably taken care of adequately; there is plenty of wheat, rice, and potato in store, for example. But if we are truly to get to grips with the mass – the 99.9 per cent of plants that are not prime food crops – then a great deal more needs to be done, and quickly. Kew's 5 000 species in store represents only 2 per cent of the 250 000 species of flowering plant. And although some species at Kew are represented in stores by many hundreds or thousands of samples – accessions – few species have been comprehensively studied. Some of Kew's projects, such as the collection of legumes and grasses from the Mediterranean, have an air of almost desperate urgency. Legumes and grasses include some of the world's principal crops. Wild relatives of those crops could be of enormous significance in the future. But the wild and agriculturally primitive areas of the Mediterranean are under enormous pressure.

It is one thing to establish a gene bank, and another to make it work. Technically, and administratively, there are great many problems.

Collecting for a gene bank

The first question is what to collect. An ecologist, trying to get an unbiased view of what is growing where, would sample the various plants randomly; randomness seems close to objectivity. But the collector of seeds is seeking, rather, to collect as broad a range as possible of the different types within a particular population of plants. If he simply selects randomly, he may well miss the rarer types; but the rare ones might be those of most value. In particular, he could well miss those characters that have a very localized distribution. Professor Hawkes cites the gene that confers resistance to bacterial wilt, *Pseudomonas solanacearum*. This is found in the wild potato *Solanum phureja* – but only among individuals in a small area of the plant's total range. On the other hand, if the collector is too biased, he might concentrate upon the most spectacular or wayward specimens, and yet miss those cryptic characters that are not immediately obvious – such as resistance to disease. In short, the ideal collection strategy is probably based on randomness, but modified (and biased) by as much useful information as the collector can bring to bear, and about the range and distribution of different characters within a particular population.

But it is one thing to have an ideal strategy for collection, and quite another to be able to carry it out. Collections are made largely from areas where agriculture is still primitive, and where relatives of the crops are still living in the wild – places such as Peru and West Africa, in the Middle East and South-East Asia, in Ethiopia and around the Mediterranean. To collect seed, or tubers, the collector should be on the spot when the seed is ripening. One problem is that crops that are not highly bred tend to ripen their seed over prolonged periods, particularly in some areas of the tropics, where there may be little distinction between seasons. In practice, then, collections are often made under less than ideal conditions, by methods that may range from scouring the roadsides, to visiting scores of farms, to exploring the local markets. The collections that actually get sent back to the seed banks may occasionally come close to the ideal. But in any one year they are likely simply to reflect whatever compromise the collector can make.

Storing the germplasm

Seed storage is not always straightforward. There are basic principles, but no universal method, applicable to all seeds. In general, seeds last longest when dried, and stored at low temperatures.

Seed may be dried by gentle warming, or by removing moisture with silica gel. In either case, the aim is to reduce the moisture content to around 4 per cent. The rule of thumb is that for every 1 per cent of moisture that can be removed below 14 per cent, the life of the seed is doubled. For example, onion seeds with a 4 per cent content of moisture are said to last 1 000 times longer than those with a 14 per cent moisture content. But if seeds are dried below 4 per cent moisture they may be damaged, because the fats they contain undergo auto-oxidation.

Low temperatures means +4°C down to −20°C, though there is increasing interest in the possibility of keeping them at the temperature of liquid nitrogen, −196°C. One advantage is that storage in liquid nitrogen gives plenty of leeway. Many germplasm banks are in tropical countries where normal temperatures are high and where power supplies are sometimes suspect; but liquid nitrogen, when in suitable canisters, will stay cold for long periods. The only question is whether seed can indeed be taken to such low temperatures, and then restored.

But these rules for storing seeds cannot be applied to all kinds. A large number are in the category known as 'recalcitrant', and these − perversely − are damaged by drying. Recalcitrant seeds, in large part, often include those of tropical trees. After all, the 'reason' why a plant produces seed is partly to reproduce itself, partly for the purposes of dispersal, and partly to tide it over hard times − such as the winter. In a tropical forest there are no hard times and the best strategy for a seed is to germinate immediately, so avoiding the perils of being eaten as a seed. Unfortunately many of the world's most valuable crops are tropical or sub-tropical trees. The recalcitrant types include coffee, cacao, citrus, rubber, and many palms, including oil palm and coconut.

153

Professor Hawkes describes a possible solution to the problem of recalcitrance. Tropical trees may not care to remain as seeds. But many are able to remain as seedlings or as young trees after they have germinated; effectively standing still until a space appears in the forest canopy. So perhaps they could be stored in the form of seedlings. Or perhaps pieces of meristem might be stored in frozen form, rather than the seeds.

Then there is the question of bringing the seeds round after storage. The scientists in charge of the gene bank at Kew Gardens, led by Roger Smith, are seed physiologists. They are interested not so much in the genes that particular seeds may contain, but in perfecting methods of storage. Their problems are different from other seed banks in that many of the species they deal with are unstudied; nobody has looked at their storage requirements. Many of the non-recalcitrant seeds will remain alive in storage for many years, even for centuries. Some will germinate as soon as they are warmed and moistened.

But some seeds enter a distinct physiological state of dormancy when they are stored. These will not 'come to life' unless they are first given some specific stimulus, in addition to the basic requirements of warmth and moisture. Dormancy is an evolutionary device, the purpose of which is to prevent premature germination, at inappropriate times or in inappropriate places. Thus, many cereals will not germinate unless they are first subjected to cold – cold that simulates winter. This ensures that they do not germinate until after the winter. 'Winter' cereals – those that are sown in autumn – are varieties that have lost this natural reluctance to germinate. Other species need to be exposed to light before they will germinate. This is true of many weed species, that are doomed unless they germinate close to the soil surface. The Kew Gardens physiologists take it upon themselves to discover the precise germination requirements of each of their charges. Then, when other scientists ask them for specimens to work on, or to breed from, they can give the necessary instructions.

When seed banks were first established, it seemed necessary to plant out all the stocks every few years, to renew the stocks of seeds. Otherwise, those in store could simply pass quietly away. There are hazards in replanting, however. A crop may be wiped out by disease when replanted. Some of the original genes may be lost by genetic drift, and others may be introduced by cross-pollination. But as knowledge and techniques of storage increase, the requirement for constant re-planting is reduced. Most seeds now can in theory be kept safely in store at least for decades, and probably for centuries.

One problem that will always be with us, however, is that of keeping track. In any one gene bank there may be tens of thousands of accessions, perhaps representing thousands of varieties, landraces, and wild species. Each accession will contain genes containing some particular character – resistance to this pest or that, long growing season, high-quality grain, or whatever. All these characters in all the accessions must be characterized and the information stored so that it is instantly available. Without the computer, this task would hardly be feasible. With computers, it is possible simply to key in a list of requirements and obtain a printout within minutes of all the accessions that contain the required characters.

For the future, we can expect to see seeds kept ever more safely. Increasingly, they may be stored at the temperature of liquid nitrogen. Where appropriate, the banks may contain parts of the plant other than seed. It is already possible to take meristem tissue of potato and of cassava down to $-196°C$, and bring it back again safely to normal temperatures. Plant physiologists will eventually master all the recalcitrant species, and perhaps contemplate long-term storage of seedlings.

But species and varieties are becoming extinct much faster than they are being coralled into seed banks. Many characters that are thought to be of no value often prove to be of use. Thus, as Professor Hawkes says: 'when I look back on my work with potatoes over some 20 or 30 years, I now know that much of what I regard as interesting and important today was then regarded as of little or no consequence. How can we be certain of what we will need in 30 years time?'

However, there is enough material even in present seed banks to keep breeders employed for many a decade. The kinds of things they might do with that genetic wealth are the subject of the next chapter.

9   Tasks in Hand

Introduction

The crops that breeders release for farmers to grow are never perfect. They merely represent the state of the art. There is always room for improvement.

One problem, as we discussed in chapter 1, is that improvement can be defined in many different ways, and some ambitions conflict with others. The needs of the packer may conflict with those of the gourmet. Yield may conflict with protein content, because more energy is required to produce a gram of protein than to produce a gram of starch. A plant tailored for the garden may not suit the arable farmer, and vice versa.

In practice, market forces tend to prevail. Breeders strive to produce whatever people care to ask for, provided only that what is asked is biologically possible, and that the customer is able to pay. The principal flaw, of course, is that people who are most in need are often the ones least able to pay, so that tropical subsistence crops have been sadly neglected through most of this century. Various institutions are now helping to make up for lost time, however, such as ICRISAT, which brings some of the most advanced techniques of crop improvement to bear upon crops that are grown by some of the world's poorest farmers.

In practice, the improvements that breeders contrive to make fall into four main categories. Firstly, they try to make crops more compliant; to improve their level of adaptation to the general conditions they will be provided with, and the exigencies of harvesting or processing. Secondly, they strive to improve quality, as defined by consumers and nutritionists. Thirdly, they endeavour to increase resistance to stresses of all kinds, including disease. And finally, they strive to increase yield. A fifth ambition – to enhance the ability to fix nitrogen, or to create new classes of nitrogen fixing crops – is discussed in the next chapter. Here, we should discuss the main four lines of approach.

Compliance

Many of the most important qualities of a crop are of the kind that are easily taken for granted. For example, the seeds of spring cereals germinate only in spring. They do not sprout as soon as they fall off their parent plant in the previous autumn. They do that because they have a requirement for *vernalization*. They need to be cooled, as a signal that winter has passed, before they germinate. Winter cereals, by contrast, are actually planted in autumn, and put on growth before the winter, so that they are ready to race away in the following spring. They do not require vernalization.

Temperate crops in general are liable to be nipped by frost at the beginning and end of their season, and must adjust their cycles of germination, growth, and ripening to take account of that fact. They do this, in general, by responding appropriately to the lengthening days of spring, and the lengthening nights of late summer. Many temperate crops simply will not flower or ripen at all unless the changing day-length stimulates them to do so. Crops from low latitudes, by contrast, face a 12-hour day all year round, and often have lost or perhaps never evolved the ability to acknowledge changes in the length of day. So when crops are taken from the tropics into more temperate lands, or vice versa, they must be given the genes that will allow them to respond appropriately to the signals of the region. Neither potatoes nor wheat travel easily between latitudes.

More specifically, farmers like plants of any one variety to ripen all together, so that all can be harvested together by machine – or all sold *en masse* to the processor. But they may often prefer different varieties to come to fruition at different times, so that they can spread the task of harvesting over several weeks. Thus breeders provide early and late varieties of soft fruits and vegetables. Again, crops must be bred that 'read' the time of year accurately.

Similarly, some crops are natural *annuals*, and complete their life-cycle in a single year. Others, known as *biennials* spend one year in growing, and come to fruition in the following year. *Perennials* persist for many years.

Sugar beets are natural biennials. They lay down storage tubers to carry them through the winter, and produce seed in the following year. Farmers harvest this tuber – half way through the beet's natural cycle. Some beets, however, known as 'bolters', miss out the tuberous phase, and produce seed in their first year. It probably pays natural species of biennials to pursue 'mixed strategies'. The longer a plant stays in the ground, the greater the chance that it will be destroyed before it reproduces. But a plant that does take two years to grow can in the end produce more seed than one that takes only one, because it has greater reserves of nutrient to draw upon. On the other hand, the presence of a

157

few individuals that produced just a few seeds at the end of the first year, would provide a form of insurance. For farmers, however, bolting sugar beet are simply a waste; and indeed, bolters are regarded as weeds, and invade other arable crops, besides corrupting the beet crop itself. Bolting in short is a 'vice', that must be eliminated as far as possible by breeding.

Some crops, however, are best grown as annuals in some circumstances, and at other times are most useful as perennials. The breeder may therefore be called upon to develop two different sets of varieties, pursuing different cycles. Thus, one of the principal pulse crops of the dry lands of India is the pigeon pea. In the better areas, where water is available, this is best grown as an annual. Energy is then diverted into pod production, rather than into producing big woody stems. But in the drier areas, perennials are better, because the growing season is too short to allow a good crop to be produced in a single season. In addition, the woody stems produced in the subsequent seasons are a useful source of fuel. However, pigeon peas tend to accumulate viruses as the years pass, and perennials tended to produce very uncertain yields until breeders at ICRISAT developed resistant strains.

It is often necessary, too, to adjust the physical form, or *habit* of the plant. Thus in chapter 1 we discussed the possibility of producing winged beans in more than one form: a short stiff form for growing in the field; and the trailing form, which is the natural habit, for gardens.

In general, the habit of a plant may be *determinate*, or *indeterminate*. Those of determinate habit grow to a certain 'predetermined' size, then mature, become senescent, and die. Wheat is of this kind. Other plants simply go on growing until they die.

Field beans, *Vicia faba*, which are a form of broad bean, have indeterminate habit. They produce an inflorescence, from which beans will develop, and then the stalk continues to grow and produces more leaves. Broad beans do this as well, of course, and the gardener simply removes the tops. But farmers have no time to prune each plant individually. Field beans therefore may grow to two metres in height and at the end of the season they look an untidy mess: a pile of rotting stalks. Yield is highly variable, as might be expected, with so much photosynthetic energy devoted to superfluous vegetation. Accordingly, field beans have long been grown in the United Kingdom, but only in small amounts: about 30 000 hectares – comparable with linseed or lupin.

David Bond at the PBI in Cambridge has now bred a 'topless' bean. This produces no leaves after it has laid down its inflorescence. Its habit is therefore determinate. Yields so far are no higher than with the indeterminate beans, but as the breeding programme continues, they should increase. When the crop is tidier, it may be worthwhile improving the seed quality of the field bean, to bring it more in line with that of the broad bean. One requirement is to breed varieties with a lower content of tannin; field beans should not only be animal fodder. In a more rational world, making better use of resources, they would be an important food for humans – just as the broad bean is in the Mediterranean and Middle East.

The gene that produced the topless bean is an artificial mutant, created in Sweden by exposure to X-rays. Examples of successful mutants are not common, but some are very valuable indeed.

The list of such refinements could be extended indefinitely. In general, however, we may note that the business of adjusting the habit of the plant and its responsiveness to time is part of the general problem of domestication. Any wild plant that is a potential candidate for cultivation, or any crop moved from one latitude to another, must be suitably adjusted. To the extent that their habit is indeterminate, field beans may be considered 'primitive'. Until the recent work at PBI, they had failed to cross one of the basic hurdles of domestication.

Another primitive quality of many crops that has yet to be eliminated is toxicity. The toxicity doubtless evolved as a means of repelling predators, but what served for survival in the wild is a severe disadvantage in a domestic crop. This takes us to our next category of improvement: consumer quality.

Quality improvement: toxicity

Many plants that have become major crops have innate leanings towards toxicity. The members of the Solanaceae tend to be versatile organic chemists and many wild species of potato produce dangerous compounds. Even the domestic *Solanum tuberosum* produces toxic solanins if exposed to the light. Cassava, of the equally versatile Euphorbiaceae, contains cyanogenic glycosides: sugar-derivatives that generate cyanide. Breeding has reduced the amount of cyanogenic glycosides, but no varieties are entirely free of them. Besides, farmers in poor areas prefer the bitter, cyanogenic types, because they tend to be more resistant to pests.

Cassava is not toxic if it is heated or fermented, however; but many problems of toxicity in pulse crops can be eliminated only by breeding. Thus, though broad beans are an admirable food, they cause a form of acute anaemia in some people; a condition known as favism. Only some people are susceptible, and the reasons for this are not clear. Victims do tend to be deficient in the enzyme glucose-6-phosphate dehydrogenase (G6DP), and the defective allele that leads to G6DP deficiency happens to occur most commonly among people of the Mediterranean and Middle East, where the broad bean is most commonly eaten. G6DP deficiency cannot be the only cause of the disease, however, because

American blacks also tend to be G6DP deficient, and do not suffer from favism.

One possible solution was suggested by Pythagoras – avoid broad beans. More promising is the research at the Hebrew University of Jerusalem by Jacob Mager. In the 1960s Professor Mager isolated two compounds from broad beans, vicine and convicine, which are among the toxins responsible for triggering favism in susceptible people. Once the culpable agents are discovered, then it becomes possible to breed lines that lack them. At its simplest, all that is required is to take small samples from individual seeds to find those free of the toxin, and then plant only those seeds. Work continues at the Hebrew University, under Professor Mordechai Chevion.

Even more serious than the toxicity of the broad bean is that of a minor pulse: the grass pea, *Lathyrus sativus*, which is widely cultivated and eaten in Northern India. *Lathyrus* contains a very peculiar amino-acid (not one that normally appears in proteins) known as beta-N-oxalyl-L-alpha beta diamino-proprionic acid, or ODAP. This compound causes lathyrism, a crippling condition of the legs. The victims, mostly young men, are reduced to crawling on their bellies. Perhaps Pythagoras' advice should in this case be taken. Perhaps *Lathyrus* really is beyond the pale. But *Lathyrus* is a potentially valuable crop, and breeders at the Indian Agricultural Research Institute in Hyderabad are striving to develop low-toxin varieties. At present, however, the lines that are least toxic produce very poor yields.

In practice, the more closely crop plants are examined, the more potentially injurious compounds they prove to contain. Even parsnips are potentially dangerous. In 1981 Wayne Ivie, Douglas Holt and Marcellus Ivey at the Veterinary, Toxicology, and Entomology Research Laboratory in Texas, reported in *Science* that those sweet and pleasant taproots contain 40 parts per million of agents known as psoralens, which are potent carcinogens. The concentration may not sound impressive: but 100 grams of parsnip (about a quarter of a pound) contain 4 milligrams, which is a heavy dose. Again, breeding could in theory eliminate this vice.

Mercifully, the world's principal staples, the cereals, do not raise problems of toxicity – except of course when the seed is contaminated by moulds and other fungi. The Gramineae are not exuberant chemists, as are the Solanaceae, the euphorbs, the legumes and the umbellifers. With them, the prime consumer problem is to adjust the protein content.

Quality: cereal protein

Protein should be considered under two headings: concentration, and quality. Quality in turn has two connotations. It may refer to the physical properties of the proteins, or to their chemical composition.

High protein concentration or low?

The concentration of protein in a cereal depends partly on breeding, and partly on how the crop is grown. If a cereal has a short breeding season but is heavily plied with fertilizer, then it will tend to produce small yields with a high protein content, as is the case with spring wheats grown in Canada. A long growing season with high application of nitrogen at appropriate times results in much heavier yields, with a lower protein content – as in British winter wheats.

In some special instances a high protein content is a disadvantage. Brewers, for example, favour barley with a low content of protein nitrogen. In general, however, a high protein content is desirable.

However, as noted in chapter 1, there is a conflict between protein concentration and yield, because more energy is required to produce a gram of protein than to produce a gram of starch, and every increase in protein content carries a 'yield penalty'. This raises a serious dilemma. On the one hand, there can be no doubt that the potential for raising the protein content of cereals is stupendous. The average commercial wheat contains between 8 and 14 per cent protein, but Moshe Feldman and his colleagues at the Weizman Institute in Israel have found wild species in the hills of what was once the 'Fertile Crescent', that contain 20 per cent or more: a level more usually associated with pulses.

In the 1960s, few nutritionists would have doubted that ultra-high protein cereals were desirable. Then, it was widely believed that the chief nutritional deficiency in the world at large was a lack of protein. Nowadays most nutritionists argue that a specific deficiency of protein is rare. People are malnourished not because of a lack of protein in particular, but because of a lack of food in general – deficiency of protein-plus-energy. Many now feel that the 10 per cent of protein contained in present-day cereals is adequate, especially when the cereal is augmented with pulse and with small amounts of meat or fish. The chief requirement, then, may not be to raise protein content but to increase yield. Yet as we have seen, the two aspirations are not entirely compatible.

Perhaps breeders should strive to pursue all options: on the one hand to produce very high-yielding varieties of cereal with a modest protein content, and on the other to provide a few specialist cereal varieties with a very high protein content.

The quality of protein

What clearly is of great significance, however, is the quality of the protein: its physical properties and chemical composition.

Wheat contains proteins of high molecular weight known as

glutenins, which become very springy when wet. Because of this property, dough can be leavened; the bubbles of carbon dioxide produced by yeast are contained in elastic membranes. Other cereals contain little or no glutenins, and cannot produce leavened bread. Among wheats, some are far richer in glutenins than others.

All hexaploid domestic wheats of the species *Triticum aestivum* are known loosely as 'bread wheats', but only some, in practice, produce good bread. Those grown in the long cool summers of the United Kingdom tend generally to be low in appropriate proteins, and although British wheat farmers produce some of the highest yields in the world, and Britain is an important wheat-growing country, it has been necessary in the past to import wheat for bread-making from North America. The home-grown grain was made into biscuits, or fed to livestock. As late as the 1950s, the United Kingdom imported 80 per cent of its bread-making wheat from North America.

However, scientists are the PBI have now identified a great many glutenin-rich varieties of wheat, from a wide variety of sources, and introduced them into their cereal breeding programmes. Now, United Kingdom farmers provide 80 per cent of the wheat that goes into the United Kingdom loaf. Soon they should provide 100 per cent.

Scientists at Rothamsted, led by Dr Peter Shewry, are now making a particularly subtle contribution to improvement of glutenins. They are seeking to relate the behaviour of glutenins to their physical structure, and suggest that innate springiness is conferred by a sequence of amino acids arranged in a spiral – literally in a spring – that occupies the centre of each glutenin molecule. Each end of the molecule, they suggest, attaches to neighbouring glutenin molecules, so that the mass together form a collective spring.

They are now testing this 'model' of the glutenin molecule by isolating the gene that produces it. Then they can alter the sequence of nucleotides within the gene and thus produce a *controlled mutation*. The altered gene will then produce a protein with a different sequence of amino acids. By comparing the physical properties of this new, altered protein with that of the original the Rothamsted scientists will be able to test whether their original model was correct. More importantly and generally, they will be able to relate the physical properties of the protein to its amino acid sequence. In theory, eventually, they should be able to construct genes (by altering existing genes or synthesizing new ones) that produce precisely the sequence of amino acid needed to produce a protein with precisely the required physical characteristics. This altered gene might then be reintroduced into wheat.

Nutritional quality is a separate issue. Cereals in theory contain enough protein to satisfy most human needs, but that cereal protein is not of the highest nutritional quality. In particular, it contains a low concentration of the essential amino-acid lysine. If only one essential

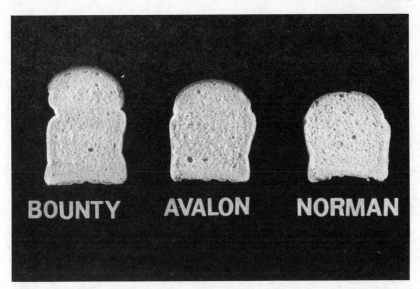

Figure 9.1 The extent to which bread will rise depends upon the elasticity and strength of the glutenin proteins in the wheat from which it was made. Norman is a British wheat intended not for bread but for biscuits. Bounty is a high quality British bread wheat, now succeeded by Avalon, which yields more heavily.

amino-acid is lacking, then the quality of the whole protein is deficient.

In practice, it is hard to judge the overall importance of that defect. People in poor countries derive a high proportion of their protein from cereals, so a lack of quality could be important. Even in poor countries, however, cereals are generally accompanied by other foods, including pulses and small amounts of meat or fish. Animal protein is usually of extremely high quality, and pulse proteins are particularly rich in lysine. In either case, then, the cereal deficiency would be made good.

However, it does seem desirable to raise the nutritional quality of cereal storage proteins, provided this can be done without compromising other qualities. This is certainly desirable in cereals destined to be fed to livestock.

Barley has been the chief target of scientists at Rothamsted. The storage proteins of barley are many and varied. Some have an excellent balance of amino acids, and indeed are similar in chemistry and in nutritional qualities with those of legumes. But the dominant storage protein is hordein, which is very low in lysine, and reduces the nutritional quality of the grain as a whole.

The aim at Rothamsted is not to seek to alter the genes that produce hordein, but to suppress the genes that code for hordein and enhance the genes that code for other, more desirable storage proteins. The idea is to identify and isolate the regions on the barley DNA that regulate the expression of the storage-protein genes. These can then be altered – another example of 'controlled mutagenesis' – so that they either damp down the activity of the hordein genes, or encourage the activity of the non-hordein storage genes. This is genetic engineering on a new conceptual plane: a matter not of directly altering or introducing genes that produce particular proteins, but of changing the genes that *regulate* the genes that produce those proteins.

When methods of adjusting the protein quality and content of cereals are perfected, then it might be profitable to direct efforts in particular towards sorghum. In West Africa, sorghum farming is being held back largely because there is little incentive to produce high yields, as surpluses cannot readily be sold on the open market. One reason for this is that rich West Africans are developing a taste for springy, western-style bread, which can only be produced from grain with a high gluten content, that is, from wheat. But if sorghums containing gluten genes could be developed then the farmers of the semi-arid lands of West Africa could produce crops that would satisfy their own countrymen, thus providing themselves with a more satisfactory living. Genetic engineering could, in theory and in time, provide such crops.

Even in the short term, genetic engineering might be used to produce high-protein potatoes. The quality of potato protein is excellent, but the concentration is low. A protein-rich potato would be a very fine meal indeed.

Breeders of potatoes at present are more concerned with other consumer qualities, however.

Quality: potatoes for all predilections

Potatoes find their way into human beings by many different routes. Some are canned, some are crisped, some are baked, some are boiled and some are sliced thin in salads. Different methods of preparation require different qualities; and, of course, different individuals prefer different flavours (strong or bland), textures (waxy or floury), and colours (white- or yellow-fleshed, white-, red-, or blue-skinned). The world's seed banks between them have about 40 000 accessions of potato in store, including most of the world's 154 wild species, and the countless cultivars within the 7 or so species that have been cultivated. The genus *Solanum* has enough variability to suit every human requirement and more besides, but to incorporate the required qualities into plants that farmers in Europe and North America can actually grow in reasonable amounts is not easy; and to incorporate quite contradictory properties into the same potato is of course impossible. At PBI, Dr Alan Thomson and his colleagues have various priorities in mind.

Everybody, fortunately, wants tubers that have a good, regular shape, although some prefer them small and round for canning, and others like them big and oval for baking. Many of the potatoes grown in the Andes are knobbly or formed like misshapen sausages. Many, too, have very deep eyes, and so do many cultivated varieties. Though one may cry *vive la difference*, the fact is that such eccentricities of form complicate preparation. Clearly, when the breeder incorporates genes from new species or from a deep-eyed cultivar, he must back-cross to eliminate ill-shapenness.

Nobody who boils potatoes likes them to turn black. This too is a heritable characteristic, which can be eliminated by breeding. The fact that it has not been eliminated reflects the fact that it has not been possible, in the decades in which potatoes have been intensively bred in the West, to combine every required quality in a single plant, while eliminating the vices. Some people who like potato chips (what the Americans call French fries) prefer them to be brown; but the manufacturers of crisps (what the Americans call chips) wish them to remain pale (or 'golden' as the jingle has it), and in the harsh commercial world, the voices of the powerful crisp manufacturers are likely, unfortunately, to prevail. The chemical basis of this is clear: potatoes turn brown when they are rich in reducing sugars. When the chemical basis of a quality is known, then screening for that property is easier, and breeding is more straightforward.

Everyone should take the side of the crisp manufacturers in their demand for varieties that take up very little fat when fried. This quality again is heritable: some varieties take up more than 40 per cent of their own weight of fat when fried, while others take up less than 30 per cent. The crisp manufacturers are interested primarily in cost: fat is more expensive than potatoes. The consumer should be interested in health; the low-fat French fry would be a very important innovation.

Colour is important, too, in the breeding of potatoes. The British prefer reds and whites; so far they have not appreciated the odd splashes of purple that appear from time to time. But the colours of Andean potatoes can be truly wonderful: red, blue, yellow, white, orange and purple. We should bury our conservatism, and transmit to the breeders the notion that blue, or purple, or orange, would be good to see.

The breeders at PBI even care about flavour. After all, the flavour of some potatoes is 'out of this world', as Nigel Smith has commented. It is thus in sharp contrast to much of what is now on offer. Even those who have not shared Dr Smith's experiences in Bolivia may properly regard the first Jersey potatoes of summer as one of the gastronomic highlights of the year. The wild species and ancient cultivars are still available in the Andes, and the old-fashioned European varieties are still retained at places like the PBI, even if they are no longer grown commercially. Among the potatoes now being tested for flavour at the PBI is the lumper, which succumbed to blight in the Irish potato famine. If the lumper, or others, do indeed have genes for delectability, then these genes could be bred into some modern variety which yields more

Figure 9.2 European potatoes are all developed from just one species, *Solanum tuberosum*. But at least seven species, each divided into scores of landraces, are still grown in the Andes, and offer an extraordinary variety of colour, shape, texture and flavour.

heavily and is more resistant to disease.

In the fullness of time it would be possible, following Mendel's law of separate inheritance, to employ skin colours as markers of different flavours and textures: a blue might be strong-flavoured and floury, a purple floury and bland or an orange strong and waxy, for example. This would not merely be caprice. It would be good for the world's economy and nutrition, if people were to eat more potatoes, and the potatoes should be made as interesting as possible. The potato, as we have seen, has the potential to be very interesting indeed.

The same principle applies to all the staple crops, and indeed to all plant crops. The reality is that most people in the world will always have diets that are very heavy in staples, and in which meat is added mainly for flavour; and such a diet would be desirable for Westerners, who at present have moved too far from this simple foundation. But if diets are to be heavily dependent on staples, then the staples themselves must not be merely nourishing, but good to eat as well.

The fundamental requirement, however, is for varieties that will grow in conditions the farmer is realistically able to provide. Crops must be resistant to stress.

Resistance to stress

Farmers and growers seek to meet all the physiological needs of their crops and to protect them from adversity. This is what 'cultivation' implies. In the greenhouse, every whim may be catered for: temperature and light can be adjusted; minerals provided at precisely the right concentration; pathogens banished. But this is feasible only when the crop has an extremely high market price: a cucumber sold out of season, for example, or a melon rushed from Israel to the supermarkets of London. Crops of lesser market value canot be so cosseted. All crops must endure some stress. Those grown in the world's harshest environments by the world's poorest farmers have to put up with a very high degree of stress indeed.

In practice, stresses are of four main kinds. Crops inevitably are exposed to predators, parasites and pathogens – rats, birds, insects, slugs, nematodes, mites, bacteria, fungi, and viruses. Most crops at some times must endure drought – 'water stress' – and for those in the vast areas of the semi-arid tropics, this is inevitable. Some must endure extremes of temperature: some must stand through the frost, and others must germinate through soil on which it is possible to bake an egg. Many are called upon to endure 'mineral stress': deficiency of some essential nutrient, or surplus of another. In particular, many crops are exposed to salinity.

Parasites

There are two ways in which plants may increase their resistance to parasites. The first is to be variable and the second is to contain genes conferring specific resistance.

Variability is an important safeguard. Indeed, as we saw from chapter 4, Professor William Hamilton has suggested that the whole point of sex is to produce variability, thus undermining the ability of parasites to become too well-adapted to their hosts. Crops of primitive landraces generally avoid being entirely eliminated by a particular pathogen in any one year simply because they are variable. Only a proportion of the plants are outstandingly susceptible to a particular strain of pathogen in any one year.

Variability may be introduced deliberately. Dr Alan Thomson at the PBI is at present producing 'varieties' of potatoes suitable for the Third World. However, he is not delivering these potatoes in the form of tubers, as is usual, for tubers develop into identical clones. Instead he is preparing collections of true seed, as contained within the fruits. True seed does not breed true, but a suitable mixture of true seed can produce a crop of reasonably uniform phenotype, but varying sufficiently in its physico-chemical details to avoid elimination by a single parasite. The dangers of excessive uniformity in potatoes were illustrated all too clearly in the 1840s, when the lumper potato variety found in Ireland and West Scotland succumbed almost totally to the depredations of the blight fungus, *Phytophthera infestans*.

Maize, in the United States, provides a more recent example of the perils of uniformity. As described in chapter 5, maize breeding was greatly advanced by the discovery of a gene for male sterility in the variety Mexican June. By the late 1960s, therefore, most of the maize grown in the United States contained genes from that single variety. Maize is not anything like as uniform as an inbreeding crop can be, but such a concentration on a few genes reduced the range of types – which had already been greatly reduced by a century of intensive breeding. The danger was exposed in the summer of 1970 when the United States maize crop was attacked by a race – race T – of the southern leaf blight fungus *Helminthosporium maydis* which spread northwards at an astonishing 150 km per day. Maize breeders today are particularly anxious to recover some of the lost variability.

Again, however, we see a conflict of aspirations. Variability reduces the impact of any one epidemic, but farmers and consumers prefer crops to be uniform. One solution is to produce crops that are similar in the properties that are conspicuous – in their response to fertilizer, in their size and form and nutritional qualities – but are as variable as possible in characters that are of no direct concern to the grower or consumer. This is not impossible. All it implies is that genes determining essential physical characteristics should be 'fixed' in the population – that is, reduced to one allele – while other, less important genes should exist in several or many different alleles.

Alternatively, or in addition, the breeder can endeavour to endow crops with genes conferring specific resistance to disease. Sometimes he finds these by screening existing varieties. Such searching has provided mildew-resistant sorghum and millet, and pigeon peas resistant to various fungi and viruses. But often he has to cast the net more widely.

And excellent example is again provided by the potato. In the 1950s the entire potato-growing industry in the Fens, one of the chief growing areas in England, was almost brought to a halt by the potato cyst nematode, *Globodera*. However, three species that are exotic to Britain all showed resistance: *Solanum vernii*, *S. cruzianum* and *S. andigena*, which is the ancestor of the European type, *S. tuberosum*. A cross made in 1955 between *S. tuberosum* and *S. andigena* eventually produced the famous variety Maris Piper, which was released in 1966. By 1980 Maris Piper was the leading variety in England and today it occupies 60–70 per cent of the Fenland potato fields.

Crucial to the development of resistant varieties are methods of monitoring the ability to ward off attack. Breeders of potatoes at the PBI grow plants in pots, and infest each pot with a standard number of *Globodera*. Then, resistance can be assessed simply by counting the

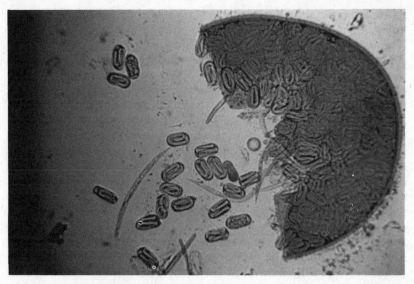

Figure 9.3 Potato cyst nematode, *Globodera*, once threatened the entire potato crop of Britain's fenlands, before the partially resistant Maris Piper was introduced. Breeders are still trying to develop a potato variety resistant to all types of *Globodera*.

number of cysts subsequently forming on each tuber.

Worldwide, the acknowledged catalogue of potato pests includes 128 insects, 68 nematodes, 38 fungi, 23 viruses, and 6 bacteria. Some of these pests, unlike *Globodera*, yield to conventional pesticides, but increased resistance is always desirable. Among the fungi, blight is still extant; so too are various rots, including gangrene and dry rot, which attack during winter storage. Bacteria, such as blackleg, rot the potatoes in the fields. But the most important pathogens of all are the viruses; in particular, potato virus Y and potato leaf-roll.

One way to increase resistance to viruses is to find specific virus-resistant genes; and genes conferring resistance to potato virus Y are to be found in *Solanum stoloniferum*. The search continues for genes that will offer resistance to leaf-roll virus.

Viruses are usually carried by aphids and an alternative ploy is to breed potatoes resistant to those insects. This again is being attempted through programmes at the PBI and at Rothamsted and involves crossing with the wild species *Solanum berthaultii*. *S. berthaultii* has hairy, sticky leaves, and it was once thought that it was resistant to aphids simply because the insects entangled in the leaves. It is clear now, however, that the potato's resistance has a far more subtle basis. At Rothamsted, Drs R. W. Fibson and J. A. Pickett have shown that some of the leaf hairs exude a substance called *(E)*-beta-farnesene, which is very similar to a pheromone produced by aphids. When aphids exude this pheromone it provides an alarm signal – a warning to other aphids; in short, aphids are 'scared' by *(E)*-beta-farnesene. Experiments showed that the aphids are not simply entangled by *Solanum berthaultii* leaves, but are reluctant to land on them. Indeed, air blown from syringes containing such leaves was also repellent.

The aim, therefore, is to breed *Solanum tuberosum* varieties containing appropriate *S. berthaultii* genes. In principle this is not too difficult and some such varieties have already been produced. However, the required breeding programmes vividly illustrate one of the problems of crossing with wild species. *S. berthaultii* is adapted to life in semi-desert. One characteristic of dry land plants is that they tend to spread themselves out, so that their offspring do not compete with each other for water; the underground pods of some wild groundnuts, for example, are two metres in length, with tiny seeds at the ends. *S. berthaultii* produces its tubers at the ends of stolons that are two to three metres in length; precisely the opposite of the compact habit which farmers prefer. Thus, after the first cross between *S. tuberosum* and *S. berthaultii,* the breeder must undertake a prolonged series of back-crosses to eliminate undesirable qualities.

However, *S. berthaultii* does have one other quality that might be turned to advantage; another adaptation to life in the desert. Its tubers tend to remain dormant for prolonged periods – a way of ensuring that they do not begin to sprout before the rains come. Prolonged dormancy might embarrass the farmer, but it could be of great advantage to the processors. The processors are obliged to buy their stocks when the crops are lifted, but need to feed the potatoes into their machines in a steady stream, all year round. Hence they require varieties that are easy to store.

One essential in breeding disease- or pest-resistant crops is to find appropriate genes. The second essential is astute monitoring.

Disease resistance: monitoring

It has sometimes been argued that primitive landraces are bound to be more resistant to local pests than modern cultivars, because they have evolved in contact with those pests and have been selected over many centuries. There is some force in this argument, and it is clearly ridiculous to introduce a cultivar into any new area unless it has been shown to be suitably resistant. However, landraces may not contain all the appropriate genes; as we have seen, genes for specific resistance may have to be sought in other species or genera, in other continents. Often, indeed, their apparent resistance is highly deceptive. They are saved from total elimination in any one year by their variability, but 'primitive' farmers in general expect to lose a high proportion of their crops each year from disease and pests.

Even when a landrace contains some individuals with specific resistance to a specific disease, the state may never be reached when *all* the individuals contain those specific genes, however rigorously the farmer selects. The reason is that in the field, crops are exposed to several pests and diseases at once, every year. Plants resistant to mildew, say, may succumb in any one year to an insect pest or another fungus; and plants that are extremely susceptible to mildew may thrive in years in which the climate does not favour that particular fungus. In short, it is extremely difficult to select for resistance for more than one disease at once, and it is theoretically impossible to fix a wide variety of resistance genes in an outbreeding population of plants simply by the informal methods of improvement adopted by farmers and craftsman breeders.

Modern breeders instead expose plants to one disease at a time, and when they have produced resistance to one type, they turn their attention to the next. Maris Piper is resistant to *Globodera*, but it is susceptible to scab, so scab-resistance is the present priority. But the two forms of resistance could not have been developed together.

Breeders do not simply expose their plants to disease; they infest them with known doses of disease – sometimes very heavy doses – and then compare their performance with controls. John Whitcombe's endeavours to produce mildew-resistant millet at ICRISAT illustrate the principle very well. He first plants the putatively resistant strain in a row and on either side of this row he plants several rows of varieties that are known to be very susceptible indeed. He also plants rows of 'control' plants, of medium susceptibility; probably those of a current, popular variety of millet. He then infects the whole plot. The candidate plants thus grow up in a hotbed of disease; the degree of exposure is known, and is massive. Their performance can be gauged accurately by straight comparison with the nearby controls. Those candidates that survive are therefore known to be truly resistant to mildew and already, mildew-resistant strains are emerging. Now different mildew-resistance genes can be superimposed on the existing genes and genes conferring resistance to other diseases can be added.

The acquisition of disease-resistance genes from alien species is likely to be one of the first tasks tackled by genetic engineers. Resistance is sometimes conferred by one, or only a few genes, and as we saw in chapter 7, resistance genes might usefully and relatively easily be introduced into mitochondria or chloroplasts, rather than into the nucleus of the cell. Already, techniques of tissue culture are offering a speedier route to disease resistance. Thus, as discussed in chapter 6, breeders at PBI are endeavouring to produce somaclonal variants of Maris Piper that are resistant to other parasites, particularly scab. In Bombay, scientists at Hindustan Lever are hoping to find somaclonal variants of sugar cane that are resistant to the devastating fungus disease, red rot. They are also hoping to produce elite somatic hybrids of coconut that are resistant to root wilt, by introducing the nuclei of elite lines into the cytoplasm of resistant types. The genes conferring resistance to this particular disease are borne in the mitochondrion.

The task of producing pathogen and predator-resistant crops will never cease. It is doubtful whether aphids could ever evolve the ability to overcome their 'fear' of *(E)*-beta-farnesene, but it is all too clear that micro-pathogens – fungi, bacteria, and viruses – can quickly produce new mutant strains able to break down resistance. Breeders are involved in a constant race to stay ahead of rusts in wheat, for example.

These are early days, however; the breeders of a hundred years hence will consider present attempts to produce resistance varieties to be extremely primitive. By then we may expect that the major crops will each contain several different genes, each conferring a different form of resistance to each of its major pathogens. Probably, too, breeders will provide different strains or mixtures of the same variety, each with different combinations of resistance genes. Each strain will be grown for only a few years and as soon as the local pathogens seem to be acquiring the ability to overcome particular forms of resistance, the farmer will simply switch to a different strain, and confront the pathogen with a new range of problems. When a pathogen is not exposed to a particular form of opposition, natural selection no longer favours the means to overcome that opposition, and virulence diminishes. When it is diminished, the original form of resistance can be re-introduced. The principle is already employed with some pesticides.

Pests and diseases are a hazard everywhere and in addition, every crop must face the hazards of local climate. One of the greatest hazards worldwide, of extreme importance to the 750 million people of the semi-arid tropics, is drought.

Drought

With all forms of stress, there are two possible approaches. One is to remove the stress, and the other is to produce stress-resistant crops.

In the case of drought, there are many possible ways of reducing the stress. Some are very expensive, and raise theoretical and practical difficulties. Others are far simpler. Major dams are expensive, and change the ecology of entire regions in ways that are largely unpredictable, and with side-effects that range from the spread of water-borne parasites to the destruction of fisheries. Artesian wells may eventually cause subterranean water to become saline, as fresh water is removed and saline water is drawn in from further afield. Far cheaper, and with no such side consequences, are some of the many techniques now being developed for the preservation of surface water. In the Negev desert in Israel, shallow depressions are dug around favoured crops that channel the minutest quantity of moisture, even dew, to the plant. This technique is now being taken up in much of Africa, and being applied not merely to crops of great cash value, but to sorghum and maize. The rain that falls in sudden squalls in semi-arid areas is largely wasted because it runs off the surface before it can sink in. Minute 'terraces', barely a few centimetres in height, can critically reduce the rate of run-off and hence the amount of rain that permeates below the surface. Again, this technique is spreading within Africa. At ICRISAT, techniques are being developed for catching flash-flood water in ditches, and running it back slowly into the fields, thus prolonging the growing season by a precious few weeks. In Israel, valuable crops are fed by water in polythene tubes, doled out a half-litre at a time, so that little water is lost by evaporation. The scope for such techniques has barely been realized. Water conservation, world-wide, is still haphazard.

Often, the solution to drought is simply to change the crop. South Africa is only now emerging from a drought that in some areas has lasted for five years. Maize is the chief crop and in many areas it could probably give way to sorghum. In other areas of Africa, sorghum may have to be replaced by millet. In places too dry even for the groundnut, *Arachis hypogaea*, there is scope for the bambara groundnut, *Voandzeia subterranea* and as we saw in chapter 2, the problems of drought offer particular scope for introducing new crop species, such as the marula and mongongo trees as advocated by Dr A. S. Wehmeyer, of the National Nutrition Research Institute in Pretoria, South Africa.

It is not easy to increase the drought resistance of existing crops, but this is a priority at ICRISAT, where there are two standard approaches. The first is simply to select the most drought-resistant strains, and the second is to analyse the mechanisms that lead to drought resistance, and then seek out individuals that possess those mechanisms.

The method of selecting drought-resistant lines is comparable to that employed in selecting for disease resistance. The plants are exposed to the particular stress in an acute, but highly controlled form. Thus, at ICRISAT plants of all species may be found being 'cooked' in incubating chambers, at precisely controlled temperatures, with a precisely monitored supply of water, at various stages of development from germination to maturity.

Already ICRISAT scientists have identified genotypes of a groundnut that in 1982 produced more than 1 000 kg a hectare, even when stressed by drought, compared with 500–800 kg achieved in the same year by commercial cultivars that were not stressed. ICRISAT plant-breeders have also identified six drought-resistant lines of sorghum which yielded two to three times as much during a severe drought in southern India as one of the recent recommended varieties; the sorghum produced 430–630 kg per hectare, against 200 kg for the present commercial type. Most important, perhaps, is the success of some of the resistant lines during severe droughts in the Upper Volta. The current aim, a realistic but not easy target, is to provide sorghums for the Sahel that could reasonably be relied upon to produce one tonne of grain per hectare.

The mechanisms of drought resistance evidently vary from species to species. Some species simply become dormant when there is no water, and resume growth when it returns. Others are genuinely resistant, and continue to grow whatever the supply of water. As knowledge of mechanisms increases, it should become possible to produce crops that combine different strategies, or transfer strategies from crop to crop.

But where there is drought, farmers are obliged to make greater use of ground water. When ground water is brought to the surface, it tends to bring salts along with it, and so raises problems of salinity. It is in the already beleagured semi-arid tropics that such problems are most serious.

Salinity

Soil contains minerals that are essential to the life of plants: nitrogen, phosphorus, potassium, sulphur, calcium and magnesium, which must be absorbed in fairly large amounts; and iron, manganese, zinc, copper, boron, chlorine, molybdenum and, possibly, nickel, needed in trace quantities. Plants that fix nitrogen (see next chapter) also need cobalt, and a few need, or at least benefit from, sodium and or silicon.

If these elements are not present in adequate amounts, then the plants languish, and are replaced, in nature, by other plants that are less demanding. If the minerals are present in excess, then in various ways they may prove toxic. Some may be directly toxic to some plant tissues; some may inhibit the uptake of other minerals; and some (such as nitrogen, if excessive) may cause some plants to out-grow their strength and fall over, or become prey to disease. In addition to the list above, a few elements are not essential nutrients, but are sometimes present in toxic amounts. Notable among these, in acid soils, is aluminium. According to Professor Emanuel Epstein at the University of California, Davis, almost four billion hectares world-wide – that is 30 per cent of the total land mass – present plants with some type of mineral stress: either deficiency in minerals, or toxicity. About a quarter of that blighted land – one billion hectares – is affected in particular by salinity, which in particular means excess of sodium, or by excess alkalinity.

The life of a plant depends absolutely upon its ability to absorb essential minerals, but at the same time to ignore or overcome the effects of minerals present in unacceptable amounts. These abilities are determined genetically, as indeed are all other aspects of the plant's physiology. They are therefore, in theory, amenable to improvement by breeding. In the past, however, very few breeders tried specifically to alter the response of crops to minerals; instead, the farmer was expected to adjust the soil to suit his crops. A few breeders, however, have long since appreciated that to adjust the soil to the crop was, in many circumstances, too expensive; and that in all circumstances it was a good principle to try, as far as possible, to adjust the plant to the soil. At Davis, Professor Epstein and his colleagues have pursued this particular philosophy since the 1960s. In particular, they have sought to develop crops that are resistant to salinity, the greatest single cause of soil toxicity.

'Salinity' does not refer exclusively to an excess of sodium salts; magnesium also tends to be present, for example. But sodium is invariably involved, and is the chief culprit. The first question, then, in contemplating the development of saline-resistant crops, is whether, in fact, plants can tolerate sodium at all in amounts that are greater than they need for nourishment, or whether salinity is innately and inescapably toxic.

The answer is, of course, that a great many flowering plants tolerate salt perfectly well. Many live on dunes and salt-marshes, and *Zostera* flourishes at the bottom of the sea. Furthermore, plants that grow in salty conditions come from a wide variety of plant families, and most of the major crop plant families contain some salt-loving or salt-tolerant species. In particular, there are many salt-tolerant grasses of the same family as the cereals, the Gramineae. Notable, and very common on the salt-marshes of Europe and North America, is *Spartina*. (*Zostera* is not a true grass, of course.)

In addition, there is no doubt that among the world's established crops and their close relatives, there are many individual lines that display at least some tolerance to salt. But as Professor Epstein commented at the 1983 CIBA symposium on *Better Crops for Food*, 'it is a reflection on the yet early state of this art that of the existing banks of germplasm of existing crops, especially the world collections, not one has been extensively screened for salt tolerance.'

The potential of such screening has already been demonstrated by Professor Epstein's and his colleagues' work on barley. Farmers have long recognized that barley tends to be more tolerant of salt than many crops, but the scientists at Davies have now developed lines that will germinate and grow in water that is not far removed from sea water. This has been achieved by growing successive generations of barley in water that has been made more and more brackish, and then by breeding only from the survivors; the same kind of principle that is employed to develop crops resistant to disease.

In the barley experiments, Professor Epstein simply exploited the potential of an existing crop. But he and his colleagues have also shown what might be achieved by cross-breeding existing crops with salt-resistant relatives. In particular, they have produced salt-tolerant tomatoes by crossing *Lycopersicon esculentum*, the edible tomato, with *Lycopersicon cheesmanii*, which is commercially useless, but is salt-resistant.

Scientists from the PBI in Cambridge are now collaborating with CYMMIT scientists in Mexico to produce a salt-tolerant wheat. The wild grass *Agropyron* contains genes that confer salt tolerance, and these have already been transferred into wheat by the kind of chromosome manipulation described in chapter 5: developing addition lines, then leaving the relevant fragment of chromosome from the wild grass within the genome of the cultivated wheat. Dr Mike Gale recently suggested that a realistic goal is to develop wheats which can tolerate brackishness of roughly half the concentration of sea-water.

Another way of developing salt-resistant lines is being developed at Hindustan Lever in Bombay, as already noted in chapter 6, where the idea being pursued is to find somaclonal variants of sugar cane that can grow in salt conditions.

The development of salt-tolerant crops should eventually benefit from increased knowledge of the mechanism of salt tolerance, just as is the case with the development of pest-resistance. Salt seems to present plants with at least two problems. One is that excess sodium can alter the electrical properties of cell membranes, and so compromise the behaviour of the whole cell. The second problem is that salty water has a high osmotic potential, thus tending to draw water from the plant.

Salt-tolerant plants counter the osmotic potential of water in two ways. The more complicated course is for the plant to produce high concentrations of organic material which provide an osmotic potential equal to that of the surroundings. The drawback, however, is that a fair amount of photosynthetic energy must be squandered to produce such organic molecules. The simpler method – and the method preferred by true salt-loving plants, or 'halophytes' – is to allow the sodium to invade, so the entire plant is brackish. This requires no energy, but it does raise the question as to how the true halophytes protect their cell membranes. In the fulness of time, however, when the skills of genetic engineering are perfected, it might be possible to produce crops that are not merely salt tolerant, significant though this would be, but are truly halophytic.

It might be objected, of course, that it is considered dangerous to consume too much salt, because excess appears to predispose to hypertension. So salty crops might be a somewhat equivocal commodity. Professor Epstein points out, however, that the crops for which salt-tolerance has the most relevance are the grains, and perhaps the fruits. Most of the material in seeds and fruits enters by the vessels of the phloem, whereas sodium salts are carried mainly in the xylem, so it seems that seeds provide their own filters.

It is impossible to predict what kinds of crops will be growing in, say, a hundred years' time. One thing that does seem certain, however, is that the crops will be growing in locations that now seem impossible, not to say ridiculous: thrusting their way through blatant crystals of salt as they are beaten by the Sun, with no protection from the fungicides and pesticides that present crops so often need.

Another reasonable prediction is that whatever yields are now considered to be acceptable could, by then, be surpassed several-fold. But yield is the most complicated quality of all.

Yield

In recent years there have been many reasons for doubting the value of trying to increase yields. Europe has a grain mountain – so why produce more? Third World farmers have all too often found that when they do raise significantly more produce than they or their village can consume, that the surplus is simply wasted. Such arguments are not trivial, but they are easily countered. The proper answer to Europe's surplus is simply to take land out of production, and return it to our fellow species. There is no excuse for mediocre arable farming practised on a lavish scale and if it is the case that poor farmers sometimes do badly by being more productive, then the answer lies in economic reform, not in perpetuating the poverty of subsistence farming.

However, there are four legitimate reasons for not rushing headlong into breeding programmes designed specifically to increase yield. The first, as we have seen, is that there can be conflict between yield and quality. Sometimes the conflict is apparent rather than real. For example, some high-yielding varieties of different crops have been found to be lacking in flavour; but there are few innate reasons why high-yielding crops should not taste good. Sometimes, however, the conflict is real, as between protein content and total biomass.

Secondly, for farmers working under difficult, unpredictable conditions, extremely high yields are less important than consistency. In the Sahel, for example, the aim should be to produce yields that are at least acceptable even in the bad years. A tonne of millet or sorghum is a good yield in a bad year. To strive for Western-scale yields – eight tonnes or so – would simply be a waste of fertilizer, if the rains failed.

Thirdly, as discussed in chapter 1, it should not be assumed that intensive farming, or farmland dedicated to only one purpose, is the only proper course for agriculture in a crowded world. There is a case for well-managed, but essentially old-fashioned meadows or farms, run partly for conservational purposes, and for integrating farming with wild-life management, as is pursued around some of the reserves in Africa and India. In such cases the highest possible yields are not the first priority. As also noted in chapter 1, however, there is a difference between relaxed farming and sloppy farming. If fields are used exclusively for arable crops or intensively managed pasture, then the yields should be very high indeed to justify the banishment of all other living things. By the same token, an old-fashioned meadow should contain a varied flora, and not be allowed simply to fill with thistles.

Finally, there would be less need to increase yields if less food was wasted after harvesting. In the Third World this waste is literal; in some countries in some years up to 40 per cent of the harvest may be ruined by insects and fungi. In the West the waste is more discreet. At least half the grain grown in Europe and the United States is fed to livestock, which then provide high-fat food that corrupts the Western artery. It is permissible to feed at least some grain to livestock, but there can be little doubt, on grounds of nutrition, economy, humanitarianism, and plain common-sense, that we feed too much. I have always felt that a serious research priority should be to develop strains of wheat with soft, bland grains that can be eaten like rice. This would facilitate the good intentions of some Westerners to pursue a more grain-based, less meaty diet; and a wheat yielding only three tonnes per hectare, able to be eaten like rice, would be worth at least as much as a wheat yielding eight tonnes per hectare (roughly the national average in the United Kingdom), of which half was fed to livestock.

Despite these conditional clauses, however, we must increase yield if we are to feed the future population of the world, and yet leave room for our fellow species. It may be a nonsense to produce more grain in Europe than people can eat, at great expense, but it is theoretically possible to produce twice as much wheat per hectare as we do at present; if we did, we could release half the land now given to the crop for other purposes. The United Kingdom could feed itself if it chose, and still leave room to re-plant Sherwood Forest, and to reintroduce the boar and the wolf. Many Third World countries lack the financial and commercial infrastructure to deal sensibly with high yields, and to deal fairly with the people who produce them, but the fault lies with the infrastructure, not with the technology. It is both nonsensical and cruel to perpetuate systems that are clearly inadequate.

Despite the conditional clauses, then, it must remain a prime ambition of all breeders to increase yield, within whatever context they are working.

Components of yield

Breeding can affect yield in many ways. A breeder may increase or reduce yield while working on some quite different characteristic. If pest resistance is increased, then the yield should be raised, unless the original crop was otherwise protected from the particular pathogen. In other cases, the development of different qualities may depress yield, as is bound to happen when crops are developed for the highest possible protein content.

Sometimes – often, indeed – yield is increased by lengthening the growing season, and this will depend on several factors. The first, in temperate climates, will be to develop crops that are less vulnerable to cold. Winter cereals are planted in the autumn, and yield more heavily than spring cereals because they are in the ground for nine months or more, rather than for six or seven. But they have to be able to survive as young plants through the worst months of winter. They also need to be particularly resistant to disease, because the longer they are in the field, the more they are exposed to pathogens. The same applies to the pigeon pea, which can be grown as a perennial only if it is resistant to virus.

However, in addition to such 'non-specific' contributions to yield, breeders can and do strive specifically to develop high-yielding varieties. Here there are two general approaches. The first is to increase the total mass of the crop – the *biomass*. The second is to increase the proportion of the biomass that actually serves as useful crop: that is, to raise the *harvest index*. We will deal with the second of these considerations first.

Harvest index: wheat and rice

The wheat that Breughel painted grew shoulder high; a donkey could have been lost in it, and doubtless many were. The wheat that grew in Britain before the First World War stood about 140 cm tall. Yields were around two tonnes per hectare, and it was assumed that only the biggest plants could produce the biggest yields. by the Second World War, British wheats had shrunk, to around 120 cm. Today they stand at 75–90 cm, yet the average yield is approaching eight tonnes per hectare. Plants that are only two-thirds or less the height of those of the turn of the century, yield four times as heavily.

Figure 9.4 The wheat depicted by Breughel was as high as a man's shoulder: in the old days, the wheat plants that yielded most heavily were big. Modern varieties are 'semi-dwarf' – hardly waist high – but they have bigger heads than the old kinds.

Two things have changed. The first is the amount of fertilizer applied, and the second is the harvest index. In practice, though not necessarily in theory, the two are closely linked. We will take the first point first.

Perhaps the single greatest advance made in agriculture during this century is in the increased application of nitrogen fertilizer. Plants need a great many other minerals besides nitrogen, but nitrogen is the one needed in greatest amounts. As outlined in chapter 10, nitrogen was supplied in the past only in the form of manure, or by nitrogen-fixing plants such as clover. In the last century, farmers also added nitrogen in the form of potassium nitrate. But it was in this century that artificial fertilizers were first produced by combining nitrogen gas with hydrogen, to form ammonia. Twentieth century farmers have thus been able to make their fields more fertile than ever before.

There are various snags, however. Plants cannot make use of the additional nitrogen unless they are adapted to do so. Some cannot utilize more than a limited amount. Others do take it up, but having done so, they suffer, becoming elongated and straggly, or soft and fleshy. Adaptation to high nitrogen inputs is, indeed, part of the process of domestication.

Some cereals have been cultivated for tens of thousands of years, but only in recent decades have they been expected to respond constructively to huge inputs of nitrogen. Such ability has not been selected for. Thus, when farmers first began to apply artificial fertilizer to wheat, after the First World War, they found that it responded badly. It grew well enough, but out-grew its strength. The stalks grew longer and longer, and at the first puff of wind they fell over, or *lodged*, as the expression is. It was all deeply frustrating. Here, with the artificial fertilizers, was the means to increase yields as never before; indeed to double or triple them, but when the fertilizer was applied, the plants collapsed and in wet and windy years the yields could be disastrous. In Asia, after the Second World War, farmers experienced the same frustrations with rice. Extra nitrogen could increase yields, but when the extra was added, the plants shot up and keeled over. In both cases, what was needed were plants that had short straw, which would remain of tolerable length even in the face of heavy fertilization.

As we have already seen, when breeders seek a new quality their first tactic is to screen known varieties to see if any possess the quality required. In this particular case they sought varieties of wheat and rice that were short, or 'dwarf'. Such varieties might not themselves be useful as crops, but, with luck (or more particularly, with patience) the required quality could be bred into commercial varieties.

The search for a dwarf wheat ended in Japan, with the dwarf, or fairly dwarf, variety Norin 10. In 1947 Dr Orville Vogel of the United States Department of Agriculture introduced the Norin 10 gene into North American wheats, and soon afterwards released the first commercial semi-dwarf wheat into the United States. This was Gaines, which produced world record yields in irrigated land in the Pacific north-west.

Gaines, however, was adapted to temperate zones, with the long days of summer and the short days of winter. Dr Norman Borlaug, working for the Rockefeller Foundation, perceived that farmers nearer the Equator needed a semi-dwarf wheat adapted to days of near-constant length. He combined Gaines in a breeding programme that included other varieties from the United States, and from Japan, Australia, and Colombia, and so developed semi-dwarfs that could be grown at low latitudes. Such varieties were first grown in Mexico, and through the 1960s and 1970s were distributed through Turkey, Pakistan and India.

The dwarfing genes from Norin 10 reached Britain in 1964, via Dr Francis Lupton of the PBI. The first variety that contained the genes, Maris Fundin, was released in 1974. Maris Fundin did not make a huge impact but its immediate successors did. By 1982 more than 80 per cent of wheat grown in the United Kingdom was semi-dwarf, containing Norin 10 genes. Since 1974, average yields in the United Kingdom have practically doubled.

The rice story is comparable. In the 1940s and 1950s breeders sought dwarf varieties, and discovered the likes of Fee-geo-woo-gen, in China. The early 1950s saw the first semi-dwarf rice bred outside mainland China: Taichun Native 1, which was released in Taiwan. In 1960 the

Figure 9.5 Yields of wheat in Britain have increased roughly four-fold since the turn of the century. Yet the plants have become smaller; what has increased is the 'harvest index', the ratio of head to stem. The varieties shown are all from the Plant Breeding Institute in Cambridge. From left to right: Little Joss dates from 1910; Yeoman from 1916; Holdfast, an excellent bread maker, was released in 1936; Maris Widgeon was a high quality bread wheat of the 1960s; and Maris Huntsman, still on the recommended list, dates from 1972. Hobbit, from the late 1970s, Avalon (1983), and Norman (1982), all contain semi-dwarfing genes.

Ford and Rockefeller Foundations collaborated with the Government of the Philippines to establish the International Rice Research Institute (IRRI), with Dr Robert Chandler as director, and the pace of research accelerated. By 1966 the IRRI breeders released IR8, and it was this variety that earned the soubriquet 'miracle rice'. It yielded as no rice had ever done before. Others followed, all semi-dwarfs but with a shorter and shorter growing season, and ever more able to respond to good management: IR5, IR20, IR22, IR24, and others. Top yields are very comparable with those of wheat: around 8 tonnes per hectare, with yields of over 13 tonnes recorded.

The new varieties of wheat yield more heavily partly because they are able to respond appropriately to very high applications of fertilizer. But this is not the whole story; they do well even when they are fed relatively poorly. This was demonstrated, in wheat, in an experiment at the PBI in 1978, by Dr R. B. Austin. He and his colleagues grew a range of varieties, modern and not-so-modern, under the same conditions. They held the wheat plants up with nets to prevent the older types from lodging, protected them with fungicide, and gave them either low doses or high doses of fertilizer.

The new varieties, such as Norman, which was released commercially in 1980, out-yielded the older types such as Little Joss (released in 1908) by 45–49 per cent. The difference was most marked at high doses of fertilizer, but was apparent too at the lower doses. This was serendipitous. After all, it would theoretically be possible to breed a plant that yielded extremely well at high levels of fertility, but did less well than the older varieties when fertility was low. In such cases, farmers who did not fertilize their fields heavily would need to grow varieties different from those who did. In this case, however, this theoretical drawback was not encountered. The modern varieties out-stripped the old-fashioned ones, whatever the level of nutrients. At ICRISAT, Dr John Whitcombe and his colleagues have found that the same principle applies to their high-yielding millets. Those that yield best at high levels of fertility, also yield best when fertility is low.

Indeed, the improved performance of dwarf wheats at virtually all levels of fertility is not surprising, for the secret of their success is that they divert more of the available nutrient towards the production of grain, and less to making straw; and they do this however much nutrient there is. In short, old-fashioned varieties of wheat have a harvest index of less than 40 per cent, whereas modern types have surpassed 50 per cent.

Over the past 30 years, yields of wheat in the United Kingdom have increased by about three per cent per year, and there is no sign of slackening off. The proportion of increased yield due to breeding has been achieved entirely by improvement of harvest index; indeed, the modern plant is smaller than those of past decades. However, there is a limit to the increases that can be made simply by such means. The wheat plant cannot be too small: it needs good big leaves in order to photosynthesize efficiently, and if the stalk were significantly shorter than 30 cm, machine harvesting would be difficult. Furthermore, theoretical calculations suggest that the maximum possible harvest index is around 60 per cent. The time will come, eventually, when the only option open to the breeder will be to begin breeding again for bigger wheat plants – albeit plants with strong, thick stalks. We may again see Breughelesque wheat fields; only next time the heads will stretch half way down the stalks, like pampas grass, and the stalks will be like pokers.

But that lies in the future. I know of no wheat breeding programmes world-wide that at this moment are specifically concerned with increasing the biomass of wheat. At PBI, scientists such as Dr Mike Gale have three priorities. The first is to unravel the precise mechanisms whereby Norin 10 dwarfing genes achieve their ends. Evidently the genes inhibit the action of giberellin, which is effectively the 'growth hormone' of plants. Plants that possess the Norin 10 genes produce normal amounts of giberellin, but they do not respond to it; either they also produce an inhibitor, or their cells have inadequate giberellin receptors, and so do not recognize the presence of the hormone.

The second priority is to find new dwarfing genes. So far breeders have identified 14 such genes among cultivated wheats. Some seem merely to have a general stunting effect, and hardly merit further investigation, but others certainly demand study. One purpose of this exercise is to reduce dependence on just one single gene, and another is to see what else it is, besides dwarfing, that these other genes have to offer. In chapter 3 we noted that some genes affect many different characters – that is, are pleiotropic in their effects. This is particularly likely to be true of genes that affect the entire character of a plant.

Thirdly, it remains to be seen whether dwarfing genes are always advantageous. Are there conditions – drought, for example – where they reduce performance? Semi-dwarf wheats and rice are still new. They have already transformed the agriculture of the world, and the prospects of the human race, but there is still a great deal to be found out about them.

In the immediate term, then, interest in increasing the yield of wheat and rice still focuses on harvest index. Biomass can be left for the future. But with some crops the harvest index cannot be increased because it is already close to 100 per cent. In these cases the only option is to raise biomass. This is the position with many forage crops, of which the chief, by far, is grass. In discussing biomass, then, grass is the best subject.

Biomass: grass

Fodder crops, by definition, are grown to feed livestock and though some countries keep too many animals, and their people eat too many, there are also many good and legitimate reasons for keeping them, as we outlined in chapter 2. The chief of all the fodder crops, and indeed the single most widely grown crop in the world, is grass.

World-wide, indeed, grassland, or at least permanent pasture, occupies just over 23 per cent, or just under a quarter, of the total 13 billion hectares; and short-term leys are also grown as rotations on some at least of the 1 300 million hectares (10 per cent of the world's total land) that are devoted to arable crops. In Britain, grass occupies 12 million hectares, compared with less than 4 million devoted to cereals, and 1 million expended on all other crops. The United Kingdom has a greater proportion of grass than most other countries; and considerably less forest.

Of all crops, grassland most clearly illustrates the point that a spectrum of cultivation is reasonable and desirable, ranging from grazing by nomadic tribespeople all over the world, through informal grazing of moors, downs, and mountainsides, to the highly intensive production in which grass is grown in short-term, one-, two-, or three-year leys as part of a rotation. All methods of cultivation are legitimate, but all should be done well. The secret is to allow sufficient animals to graze to keep invading scrub at bay, and to prevent the grass itself becoming senescent and 'rank'; but not for the animals to graze so much that the grass is reduced to the point where the blades are too small, or too sparse, to capture the light. It is then that land is said to be over-grazed, and productivity falls practically to zero. Alternatively, stock may be kept off the pasture altogether, at least for part of the year. The grass is then harvested at intervals and fed fresh, or else conserved in various ways: dried artificially to make dried grass biscuits; dried naturally to form hay; or fermented into silage. But even when stock are not allowed on the pasture (*zero-grazing*) the principle of management is the same; keep the grass at the right length, and make sure that what is in the field is youthful rather than senescent, to evoke maximum growth. To this basic principle can be added various refinements; mixed stocking with different species (sheep and goats, sheep and cattle); mixed stocking with young animals (calves) being succeeded by adults; various forms of rotational grazing, with only certain animals being allowed on certain areas at any one time; and fertilization and irrigation – ensuring that when fertilizer is applied, the grass is in the right stage of growth and has enough water to make use of it.

World-wide, however, grassland is not managed particularly well. The common grassland of much of Africa and India is often patently overgrazed. In the United Kingdom, intensive grassland (that is, land dedicated to grass and containing very few wild species or their attendant fauna) is rarely managed to anything like its full productive capacity. Often the reason is that farmers cannot afford to keep sufficient animals to make full use of the land if they did maximize production. Again, in such circumstances the question is raised as to why surplus land is not simply taken out of production, and given back to the forest.

Even though the chief desideratum, world-wide, is for better management, it is still worth trying to produce better grasses, than can respond to good management. In particular, it is worth asking how the biomass can be increased.

Farmers can raise the yield of grass by increasing the supply of nitrogen, and supplying water in times of drought. But what ultimately determines yield is the use the plants make of available light in the process of photosynthesis. In general, grasses use only a small proportion of the light that falls on the fields. So how can this be increased?

High-efficiency grass Dr M. J. Robson, of the Grassland Research Institute in Berkshire, England, summarized the possibilities for increasing the efficiency of grass at a recent meeting of the British Association for the Advancement of Science.

There are, he said, some innate contradictions. For example, grass would in theory yield more heavily if it grew during the winter, as well as through the summer, just as winter cereals may yield more heavily than spring cereals because they are in the ground longer. But grass that grows through the cold of winter is likely to be killed if the temperature falls very low. Grass that is dormant in the winter is far hardier. So the farmer who elects for winter-growing varieties must carefully balance the possibility of higher yields against the chances of having no yield at all.

In drought areas, it seems to make sense to breed drought-resistant varieties. This implies producing varieties that do not transpire too rapidly – that is, lose too much water through their leaves. But grass is often grown specifically to be dried, or made into hay; and for such purposes the farmer needs leaves that wilt rapidly. Here, then, is another conflict.

The efficiency with which plants make use of light depends largely on whether and to what extent they are able to intercept the sun's rays with their leaves. Here there are several considerations. When grass is cut short, much of the light passes straight through it, and is simply absorbed by the ground. The first requirement, then, is for varieties that grow back rapidly after cutting. When the leaves of the grass are young and sparse they will intercept most light if they lie flat along the ground, like daisies, but as the grass thickens the leaves will absorb a greater proportion of light if they stand upright, and avoid shading each other. Ideally, then, the breeder should produce varieties that begin horizontally, and then assume the perpendicular.

In general – indeed it seems by definition – grass yields are heaviest when the growth is thickest, but when the leaves are crowded some are inevitably shaded and when a leaf begins its life in shade, then it adapts to shade. The leaf never develops the ability to make use of strong sunlight, which may fall upon it after the grass is cut. However, physiologists at the Welsh Plant Breeding Station have now shown that some individual plants are less permanently affected by early shading than others, and quickly recover the ability to make good use of bright light, when this becomes available. Such individuals might form the basis of varieties with greater overall efficiency.

This finding, too, throws light on the question of why it is that breeders of grass have had less success in increasing yields than breeders of some other crops. Many modern varieties barely out-yield those of 40 years ago. Perhaps breeders have been looking for the wrong thing. When testing new varieties in the greenhouse, they very properly grow the plants in well-spaced pots, subject them to maximum light, and select ones that grow most quickly, but the plants that respond best to maximum light may not perform well in the field, where they tend to be shaded by their neighbours. Perhaps breeders should select the plants that grow best in shade, rather than those that show greatest potential in the brightest light.

Another possibility is to increase the efficiency of carbon metabolism. One highly intriguing statistic to emerge from research at the Grassland Research Institute is that only 25 per cent of the carbon that is fixed by grass finishes up as harvestable dry matter. How much of the remaining 75 per cent could be rescued?

In practice, about 15 per cent of the fixed carbon finishes up in the roots. The roots cannot usefully be harvested, but neither is there a great deal to be gained by breeding plants with smaller roots. Useful carbon is lost, however, if leaves are simply allowed to die, because dead leaves are of less nutritional value than those that are eaten fresh, or conserved while still growing. Management and timing play a large part in ensuring that grass is harvested while the leaves are still young, but the breeder might contribute by producing varieties with leaves that stay fresh longer.

Finally, and most excitingly, it might be possible to enhance the yield of grass – or indeed of all plants – by altering the process of photosynthesis itself.

Altering photosynthesis Photosynthesis involves two quite different processes. In the first, water is split into its constituent elements, hydrogen and oxygen. In the second, *carbon fixation*, that hydrogen is attached to carbon dioxide from the air to form organic molecules. Hydrogen is not simply joined to carbon dioxide; rather, the two are fed into a cycle, in the course of which hydrogen and the carbon dioxide are incorporated. But the net result is to combine carbon (with its attendant oxygen) with hydrogen.

In practice, the usual way in which carbon dioxide enters the cycle is by first being combined with a five-carbon organic compound, ribulose bisphosphate, to form two molecules of two molecules of the three-carbon compound phosphoglyceric acid, or PGA. PGA then effectively becomes the raw material from which all other organic compounds are synthesized.

The enzyme that first joins carbon dioxide with ribulose bisphosphate is called *ribulose bisphosphate carboxylase*, which is colloquially abbreviated to Rubisco. Rubisco is the key enzyme in carbon fixation, and may indeed account for 50 per cent of the protein in a green leaf. It is, indeed, by far the most common protein in nature.

However, this key enzyme, Rubisco, does not behave in quite the way that breeders or farmers would like it to. In fact, it behaves in two different and contradictory ways. For in addition to combining ribulose bisphosphate with carbon dioxide, it also may combine ribulose bisphosphate with oxygen. Thus the ribulose bisphosphate is simply 'broken down' – effectively 'burned' away – to form carbon dioxide. This perverse process, whereby organic molecules so carefully formed by the plant are simply squandered, is called *photorespiration*.

The reasons for the peculiar behaviour of Rubisco probably lie deep in the evolutionary history of plants. The enzyme is extremely ancient: it originated in organisms which lived at a time when the earth's atmosphere contained very little oxygen, and its indiscriminate behaviour was of little consequence. Indeed the Rubisco within primitive photosynthesizing organisms, such as the cyanobacteria, is even more wasteful than that of modern flowering plants, though that of modern plants still leaves must to be desired.

Accordingly, scientists at Rothamsted are seeking to develop plants with a more efficient Rubisco, which will fix carbon dioxide but will not catalyse photorespiration. To this end they are investigating the Rubisco molecule itself, to see which parts of it are responsible for which functions. In one experiment they have taken the major genes that code for Rubisco proteins from maize and from a cyanobacterium, and cut each one in half. Then they joined each of the two halves together to form hybrid genes. These they inserted into bacteria, where the genes formed the corresponding hybrid proteins. These experiments should reveal which parts of the maize Rubisco serve to make it more efficient than the cyanobacterium enzyme.

When they understand how the structure of the Rubisco enzyme influences its function, the Rothamsted scientists hope to re-design the enzyme: produce one in which the part that effects oxidation of ribulose bisphosphate is absent, or operates only feebly. This they will do by altering the sequence of nucleotides within the gene that codes for Rubisco – another example of controlled mutagenesis.

There is another, quite different, way of improving the efficiency of photosynthesis – at least in theory, and at least in some plants. A great

187

many plants do not simply combine carbon dioxide with ribulose bisphosphate, as described above. Instead, they first combine it with a three-carbon compound known as phosphoenolpyruvic acid, or PEP. Thus they form a four-carbon compound, oxaloacetate. They then remove the carbon dioxide again to reinstate the molecule of pyruvate, and the carbon dioxide that is thus released is joined with ribulose bisphosphate, just as described above, to form two molecules of PGA.

Plants that simply combine carbon dioxide with ribulose bisphosphate to form two molecules of the three-carbon PGA, are called C3 plants. Most temperate crops employ this simple method of carbon fixation. Plants that adopt the more elaborate route – first attaching carbon dioxide to a four-carbon compound and then releasing it again – are called C4 plants. Many tropical plants, including many tropical grasses, are C4 plants. Although the C4 route is more elaborate than the C3, it is more efficient. Given the same amount of light, and the same amount of carbon, C4 plants in general manage to fix more carbon than C3 plants. So could C3 plants usefully be endowed with the photosynthetic apparatus of C4 plants? Would this be a worthwhile endeavour for genetic engineers?

The first question is whether C4 plants could grow at all in temperate climates, for most C4 plants tend to be tropical. The answer is that they can. Maize is a C4 crop, and an exceedingly important one in Northern Europe. True, maize cannot reliably be grown for grain in the United Kingdom; here it is grown mainly for silage, to be chopped up, entire, while still green. The total biomass of maize is high, which is what concerns us here. The salt-marsh plant *Spartina townsendii* flourishes in the United Kingdom, as indeed in much of the rest of Europe and North America; and *Spartina*, oddly enough, is a C4 species.

The question of whether it is worth trying to transfer C4 photosynthesis to C3 plants is not so easily answered. C4 plants seem to do particularly well in drought. The method is seen to best advantage when concentration of carbon dioxide is low, as tends to be the case when the stomata are closed (the stomata are orifices in the leaves through which carbon dioxide enters). The closure of the stomata reduces the loss of water by transpiration. However, drought is not an outstanding problem in northern Europe. In addition, the C4 strategy is seen at its best when the light is particularly intense, and the temperature is high. Again, however, high light intensity and tempera ture are not typical of northern latitudes.

Finally, although C3 photosynthesis may seem less efficient than C4, it is extremely successful. C3 plants have not been supplanted by an invasion of C4s from the South, any more than fast respirers have been superseded by slow respirers. So although it might be possible in the fullness of time to produce C4 wheat, or barley, or cabbage, it is far from certain that such plants would be noticeably superior to the present forms.

In short, the task of improving the biomass of plants by improving their overall efficiency of carbon fixation is far from simple, but if the problems are broken down, and the components of efficient fixation are analysed one by one – the geometry of the leaves, the efficiency of metabolism, the chemistry of fixation – then each can be tackled individually. At present, the problems of enhancing carbon fixation are relevant primarily to crops such as grass, where the harvest index is already high, and where yield can be increased only by raising biomass, but the day must eventually dawn in the evolution of all crop plants when the only way forward is to increase the total size of the plant. Then, the ideas now being formulated with respect to grass might be applied to all crops.

Overall, the potential for increasing yields is immense. Farmers in the semi-arid tropics who now achieve yields of 500 kg per hectare, or even less, could reasonably aspire to produce 1 tonne, even in bad years; this has been achieved by ICRISAT scientists in the Sahel, using techniques of cultivation very little different from traditional methods. In the very best conditions sorghum can achieve yields of around 5 tonnes. This, perhaps, should be seen as a distant target, to be kept in mind. Yields of wheat and rice in the most proficient countries now average almost eight tonnes per hectare. The records for both crops stand at more than 14 tonnes, and research at Rothamsted shows that every hectare of the United Kingdom that is now devoted to wheat could in principle yield at least 10 tonnes. Modest calculations suggest that yields of at least 14 tonnes are possible even with today's methods; and if the manipulation of biomass is added to the present improvements in harvest index, then possible maximum yields beggar the imagination.

The final coup, however, would be to produce crops of all kinds that not only fix carbon more efficiently, but also fix their own nitrogen. Some plants, notably the legumes, already do this, but could do so with greater efficiency. Most crops do not fix nitrogen, but in theory could be given that ability. This is the subject of the next chapter.

10   Nitrogen

One of the principal tasks facing farmers and breeders over the next few decades is to increase the amount of nitrogen available to crops. If this is done then the increases in yields can be spectacular; provided, of course, the nitrogen is matched by other inputs, such as water, and, as with the wheats and rices of the Green Revolution, the crops are bred to make constructive use of what is available. There are three sources of nitrogen, all of which farmers exploit, or have exploited, in various ways.

The first of these sources comprises inorganic rocks. About 90 per cent of the nitrogen in the world (about ten thousand million million tonnes of it) is contained in rocks. Rocks, however, tend to be insoluble, and most are found in the wrong places. Only a few, therefore, have served as fertilizers; notably potassium nitrate, employed since the 19th century.

Organic materials provide the second source. The nitrogen contained within organisms that are still living is obviously unobtainable to plants. I say 'obviously', but this fact is not necessarily as obvious at all that. Thus many a potential rancher has cast covetous eyes at tropical rainforest, and in particular at the Amazonian forests, and assumed that where there is such opulence of growth, there must be commensurate fertility. But the truth is that the rate of growth in the Amazonian forest is such that most of the nitrogen contained within the whole biosystem is within the trees themselves, and the masses of animals and smaller plants that accompany them. When the forest is burnt or the trees are bodily removed, the nitrogen is lost. The quantity of nitrogen left in the soil is minute. The potential rancher is left with a potential desert.

The nitrogen contained in excreta or in dead organic material is, for the most part, unavailable to plants until it is broken down by fungi and bacteria, to release inorganic ions, of which the chief (after the inevitable oxidation has taken place) is nitrate; but breakdown is usually rapid unless the soil is either very cold (as in tundra, for example) or acid (as in peat bogs).

Figure 10.1a Cowpeas, being leguminous, 'fix' nitrogen. Here, at the International Institute of Tropical Agriculture in Ibadan, Nigeria, they are intercropped between maize. The legume provides the cereal with some nitrogen, and benefits in turn from the shade.

Figure 10.1b Here, at Ibadan, two legumes are grown together, between them providing a highly fertile soil. Cowpea is raised between rows of leucaena trees, in the system known as 'alley-cropping'.

In practice, farmers exploit organic material in two main ways. The first is simply to make use of the fertility that remains after wild plants are cleared away and thus United Kingdom farmers gain a year or two of relatively easy living when they plough virgin moorland to make way for crops; here they are making use of the fact that in cold, acid conditions a great deal of organic material remains in the soil, but can be released when the pH of the soil is raised by liming. Similarly, 'swidden', or 'slash/burn' farmers the world over live by hacking away a portion of forest, planting crops for a few years, and then moving on as the fertility declines. The second way to employ organic material is by bringing excreta, human or animal, to the plants, or mixing excreta with plant material so that the mixture rots to form compost, and giving that to the crops. Such assiduous use of excreta is, of course, one of the main bases of 'organic farming' and is one of the main sources of fertility in Third World agriculture.

There can be no doubt that animal (and perhaps human) excreta ought to be used as conscientiously as possible as a source of fertility. There is a great deal of it, and the fact that the nitrogen is in organic form means that it tends to be released slowly, thus reducing (though by no means eliminating) the danger of pollution by run-off. It is a mistake to suppose, however, as some organic farming enthusiasts have implied, that manure and compost alone can solve the world's fertility problems. The use of manure does not increase the total amount of nitrogen available in the world. It merely increases the rate of turnover, and ensures that the most valuable plants – crops – receive what is available. Organic farmers who achieve very high yields with manure alone are, in fact, taking nitrogen from a wide area (or rather from animals and people who have fed over a wide area) and concentrating it in one place. This obviously cannot be a policy for the whole world. Some way must be found genuinely to increase the total amount of nitrogen that, world-wide, is in a form available to plants.

The way to meet this last requirement is to exploit the third source of nitrogen, the atmosphere itself. Four-fifth's of the atmosphere of the earth is nitrogen and the total weight of the gas is around one thousand million million tonnes. That nitrogen can in various ways be combined with other elements to form various non-gaseous compounds, by processes known collectively as *nitrogen fixation*.

Nitrogen fixation

In practice, nitrogen is fixed both artificially and naturally. Artificially, nitrogen gas is combined with hydrogen at high temperatures, with the aid of a suitable catalyst, to yield ammonia, which is then dissolved and combined to form various salts (whatever is most convenient). A similar process occurs naturally, by the action of lightning, and at the surface of desert sand, which in this context is acting as the catalyst. But what is important to our theme is that a similar process is carried out at ordinary temperatures by bacteria – with enzymes providing the necessary catalysis. This is *biological fixation.*

The grinding of nitrogen-containing rocks and the fixing of atmospheric nitrogen are the only ways in which new sources of nitrogen enter the biosphere. In practice, the grinding of rocks requires too much effort, and rocks are a non-renewable resource. Fixation is the process that really keeps the world going, and ensures that fertility world-wide is maintained. And although the fertilizer industry is now extremely large, fixation by bacteria still supplies most – world-wide, about 60 per cent – of the new nitrogen made available to plants each year. On simple arithmetical grounds, then, it is clear that the greatest single contribution that could be made to improving world fertility is to enhance biological fixation. Besides, artificial fertilizer is expensive both to buy and to apply; if it is not to be washed away or oxidized before the plants can make use of it, then the correct amounts have to be applied at just the right times. Accordingly, enhancement of biological fixation is widely considered to be a priority.

Enhancing biological fixation

The bacteria that fix nitrogen belong to several distinct groups; as different from each other, perhaps, as animals are from plants. The first of these groups is the archaebacteria, some of the most ancient organisms on earth. Archaebacteria prefer to do without oxygen altogether, tending even to be poisoned by it. Thus they are confined to anoxic places, such as stagnant marshes. Indeed, archaebacteria are best known for their production of methane gas, as will-o'-the-wisp. They are a difficult group to control, largely because of their aversion to oxygen, but they will be used increasingly in biodigesters for the production of biogas, an approach that is being explored at the Food Research Institute in Norwich, United Kingdom. As this technology is developed, it is conceivable that archaebacteria-based digesters might also serve as suppliers of fixed nitrogen. At present, however, the fact that archaebacteria fix nitrogen remains a biological curiosity; evidence that the fixing of nitrogen arose very early in the evolution of living things.

The second group of nitrogen fixers are some of the cyanobacteria. These were formerly known as blue-green algae, though they are not in any way related to true algae, which are bona fide plants. Nitrogen-fixing cyanobacteria are extremely important. They include *Anabaena*, which lives within the leaves of the tiny aquatic fern, *Azolla. Azolla* floats on the surface of the paddy fields and, thanks to its cargo of cyanobacteria, supplies the rice of Asia, at least that grown by traditional means, with one of its principal sources of fertility. At the

International Rice Research Institute in the Philippines, the activities of *Anabaena* are, hardly surprisingly, a research priority. The encouragement of *Azolla*, the development of superior strains both of *Azolla* and the cyanobacterium, and of superior partnerships between the two, could significantly improve the productivity of the world's most widely eaten crop.

The third group of nitrogen-fixing bacteria include many members of the eubacteria – what might loosely be called 'ordinary' bacteria. Some of these bacteria live free in the soil. Others live specifically within the immediate environment of the roots of plants – the *rhizosphere*. Others, yet again, live actually within the roots of plants, in a close symbiotic relationship. However they live, nitrogen-fixing bacteria are potentially helpful; and each mode is the subject of present research.

For example, at the Glasshouse Crops Research Institute, in Sussex, United Kingdom, Dr James Lynch is exploring the possibilities of making better use of free-living nitrogen fixers. His principal brief was to find ways of disposing of surplus straw, without too much expense and preferably with profit. United Kingdom farmers of wheat and barley do not, in general, use a great deal of straw for fodder, as they did in the olden days when farms were mixed. If straw is left in the fields it inhibits the germination of next year's seeds, largely because acid is produced as it rots, and it harbours disease. If farmers set fire to it they attract opprobrium and, indeed, legal proceedings. To harvest straw is expensive, however; this is particularly irritating if no-one wants to buy it when it has been harvested.

Dr Lynch, accordingly, is developing what is effectively a system of super-composting. Traditional compost heaps rely on 'wild' bacteria to break down the material via whatever metabolic routes the conditions allow. The new system employs custom-designed combinations of specific bacteria working under controlled conditions, and includes free-living nitrogen-fixing bacteria. Laboratory-scale experiments already show that break-down of straw can be quick and thorough and can supply a nitrogen-rich liquor very suitable as a fertilizer.

Scientists at ICRISAT are exploring the nitrogen-fixing bacteria that live for preference within the rhizosphere, and in particular within the rhizosphere of millet and sorghum. One of the key advances has been the development of a technique for analysing the speed at which nitrogen is fixed around roots. By this means ICRISAT scientists have shown that within 15 to 20 days of planting, different strains of millet differ in the extent to which they encourage nitrogen fixation to take place around them. ICRISAT research has shown, too, by this new technique, that fixation taking place around the roots of sorghum is at least 10 times and sometimes more than 20 times greater than hitherto suspected. It does not follow, however, that increased nitrogen fixation around roots will necessarily increase yields. For one thing, the plants may not be able to absorb the extra nitrogen that they have themselves helped to engender. But in one trial the scientists showed that the yield of one particular strain of millet did increase by 17 per cent compared with controls, when the region around its roots was inoculated with the bacterium *Azospirillum lipoferum*. Clearly there is a great deal to be gained from breeding strains of millet that encourage nitrogen-fixing bacteria to live around their roots, and in developing more productive strains of bacteria.

The relationship between plants such as millet, and the bacteria that surround their roots, is *symbiotic*. The bacteria are not necessarily in contact with the roots, but the roots evidently exude carbohydrate, which provides the bacteria with their essential source of organic carbon, and the bacteria provide nitrogen in exchange. There are many other plants, however, and many other bacteria, which take symbiosis much further than this. In these cases the nitrogen-fixing bacteria actually live within the roots of the plants, in nodules specifically provided, by the plant, to accommodate them. Again, the plant provides the bacteria with carbon, and the bacteria provides the plant with nitrogen.

Plants from many different plant families form such symbiotic relationships. They tend to be species such as alder and bog myrtle living in difficult, often infertile areas. These species harbour bacteria of the genus *Frankia* in their roots. But the plants that make the most use of symbiotic nitrogen-fixing bacteria are, of course, the legumes: acacias, mimosas, clovers, vetches, and the pulses. The particular bacteria they harbour are of the genus *Rhizobium*.

Legumes and *Rhizobium*

Research again focuses on several fronts. One obvious possibility is to enhance the rhizobia themselves. Some bacterial strains fix nitrogen more efficiently than others; these could be, and are being, developed. One drawback is that rhizobia tend to be inhibited by the presence of nitrogen salts. This means that the more they fix nitrogen the less active they are; it also means that at very high levels of fertility, the rhizobia tend to be inactive. Farmers seeking bumper crops (for example of soya) need to add artificial fertilizer, and the more they do so the more they suppress natural nitrogen fixation. Similarly, gardeners 'feed' their runner beans with manure. Breeders of soya have to a large extent ignored the property of nitrogen-fixation; it hardly seemed worth worrying about, when that property was in any case liable to be swamped by fertilizer. In the modern world, however, in which it is widely acknowledged that chemistry cannot alone provide the answer to all farming problems, it could well be worthwhile to develop rhizobia which can operate even when fertility is high. This could be desirable for all crops, world-wide.

In addition, a great deal of work is being done on the plants themselves. Within every legume species we find that some individual plants form rhizobium-containing nodules more readily than others. Again, varieties can be bred that are particularly hospitable to rhizobia; and these, combined with advanced strains of rhizobia, could produce plant varieties that fix nitrogen very efficiently, and yield accordingly. Again, such work is particularly relevant to the semi-arid tropics, where money is scarce and conditions are too uncertain to justify large inputs. To take just one example, scientists at ICRISAT have identified strains of groundnut that are particularly hospitable to rhizobia; and these can increasingly be incorporated into future breeding programmes.

But the idea that has attracted most interest is that of transferring the ability to fix nitrogen to crop plants other than legumes: notably, plants such as cereals. A nitrogen-fixing wheat would be a prize indeed.

Nitrogen fixation and genetic engineering

Here there are two possibilities, at least in theory. The easier one, conceptually, is to transfer to cereals the ability to form nodules in their roots that will harbour rhizobia bacteria or other nitrogen-fixing bacteria. The second possibility is to take nitrogen-fixing genes from bacteria and transfer them directly into the cereal, or indeed into any other crop plant. Both approaches involve transferring genes between organisms that are quite unrelated (legume to cereal, or bacterium to cereal) and are exercises in genetic engineering.

One of the first to moot such ideas was Professor John Postgate, director of the Unit of Nitrogen Fixation of the Agricultural and Food Research Council, in Sussex, United Kingdom. Because he has such an advanced knowledge of the subject, however, Professor Postgate is also the first to point out the fairly spectacular difficulties that stand in the way of such gene transference.

The conceptually simple problem of transferring to cereals the genes that could enable them to form nodules encounters, in late 1986, three problems. The first is that the necessary genes would presumably be obtained from legumes, but the genes enabling leguminous plants to form nodules have not been identified, and genes that have not been identified cannot be transferred. The second problem, as we have discussed in chapter 7, is that it is only just becoming possible to put genes of any kind into cereals. Thirdly, even when the pertinent genes have been identified and transferred, there is no assurance that they would be expressed, and function. Indeed expression is likely to prove a greater problem than mere transfer.

What then of the second possibility – of transferring the nitrogen-fixing genes themselves into a cereal, such as wheat? The first problem at least has been solved. The nitrogen-fixing genes – so-called *nif* genes – have been identified. However, there is not one *nif* gene, but many:

.17, to be precise and they work in concert. It is not yet possible to transfer any gene into wheat; but to transfer 17, *en bloc*, would be a very tall order indeed.

There is no reason to suppose that this cannot be done, however, eventually. Already, the full orchestra of *nif* genes has been introduced into yeast, and the yeast cells are more similar to plant cells than to the bacterial cells that donated the genes. But here we again encounter the third theoretical drawback: *nif* genes are not expressed in yeast.

The problem of expressing *nif* genes in wheat is likely to prove far harder to solve than that posed by genes being transferred between, say, beans and cereals. At least beans and cereals are both plants, but *nif* genes come from bacteria. Plants are eukaryotes: that is, their cells contain nuclei, which contain most of their genetic material. Bacteria are prokaryotes; their genetic material is not enclosed within a nucleus, but lies free in the cytoplasm, in the form of a giant chromosome, and in the form of plasmids. The difference is profound; prokaryotes and eukaryotes are very different kinds of organism.

The genetic code is virtually identical in eukaryotes and prokaryotes, so there should, on the face of it, be no great problem; prokaryote genes should be able to fit in with the plant's DNA perfectly well. There is, however, one difference between plant and bacterial DNA that is crucial. All genes, in order to function, have to be switched on; and the signals that switch on bacterial genes are not the same as those that switch on the genes of eukaryotes. Even if wheat plants were to be endowed with the complement of *nif* genes, they could not, it seems, coax the *nif* genes into activity.

There are several possible ways around this problem, however, and one of the most intriguing is as follows. Plants carry most of their genetic material in their nuclei, but not all of it. They also carry functional genes within their mitochonrdia and their chloroplasts, contained within the cell cytoplasm. This genetic material is not dissimilar to that of prokaryotes. In fact in 1970, Professor Lyn Margulis suggested that mitochondria and chloroplasts *were* originally prokaryotes, which came to infect the cell and stayed, in degenerate and increasingly specialist form, as symbionts. It is hardly surprising, then, that the DNA in these organelles has some of the character of prokaryotes. This fact raises the possibility that the best place to insert *nif* genes is not into the DNA of the nucleus, but into that of the chloroplasts.

Such an arrangement could have considerable advantages. As Professor Postgate points out, it would be very convenient if plants fixed nitrogen in their leaves, because leaves have a plentiful supply of air (and hence of gaseous nitrogen) and because the fixed nitrogen would then be close to the newly formed carbon compounds produced by photosynthesis, and could immediately be coupled to those compounds, to form amino-acids. The leaf would be an efficient protein factory, with all the components on site. But again there is a difficulty. The *nif* genes are very sensitive to oxygen. After all, nitrogen fixation evolved billions of years ago, when the world was still young, and there was no free oxygen in the atmosphere. Photosynthesis generates oxygen. Thus, if the *nif* genes were to function in the leaf, they would need to be heavily protected from what to them is a poisonous gas. *Azolla* possesses elaborate mechanisms for protecting its resident *Anabaena*.

Nitrogen fixation re-invented

All this, so far, is in the world of fantasy; albeit plausible, and one day realizable, fantasy. We can, however, look even further ahead. Because nitrogen fixation evolved when the atmosphere contained no free oxygen, it inevitably evolved as a reducing process; hydrogen being added to nitrogen, to form ammonia. One drawback, as we have seen, is that the controlling genes are sensitive to oxygen. The other is that the process itself is inefficient: it requires a lot of energy. One theoretical limit on the usefulness of biological fixation, then, is that in order to fix nitrogen, plants have to squander a fair proportion of the carbohydrate they create by photosynthesis. Plants on soils of low fertility need to fix nitrogen if they are to produce sizeable yields, but in fixing nitrogen they have to squander organic material that otherwise would have increased the yield still further.

Thus, at the 1983 CIBA conference on *Better Crops for Food*, Ralph W. Hardy of the E. I. du Pont de Nemours & Company suggested that in the very long term, biologists might seek not simply to transfer the ability to fix nitrogen from one organism to another, but to re-invent the process of fixation. Enzymes would have to be developed that would fix nitrogen by an oxidative process: combining nitrogen not with hydrogen, but with oxygen. Such a process would not be sensitive to oxygen, and it would not require energy at all. The necessary enzymes would probably have to be synthetic, as there are none known in nature that will oxidize nitrogen. Enzymes are of course proteins, and it is already possible to synthesize proteins. Protein chemists have also worked out the chemical structure, and the physical form, of several enzymes, but they cannot yet predict what shape of protein will produce an enzymes with particular properties. In short, knowledge of the relationship between protein chemistry and enzyme structure will have to be of quite a different order if Dr Hardy's version is to be realized. But when the necessary protein was devised, it would not be difficult, even by today's technology, to produce a molecule of DNA that would code for it; and this molecule, a synthetic gene for a quite new kind of enzyme, could then be engineered into a plant. This is a long shot, but one which, in Dr Hardy's words, 'undoubtedly will occur within the next century'.

It is sometimes suggested that the study of biological fixation of nitrogen has been neglected in the past, and that this is a sign that scientists do not really appreciate what is important. Here, however, is a classic example of Sir Peter Medawar's dictum that science is 'the art of the soluble'. Efficient or not, biological nitrogen fixation involves some of the most intricate and delicate series of reactions in all nature. The most sophisticated of modern techniques, in sciences as diverse as molecular biology and physical chemistry, are required to make sense of it and it is only in the past 20 years that scientists have been equipped even to begin such an investigation. Now the study is well under way, and the possibilities for agriculture are wonderful. It is fantasy to suggest that farmers, one day, will not need to fertilize their crops, but it is the kind of fantasy that, with the passage of centuries, might come true; and centuries are a small span of time in the evolution of agriculture.

So what are our prospects? The task of ensuring a dignified life for the huge populations of the 21st century is immense. It becomes even greater if we acknowledge that we are not the sole species, and that we should contrive to share this planet with millions of other species. The problems are not exclusively technical, but they are technical in part and one among many serious questions is whether the necessary technologies are being, and can be, developed and applied in time. That is the subject of the final chapter.

11 Epilogue

Throughout most of their existence, human beings have had very little control over their own destiny. The human species evolved, it seems, in response to changes in vegetation, brought about by a shift in climate. People were probably forced into agriculture by their own biological success – and probably with great reluctance. 'In the sweat of thy face shalt thou eat bread', were the words that God addressed to Adam when He banned him from the easy pickings of Eden. From then on people were obliged to be farmers, but whether they succeeded or failed depended on forces that for the most part were beyond their control. When the harvests failed, through disease or bad weather, people died.

Now, this need no longer be the case. We do not have perfect control – far from it. But we can avoid most of the simple exigencies that so often laid waste our ancestors' harvests. We could provide enough food for the human species, even for the 10 billion people who will probably be on earth by the middle of the next century. We could indeed do this with a great deal of leeway, to insure against the droughts and disasters that really are beyond human control. And we could do that, furthermore, and still leave room for a fair proportion of our fellow creatures. (The demise of many of them is already beyond control.)

The prize, if we cared to exert our new-found power, is very great indeed: a stable and attractive world, capable of indefinite survival. The price of failure, on the other hand, is almost beyond imagining; or it would be, had we not already seen so many portents. The famines in Africa and Asia; the deforestation and the erosion that follows it, the loss of hundreds of conspicuous species and tens of thousands of smaller plants and animals, are already familiar, almost commonplace. But there is nothing we have yet experienced that could not be magnified tenfold.

The creation of good, appropriate crop plants is not all that needs to be done. But it is an important part. Modern arable land is effectively barren except for the crop it contains and is of little or no use to other species, except for the odd poppy or ground beetle. If land is to be used so single-mindedly, then it should also be used whole-heartedly. To banish every other species from the land and then to use the land only to produce half the crop that is possible, might properly be called a sin;

an offence that is not simply an offence against humankind. If yields are to be doubled on the most fertile lands, then we need better crops.

At the other end of the scale, hundreds of millions of people now contrive to live in areas that are half-way to being desert. There is nowhere else for them to live. Some are pastoralists, and some contrive to raise crops. But pastoralism is extremely difficult. It can be done well: it can indeed be sustained indefinitely, but only if the areas are vast and if the system is well organized. But if key areas are parcelled off for farming, or more people are forced into pastoralism than the area can sustain, then the system begins to break down; the land is overgrazed, and the animals and the people die. Then – which effectively means now – pastoralism can be maintained only by a subtle blend of legislation on the one hand, and practical ecology on the other.

Raising crops in semi-desert is certainly no easier. The aim in such circumstances is not to produce bumper crops of the kind that break records in Europe, but to raise a steady and tolerable quantity even in the very worst years. Again, this is largely a technical exercise. Part of the necessary technology is the provision of drought-resistant and pest-resistant crops.

However, it has often been argued that science and technology have very little part to play in feeding and sustaining the world. Such arguments pursue two main themes. The first is that much of what is wrong with the world has simply to do with inequity, and with the failure to apply present techniques for the right purposes. The second is that 'high-tech' solutions have often failed.

Both arguments are undeniable. We are technically able to feed all the world, and people do not starve in Africa simply because of drought, but because the countryside is largely neglected, and indeed bled, in favour of the towns. High-tech solutions have often failed, and for many different reasons. Sometimes the new varieties of high-yielding cereal were simply unpalatable to the people for whom they were intended; and food that people do not like to eat is of no use. Sometimes the 'new-tech' has required greater inputs than people are able to sustain, or it has produced surpluses that local markets are not able to absorb. Sometimes – often – 'mega-projects' have proved disastrous because of unforeseen and unforeseeable ecological consequences. A dam may change the ecology of an entire region. The changes may take centuries to unfold, and many of them are bound to be far from desirable.

Beyond doubt, there is little point in throwing science and technology at problems that in essence are political. Science has often been used simply to paper over cracks in social justice. Certainly, too, high-tech and high science have often been wielded with extreme clumsiness, thrown into subtle ecologies and societies with little sense of direction and little control over the consequences. Often, a few tonnes of concrete around a well-head, or a set of rubber tyres on an ox-cart, may be far more useful and cost-effective than any ostentatious exercise in 'modernization'.

However, it is possible to envisage policies that are benign and helpful; and science is just as capable of helping to enact good policies as it is of alleviating the effects of bad ones. High-tech solutions may not always be the most cost-effective, but they should not be written off. A drought-resistant, mildew-resistant sorghum is the product of high-tech. Such a plant cannot reliably be produced in the field by informal processes of selection. Disease-resistance must be developed under controlled conditions, using controlled doses; and appropriate genes must sometimes be sought from the far corners of the earth, sometimes in plants that are quite unlike the crop in hand. Drought-resistance cannot be reliably enhanced unless the candidate crops are exposed to precisely monitored stress at critical times in their lives. If, at some time in the future, the mildew-resistant, drought-resistant sorghum were also to be endowed with improved proteins, to produce a crop that city people would pay for, then the unpromising lands to the south of the Sahara could become regions of modest prosperity and security. When problems are properly identified, and realistic targets are envisaged, then it can often be the case that the most appropriate technologies of all are the very highest.

Although it is the case that high-tech clumsily applied can make things worse, that does not mean that what was there before was perfect. For example, new varieties of wheat and rice have sometimes been virtually foisted on people who before were growing their ancient landraces and the new varieties have then succumbed to some disease or to a change in the weather, of a kind that the old landraces would have survived. It has often been wrongly concluded in such cases that old-fashioned landraces are intrinsically superior. After all, the landrace is highly variable and will never be entirely wiped out by the blight of any particular year; only modern varieties, which are perfectly uniform, can uniformly succumb.

On the other hand, farmers of ancient landraces may expect in any one year to lose a large proportion of their crop. Mildew alone commonly claims half the crop of sorghum or millet. As we saw in chapter 9, variability alone does not provide enough protection; it should be abetted by specific resistance which is not necessarily to be found within any particular landrace. Sometimes the genes needed by a sorghum crop in Africa are only to be found among landraces of India. Sometimes, to cite an example given in chapter 5, the resistance genes needed in a crop of groundnut in India or Africa are to be found only among wild relatives, in the dry lands of southern Brazil. Such genes cannot be identified and gathered from the far corners of the world, and sometimes introduced across species barriers, except by dint of an extraordinary array of technologies, which include the jet plane, refrigeration, the computer, and the techniques of cytogenetics. So we may admit that to replace a landrace cavalierly with a modern crop having no proper resistance to prevailing conditions is naive, high-handed, and perhaps at times even wicked. But this does not justify the generalization that traditional technologies, developed *in situ*, are incapable of improvement.

Overall, then, there are three orders of problem. The first is to ensure that there is justice in the world and that people are not simply written off or exploited. That of course is the perennial problem of humankind. Science can do very little to bring about the necessary changes, except perhaps to point out what it is that is being squandered by human viciousness: the possibility of living well in a stable world.

The second problem is to find means by which excellent science can be brought to bear upon the problems of people who cannot afford to pay for it. Subsistence farmers will never have the money to pay for cytogenetic research. Again, this is a perennial problem of humankind, and all we can appropriately say here is that it is a challenge to all political systems. If some elect to solve it by socialism and others by charity, then fair enough: so long as the necessary things are accomplished, in ways compatible with human dignity.

The third, most general problem, is simply to solve the problem of how to use science well. Science is immensely powerful; it is the greatest single agent of change. It needs on the one hand to be handled delicately, and on the other to be wielded subtly. In general neither of these things happens. Sometimes, in some societies, euphoria prevails, and science is presented as the talisman, the solution to all problems. At other times, in other circumstances, science is presented as the enemy of the people, and research is curtailed. In general, the highest technology is wielded by the richest commercial companies, who do not necessarily have the world's best interests at heart. In general, too, there is no society on earth where more than a very few people have the smallest inkling of what science actually entails; and so long as that is so, it cannot properly be used as an agent of democracy, because most people simply will not know what is happening, or why.

As I hope is clear from this book, however, good science well applied does have a great deal to offer. The world could be fed.

References

Essential reading

Cherfas, Jeremy 1982: *Man made life*, Oxford: Basil Blackwell.
National Academy of Sciences 1975: *Underexploited tropical plants with promising economic value*. Washington DC: National Academy of Sciences.
Nugent, Jonathan and O'Connor, Maeve (eds.) 1983: *Better crops for food*. Ciba Foundation symposium 97, London: Pitman.
Prescott-Allen, Robert and Prescott-Allen, Christine 1983: *Genes from the wild*. London: Earthscan.
Simmonds, N. W. (ed.) 1976: *Evolution of crop plants*. London: Longman.
Simmonds, N. W. 1979: *Principles of crop improvement*. London: Longman.
Watson, James D., Tooze, John and Kurtz, David T. 1983: *Recombinant DNA*. New York: Scientific American Books, W. H. Freeman.

Books, articles and key papers by chapter

Chapter 1

Coughenour, M. B. *et al.* 1985: Energy extraction and use in a nomadic pastoral ecosystem, *Science*, 230, 619.
Richards, Paul 1985: *Indigenous agricultural revolution*. London: Hutchinson.
Tudge, Colin 1977: *The famine business*. Faber and Faber, London. Pelican, Harmondsworth, 1979.

Chapter 2

Borgstrom, Georg 1965: *The hungry planet*. London: Collier Books.
Crabbe, David and Lawson, Simon 1981: *The world food book*. London: Kogan Page/New York: Nichols Publishing Company.
Crawford, Michael and Crawford, Sheila 1972: *What we eat today*. London: Neville Spearman.
Cross, Michael 1984: Ethiopian farming in clover. *New Scientist*, 19.
Heywood, V. H. 1978: *Flowering plants of the world*. Oxford: Oxford University Press.
Masefield, G. B., Wallis, M., Harrison, S. G., Nicholson, B. E. 1969: *The Oxford book of food plants*. London: Oxford University Press.

L. 't Mannetje, O'Connor, K. F. and Burt, R. L. 1980: The use and adaptation of pasture and fodder legumes. In *Advances in legume science* (eds. R. J. Summerfield and A. H. Bunting), Volume 1 of the Proceedings of the International Legume Conference, 31 July–4 August 1978, Kew Royal Botanic Gardens, Kew, 537–551.

National Academy of Sciences 1979: *Tropical legumes: resources for the future.* Washington DC: National Academy of Sciences.

National Academy of Sciences 1981: *The winged bean: a high-protein crop for the tropics.* (2nd edn.) Washington DC: National Academy Press.

National Academy of Sciences 1984: *Amaranth: modern prospects for an ancient crop.* Washington DC: National Academy Press.

Smith, Nigel 1983: New genes from wild potatoes. *New Scientist*, 558–565.

Summerfield, R. J. and Roberts, E. H. 1983: The soyabean. *Biologist*, 30 (4), 223–231.

Swaminathan, M. S. 1984: Rice. *Scientific American*, 63–71.

Tindall, H. D. 1983: *Vegetables in the tropics.* London: Macmillan Press.

Tudge, Colin 1985: *The food connection: the BBC guide to healthy eating.* London: British Broadcasting Corporation.

Ward, Gerald M., Sutherland, Thomas M. and Sutherland, Jean M. 1980: Animals as an energy source in Third World agriculture. *Science*, 208, 570–574.

Weber, Edward J. 1978: The Inca's ancient answer to food shortage. *Nature*, 272, 486.

Chapter 3

Birky, Jr., C. William 1983: Relaxed cellular controls and organelle heredity. *Science*, 222, 468–475.

Lewontin, R. C. 1985: Darwin, Mendel and the mind. *New York Review*, 18–23.

Root-Bernstein, Robert Scott. *Mendel and methodology*, Science History Publications Ltd., pages un-numbered.

Chapter 4

Cherfas, Jeremy and Gribbin, John 1984: *The redundant male.* London: The Bodley Head.

Cherfas, Jeremy 1985: When is a tree more than a tree?. *New Scientist*, 42–45.

Emlen, S. T. and Oring, L. W. 1977: Ecology, sexual selection, and the evolution of mating systems. *Science*, 197, 215–223.

Haldane, J. B. S. 1985: The biology of inequality. In *On being the right size* (ed. John Maynard Smith). Oxford: Oxford University Press.

Hamilton, William D. 1980: Sex versus non-sex versus parasite. *Oikos*, 35, 282–290.

Hamilton, William D. 1982: Pathogens as causes of genetic diversity in their host populations. In *Population biology of infectious diseases* (eds. R. M. Anderson and R. M. May). Dahlen Konferenzen, Berlin: Springer-Verlag.

Harlan, J. R. and de Wet, J. M. J. 1971: Toward a rational classification of cultivated plants. *Taxon*, 20, 509–517.

Levin, Donald A. 1975: Pest pressure and recombination systems in plants. *The*

References

American Naturalist, 109, 437–451.

Maynard Smith, J. 1978: *The evolution of sex*. Cambridge: Cambridge University Press.

Price, M. V. and Waser, N. M. 1979: Pollen dispersal and optimal outcrossing in *Delphinium nelsoni*. *Nature*, 277, 294–297.

Williams, G. C. 1975: *Sex and evolution*. Princeton, New Jersey: Princeton University Press.

Chapter 5

Bender, Barbara 1975: *Farming in prehistory*. London: John Baker.

Cohen, Mark Nathan 1977: *The food crisis in prehistory*. New Haven and London: Yale University Press.

Iltis, Hugh H. 1983: From teosinte to maize: the catastrophic sexual transmutation. *Science*, 222, 886–894.

Jackson, Mike and Thomson, Alan 1984: True potato seed: a new approach to potato production. *University of Birmingham Bulletin*, 21 May, p. 484.

Lawrence, William J. C. 1968: *Plant breeding*. London: Edward Arnold.

Lee, R. B. and De Vore, I. (eds.) 1968: *Man the hunter*. Chicago: Aldine.

Mangelsdorf, P. C. 1974: *Corn: its origin, evolution, and improvement*. Cambridge, Massachusetts: Harvard University Press.

Prescott-Allen, Robert and Christine 1983: *Genes from the wild*. London: Earthscan.

Smith, Nigel 1983: Triticale: the birth of a new cereal. *New Scientist*, 98–99.

Tudge, Colin 1983: The future of crops. *New Scientist*, 547–553.

Chapter 6

Branton, Richard and Blake, Janet 1983: A lovely clone of coconuts. *New Scientist*, 554–557.

Burgess, Jeremy 1984: The revolution that failed (a discussion of somatic hybridization). *New Scientist*, 26–29.

Christianson, M. L., Warnick, D. A. and Carlson, P. S. 1983: A morpho-genetically competent soybean suspension culture. *Science*, 222, 632–634.

Cocking, E. C. 1981: Opportunities from the use of protoplasts. *Philosophical Transactions of the Royal Society of London, Series B*, 292, 557–568.

Jones, L. H. 1983: The oil palm and its clonal propagation by tissue culture. *Biologist*, 30 (4), 181–188.

Prenosil, Jiri E. and Pedersen, Henrick 1983: Immobilized plant cell reactors. *Enzyme and Microbial Technology* 5, 323–331.

Tudge, Colin 1984: Drugs and dyes from plant cell cultures. *New Scientist*, 25.

Vasil, Vimla and Hildebrandt, A. C. 1965: Differentiation of tobacco plants from single isolated cells in microcultures. *Science*, 150, 889–892.

Chapter 7

Berg, Paul 1981: Nobel Prize lecture, 'Dissections and reconstructions of genes and chromosomes'. *Science*, 213, 296–303.

Broglie, Richard *et al.* 1984: Light-regulated expression of a pea ribulose-1, 5-bisphosphate carboxylase small subunit gene in transformed plant cells.

Science, 224, 838–843.

Caplan, A., Herrera-Estrella, L., Inze, D., Van Haute, E., Van Montagu, M., Schell, J. and Zambryski, P. 1983: Introduction of genetic material into plant cells. *Science*, 222, 815–820.

Cocking, E. C., Davey, M. R., Pental, D. and Power, J. B. 1981: Aspects of plant genetic manipulation. Review article in *Nature*, 293, 265–270.

Cohen, S. N. *et al.* 1972: Construction of biologically functional bacterial plasmids *in vitro*. *Proceedings of the National Academy of Sciences*, 69, 2110–2114.

Dodds, John H. (ed.) 1985: *Plant genetic engineering*. Cambridge: Cambridge University Press.

Flavell, R. B. 1981: The analysis of plant genes and chromosomes by using DNA cloned in bacteria. *Phil. Trans. R. Soc. Lond, B*, 579–588.

Flavell, Richard and Mathias, Raymond 1984: Prospects for transforming monocot crop plants. *Nature*, 307, 108–109.

Hooykaas-Van Slogteren, G. M. S., Hooykaas, D. J. J. and Schilperoot, R. A. 1984: Expression of ti plasmid genes in monocotyledenous plants infected with *Agrobacterium tumefaciens*. *Nature*, 311, 763–764.

Horsch, Robert B. *et al.* 1984: Inheritance of functional foreign genes in plants. *Science*, 223, 496–498.

Margulis, M. 1981: *Symbiosis in cell evolution: life and its environment on the early earth*. San Francisco: Freeman.

Marx, Jean 1982: Ti plasmids as gene carriers. *Science*, 216, 1305.

Mertz, J. E. and Davis, R. W. 1972: Cleavage of DNA by RI restriction endonuclease generates cohesive ends. *Proceedings of the National Academy of Sciences*, 69, 3370–4.

Murai, Norimoto *et al.* 1983: Phaseolin gene from bean is expressed after transfer to sunflower via tumour-inducing plasmid vectors. *Science*, 222, 476–482.

Owens, Lowell D. (ed.) 1983: Genetic engineering: applications to agriculture. *Beltsville Symposia in Agricultural Research*, 7. London: Rowman & Allanheld.

Smith, H. O. 1979: Nucleotide sequence specificity of restriction endonucleases. *Science*, 205, 455–62.

Smith, H. O. and Wilcox, K. W. 1970: A restriction enzyme from *Hemophilus influenzae*. *Journal of Molecular Biology*, 51, 379–91.

Chapter 8

Plant Genetic Resources Newsletter: published jointly by the Plant Production and Protection Division of FAO, and the International Board for Plant Genetic Resources. Rome: FAO.

Hawkes, J. G. 1983: *The diversity of crop plants*. Cambridge: Massachusetts: Harvard University Press.

Chapter 9

Anon. 1983: Fighting favism. *Quest*, 10, 9–11.

Gibson, R. W. and Pickett, J. A. 1984: Wild potato repels aphids by release of aphid alarm pheromone. *Nature*, 302, 608–609.

References

Ivie, Wayne, Holt, Douglas and Ivey, Marcellus 1983: Natural toxicants in human food: the psoralens in raw and cooked parsnip root. *Science*, 213, 909–910.

Rutter, Jill and Percy, Stephen 1984: The pulse that maims (lathyrism). *New Scientist*, 22–23.

Shewry, P. R. 1981: *Is it possible to improve the nutritional quality of cereal proteins?* Paper to British Association for the Advancement of Science annual meeting September 1981, York.

Vose, Peter 1981: Crops for all conditions. *New Scientist*, 688–690.

Vose, P. D. and Blixt, S. G. (eds.) 1984: *Crop breeding: a contemporary basis.* Oxford: Pergamon Press.

Chapter 10

Beringer, J. E. and Hirsch, P. R. 1984: Genetic engineering and nitrogen fixation. *Biotechnology and Genetic Engineering Reviews*, 1, 65–88.

Downie, Allan 1983: Molecular genetics: out of the laboratory into the field. *Nature*, 306, 639.

Ela, Stephen E., Anderson, Mary Ann and Brill, Winston J. 1982: Screening and selection of maize to enhance associative bacterial nitrogen fixation. *Plant Physiology*, 70, 1564–1576.

Postgate, J. R. FRS, 1980: Prospects for the exploitation of biological nitrogen fixation. *Phil. Trans. R. Soc, Lond., B*, 290, 421–425.

Postgate, J. R. FRS and Cannon, F. C. 1981: The molecular and genetic manipulation of nitrogen fixation. *Philosophical Transactions of the Royal Society of London, Series B*, 292, 589–599.

Royal Society, 1983: *The nitrogen cycle of the United Kingdom.* London: The Royal Society.

Glossary

Allele different individuals in a population, or homologous chromoomes within a single diploid cell, may contain different versions of the same gene. Each 'version' is an *allele* of that gene.

Allotetraploid the cells of most plants contain two sets of chromosomes and are said to be diploid. In tetraploids, the basic diploid number has doubled, to give four sets. An *allotetraploid* is the result of doubling the chromosomes within an interspecific hybrid. The term applies both to cells and to individuals composed of such cells.

Aneuploid a cell containing fewer or more than the standard number of chromosomes for its particular species. The term is also applied to individuals made up of such cells.

Autotetraploid a cell containing four sets of chromosomes, formed by doubling of the normal diploid number. The term is also applied to individuals made up of such cells.

Back-cross procedure in which the progeny of a cross are recrossed with one of the original parents.

Biomass the total mass of biological material within an organism or population of organisms.

Carbon fixation in photosynthesis, green plants combine carbon dioxide gas from the atmosphere with hydrogen obtained from the splitting of water, and thus form organic molecules. This is *carbon fixation*.

Character a 'characteristic' of a plant, determined by one or several genes.

Chloroplast a structure within the cytoplasm of the plant cell where photosynthesis takes place.

Chromosome structure within the nucleus of the plant cell that contains the genes. Each chromosome consists of a single macromolecule of DNA, coiled and re-coiled, and held in place by proteins.

Clone the total population of genetically identical organisms produced from a single progenitor by asexual reproduction.

Codon a group of three nucleotides within the DNA or RNA molecule. Each codon codes for a particular amino acid.

Crossing mating between two plants of different variety or different species.

Crossing over exchange of genetic material between homologous chromosomes during gamete formation.

Cytoplasmic gene genetic material contained within an organelle, either mitochondrion or chloroplast.

Differentiation the process whereby embryonic or callus cells take on the specific form and function of particular tissues.

Diploid a cell with two sets of chromosomes. The term is also applied to organisms made up of such cells.

Dominance the phenomenon whereby an allele inherited from one parent will override the effects of a different allele of the same gene inherited from the other parent. See *Recessive*.

Double cross the procedure whereby two hybrid plants (each of which is a 'cross') are crossed.

Emasculation removal of the male parts of the flower, or suppression of pollen formation.

Eukaryote organism in which the genetic material is primarily arranged within chromosomes that are contained within a distinct nucleus, is called a *eukaryote*. Plants, animals, and fungi are eukaryotes.

Euploid A cell containing the 'correct' number of chromosomes for its particular species. The term is also applied to individuals made up of such cells.

Expression when a gene functions within a cell – that is, produces the protein for which it codes – it is said to be *expressed*.

F1 the first generation of progeny.

F1 hybrid the first generation progeny of parents belonging to different varieties.

Fix (in the context of a gene) when only one allele of any particular gene exists within the population that gene is said to be *fixed*. All the progeny produced within that population are bound to inherit that allele from both parents, and will be homozygous for that allele.

Gamete specialist sex cell.

Gene a stretch of DNA that codes for a particular protein is called a *gene*. Proteins generally function as enzymes which control the chemistry of the cell, and hence the cell's physical form and function. Thus genes code for observable characters.

Gene bank a collection of seeds or other suitable tissues which between them contain the principal genes of a particular species or group of species.

Gene library genes of any kind of organism may be introduced into bacteria which are then multiplied – cloned – to produce a large number of copies of those genes. A *gene library* is a collection of clones that between them contain all the genes represented in a particular organism.

Gene pool the totality of alleles contained with a breeding population of organisms.

Genetic drift the process whereby the proportion of different alleles changes within the gene pool as generations pass. In practice genetic drift tends to imply the loss of genes, as individuals containing uncommon alleles die before reproducing.

Genetic engineering artificial procedures whereby individual genes are removed from one organism and introduced into another.

Genome the complete complement of genes within a particular organism.

Genotype two organisms with identical genomes are said to be of the same genotype. The form of the whole organism – that is, its *phenotype* – depends partly upon its genotype, and partly upon the exigencies of environment.

Genus a group of similar species. Different species of the same genus can often be mated to produce *interspecific hybrids*, though these are usually sterile or of reduced fertility.

Germplasm bank see *gene bank*.

Habit the 'form' of the plant. Plants of *determinate habit* stop growing and begin to become senescent after they have reached a certain 'predetermined' size. Plants of *indeterminate habit* continue growing until they are curtailed by adverse conditions or simply 'outgrow their strength'.

Haploid a cell containing only one set of chromosomes. The term is also applied to individuals made up of such cells.

Harvest index the proportion of a crop that can be used for that crop's principal purpose.

Heterosis the increase in vigour obtained by crossing two different but compatible varieties and thus producing offspring with a high degree of heterozygosity. Often used synonymously with *hybrid vigour*.

Heterozygous an individual that inherits two different alleles of a particular gene – one allele from each parent – is said to be *heterozygous* for that particular gene.

Hexaploid a cell containing six sets of chromosomes. The term is also applied to individuals made up of such cells.

Homoeologous sometimes related organisms have 'equivalent' chromosomes – similar in form, although different in many of the genes they contain. In a polyploid hybrid produced by crossing such organisms the equivalent chromosomes, now co-existing in the same cell, are said to be *homoeologous*.

Homologous each chromosome within a diploid organism is said to be *homologous* with the matching chromosome inherited from the other parent.

Homozygous an individual that inherits the same allele of a particular gene from each of its parents is said to be *homozygous* for that particular gene.

Hybrid the progeny of a cross between two different varieties. An offspring of two different species is called an *interspecific hybrid* and a hybrid formed between two organisms of different genera is an *intergeneric hybrid*.

Hybrid vigour   Charles Darwin's expression for the increased vigour often observed in hybrids.

Inbreeding   sexual reproduction between two members of the same genotype, or between the male and female parts of the same flower or plant.

Inbreeding depression   the loss of vigour brought about by excessive inbreeding – which is most obvious in organisms that do not normally inbreed.

Intergeneric hybrid   see *hybrid*.

Interspecific hybrid   see *hybrid*.

Introgression   the influx of genes from a different population.

Landrace   a variety developed *in situ* through continued selection and not subject to formal breeding procedures.

Linkage   the phenomenon whereby two or more genes sited on the same chromosome tend to be passed on as a group to the progeny.

Mitochondrion   an organelle within the cell cytoplasm containing the enzymes responsible for respiration, and hence for providing energy.

Monosomic   an aneuploid cell lacking one chromosome. The term is also applied to individuals containing such cells.

Mutation   a change in a gene, which changes its code and hence causes it to produce a different kind of protein from before.

Nitrogen fixation   the process whereby atmospheric nitrogen gas is combined with hydrogen to form soluble ammonium ions, which may then be oxidized to form soluble nitrites and nitrates. Theoretically, though not in practice, nitrogen fixation could also be effected by the direct oxidation of nitrogen.

Organelle   a structure within the cell having a specific function.

Outbreeding   sexual reproduction between organisms of different genotype.

Parthenogenesis   differentiation and development of an unfertilized egg to form a complete new organism; that is, a form of asexual reproduction based upon female sex cells.

Partial dominance   the condition in which an allele inherited from one parent partly but not completely overrides the effects of a different allele of the same gene inherited from the other parent.

Phenotype   the physical form of an organism.

Plasmid   a circular piece of DNA found within the cells of prokaryotes. Plasmids can reproduce independently of the whole cell, and may pass from one organism to another.

Pleiotropy   the phenomenon by which a single gene may influence several or many different characters.

Polygenic   the term applied to a character that is determined by more than one gene.

Polyploid   a cell containing more than two sets of chromosomes. The term is also applied to individuals containing such cells.

Prokaryote an organism in which genetic material is contained within plasmids and within a 'chromosome' that does not contain structural protein and is not contained within the nucleus. Eubacteria, Archaebacteria, and Cyanobacteria are prokaryotes.

Protoplast often known as a 'naked proplast'. A plant cell stripped of its cell wall by means of enzymes, and so surrounded only by the cell membrane.

Recessive the term applied to an allele whose effects are overriden by a different allele of the same gene on the homologous chromosome.

Recombination when two broken strands of DNA are joined up again they are said to be *recombined*. Normally the term is applied to the recombination of stretches of DNA from different species.

Recombinant DNA DNA formed by recombining stretches of DNA from different species.

Restorer gene a gene that overrides the effects of any gene that predisposes to male sterility.

Restriction severance of DNA by means of bacterial enzymes.

Ribosome organelle within the cell where amino acids are joined to form proteins. Messenger RNA determines the sequence of joining.

Seed bank see *gene bank*.

Self-incompatible when two organisms of the same genotype (or the male and female parts of the same plant) are unable to reproduce sexually they are said to be *self-incompatible*.

Somaclonal variation sometimes members of a clone differ one from another, even though they should be of identical genotype. Such variation is called *somaclonal variation*.

Species a group of organisms whose members can reproduce sexually one with another to produce fully viable, sexually fertile offspring.

Sticky end a pair of nucleotides protruding from the end of a severed piece of DNA when it has been attacked by a restriction enzyme of the type that produces a 'staggered cut'.

Tetraploid a cell containing four sets of chromosomes. The term is also applied to individuals made up of such cells.

Totipotency the ability of a cell to differentiate into cell types of any tissue within the organism. Most animal cells cease to be totipotent after the early embryonic stage, but plants retain totipotent cells throughout their lives.

Transcription the process by which a molecule of messenger RNA is formed as a 'mirror image' of the parent DNA, and thus encompasses the genetic code.

Translation the process by which the genetic code contained within messenger RNA is translated into a series of amino acids – that is, into a protein.

Translocation sometimes during cell division a piece of one chromosome becomes attached to another. This is *translocation*.

True breeding   an organism whose offspring are virtually the same as itself is said to be *true breeding*. Highly homozygous organisms are true breeding, highly heterozygous organisms are not.

Vector   literally, a 'carrier'. The term is applied to plasmids or viruses that can carry genes into cells, and to insects that carry disease organisms.

Zygote   the first cell of an embryo, formed by the fusion of two gametes.

Index

Index

Index by
Jacqueline McDermott